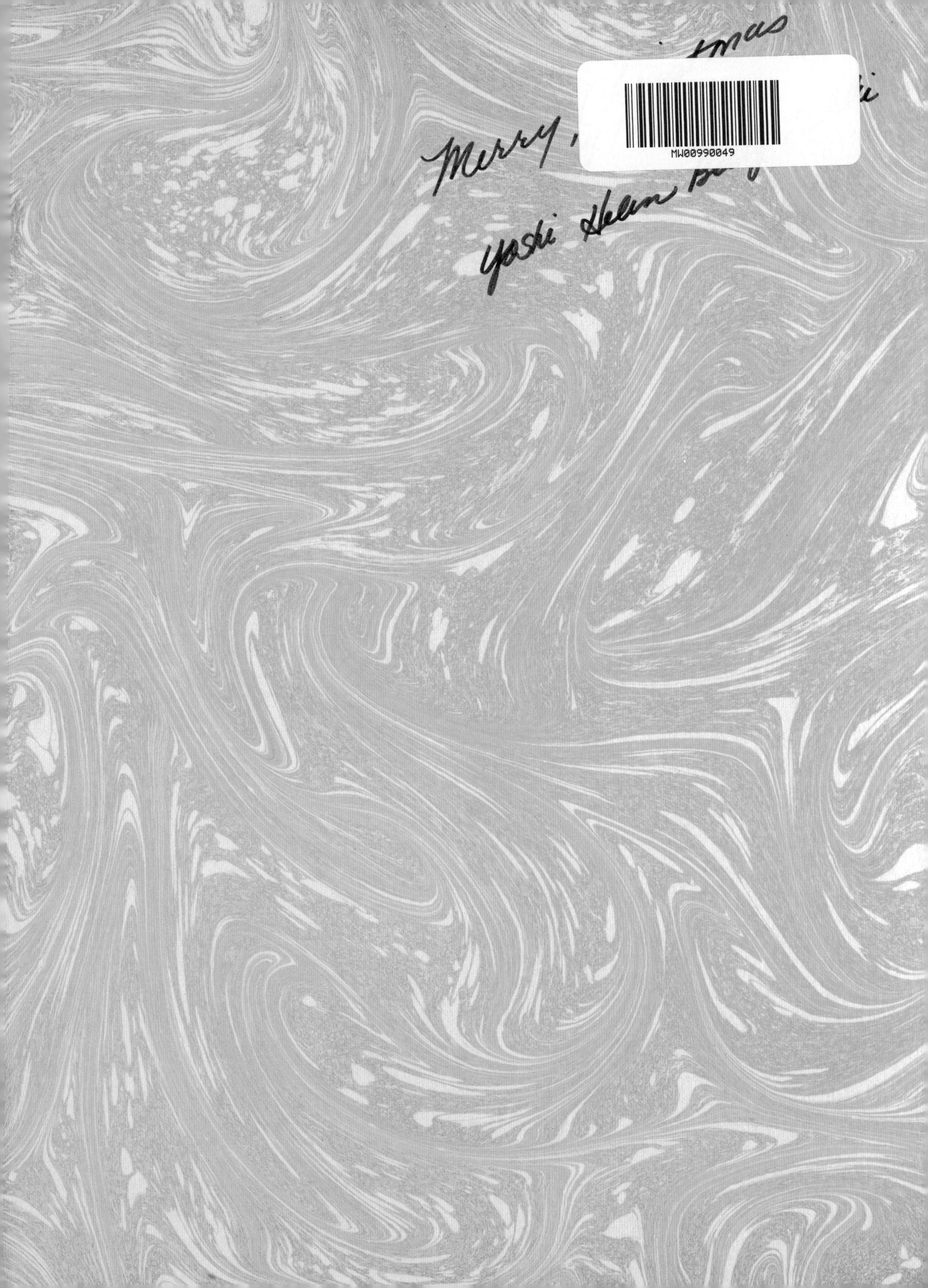
MW00990049

THE HAWAIIAN CALABASH

RIGHT: *Ancient Hawaiian calabashes are considered cultural treasures by residents, and calabashes both old and new are often prominently displayed in island homes. The 10″ tall ancient handmade umeke kou in this picture is displayed framed by a traditional maile and ilima lei.*

The early 1900s watercolor still life by Honolulu artist Helen Kelly depicts an old traditional Hawaiian wooden bowl overflowing with a floral decoration of maile and ilima leis displayed on a lauhala mat.

THE HAWAIIAN CALABASH

IRVING JENKINS

PHOTOGRAPHY
HUGO DE VRIES

A PROJECT OF

KAUAI MUSEUM
THE BERNICE P. BISHOP MUSEUM DEPARTMENT OF ANTHROPOLOGY
THE HONOLULU ACADEMY OF ARTS

PUBLISHED BY EDITIONS LIMITED

Published by Editions, Ltd.
PO Box 10558
Honolulu, Hawaii 96816

Book Design by Irving Jenkins

Library of Congress Cataloging in Publication Data

Jenkins, Irving.
The Hawaiian Calabash / Irving Jenkins; photography Hugo de Vries. — 1st ed.
Includes bibliography and index
1. Hawaiians—Material culture. 2. Containers—Hawaii. 3. Hawaiians—Antiquities.
4. Hawaii—Antiquities. I. Kauai Museum. II. Bernice Pauahi Bishop Museum. Dept. of Anthropology. III. Title.
DU624.65.J45 1989 88-36707
996.9—dc19 CIP

ISBN 0-915013-09-6

First Edition 1989
Second Edition 1995
Printed in Hong Kong

To Juliet Rice Wichman
(1901 – 1987)

RIGHT: *The large handmade kou bowl on the koa centertable is 16 1/4" wide, 6 3/4" high, and was carved by Puakoa, son of high chief Kaiana. It is still in possession of Puakoa's heirs and is the only old handmade Hawaiian calabash known to still carry with it the name of the craftsman who carved it.*

Little is known of Puakoa's life, but in ***History Makers of Hawaii*** *author A. Grove Day wrote of his illustrious father: "Kaiana's high rank, his fame in war, and his knowledge of the use of foreign weapons, gave him much prestige and he was a valuable ally to Kamehameha for several years. Kaiana was killed fighting against Kamehameha at Nuuanu Pali in 1795."*

The book in the foreground is open to a portrait of Kaiana, the first Hawaiian chief to travel abroad, done during his visit to China in 1788. He is pictured at age thirty-two, standing well over six feet tall and dressed in a traditional Hawaiian feather cloak and helmet which he wore on the streets of Canton and Macao. English Captain Nathanial Portlock wrote: "Tyaana was generally indulged in walking about wherever his inclination led him; and on these occasions he constantly wore a beautiful feathered cap and cloak, and carried a spear in his hand to denote himself to be a person of grandeur and distinction; nor did he like to wear any other dress, except the maro, which is always worn by Sandwich islanders about the waist."

Puakoa was born some five years before Kaiana's death in 1795 and lived until 1869. He lived in relative obscurity as a result of his father's defection from Kamehameha's ranks. This shift in allegiance, which took place on the eve of the decisive battle of Nuuanu, caused Kaiana's heirs to lose their standing, privileges and possessions in the new kingdom.

As this bowl recalls the life and deeds of Kaiana, so umeke in ancient times often served the same purpose, preserving and honoring the memory of an ancestor for succeeding generations.

In 1900 a newspaper in the United States described the esteem in which these bowls were held by residents of Hawaii: "It is only here that they are appreciated as the 'diamonds and gold of Hawaii.' There are some collections here which are not for sale at any price. Many of these collections of calabashes have historical value, having been handed down from generation to generation since the time of the first Kamehameha."

TABLE OF CONTENTS

PREFACE

Since the first edition of *The Hawaiian Calabash* was published a number of new calabashes of historic significance have come to light. These important pieces are illustrated in this second edition and a number of new photographs have been added. There are also some additions to the text. The few mistakes and omissions that appeared in the first edition have also been corrected.

It is hoped that these new additions and corrections will further contribute to the growing appreciation and study of this craft which ancient Hawaiians advanced far beyond any other Pacific Island culture.

INTRODUCTION

This work traces the history of traditional Hawaiian containers, called "calabashes," made of wood, gourd, coconut, and fiber. The English word "calabash" was probably derived from the French and Spanish words *calebasse* and *calabaza,* both meaning gourds or pumpkins. The source of these words was perhaps the Persian word for melon, *kharbuz.* By extension, the term "calabash" came to be used by natives and foreigners alike to refer to gourd-like containers of various materials. In 1779, ship's surgeon David Samwell referred to Hawaiian gourds as "calibashes"; Capt. James Cook, writing at the same time, is cited by the *Oxford English Dictionary* as the first source of the extended, generic use of the word calabash.

Gourds were by far the most common containers used by all levels of Hawaiian society. The most beautiful containers, however, and perhaps the most difficult to make, were the Hawaiian bowls made of wood. Perhaps because of their superb craftsmanship, beauty, and utility, they have come to represent, in the minds of many today, ancient Hawaiian culture itself. A large portion of this study, therefore, is devoted to wooden calabashes, the woods used to make them, the methods of carving and repairing these containers, and the manner in which the tradition of bowl making was continued into the twentieth century.

Unfortunately, very little of the ancient history and significance of traditional bowls was preserved, nor have records been kept concerning the craftsmen who made them. Of the few significant writings that do discuss traditional Hawaiian wooden bowls, only one, by David Malo, was written in the nineteenth century; the other three were written in the twentieth century. David Malo's discussion of the traditional methods of bowl making is included in his historic book on Hawaiian culture, *Moolelo Hawaii [Hawaiian Antiquities],* in a chapter written in the 1840s titled "Concerning Houses, their Furnishings and Decorations." His entire discussion of bowls, however, is only a bare outline, consisting of just three paragraphs:

LEFT: *Shown here are calabashes of gourd, wood, and coconut, the traditional materials Hawaiians used for containers. The lidded container in the background, with a woven covering, and the covered gourd in front of it were used for storage of both foods and dry goods. Next to the covered gourd is a tall-necked, stoppered gourd that was used exclusively to hold drinking water. The designs on this gourd were applied by a process, now lost, developed by Hawaiians. In front of the water bottle is a kou wood food bowl. These wooden bowls traditionally imitate gourd forms. However, because craftsmen were able to completely control their shapes and final finish, they are now justifiably looked upon as pieces of art. This bowl was the property of George Hueu Davis, son of Isaac Davis, an English seaman who became a high chief and intimate advisor to Kamehameha I.*

In the foreground is a coconut drinking cup that held the soporific awa. This cup would have been used only by a priest of the ancient Hawaiian religion as indicated by its shape, cut lengthwise from the nut.

The awa cup is 6 3/4" long, while the wooden food bowl behind it is 5 1/8" high and 11" wide across the rim. The covered gourd storage container is 12 1/4" high, the gourd water bottle 14 7/8" high, and the container with woven covering stands 22 3/4" high.

"The container was an appropriate thing in which to place food. The containers of the old Hawaiians were of two varieties, the wood container and the gourd container.

"Those who were skilled in the art of carving containers carved them from several woods, but kou was the wood of which most containers were carved; sections of wood were cut out and some were shaped into umeke and others into ipu kai; some were dug out deep within and for the ipu kai the wood was made flat on top [indicating a thick-rimmed shallow bowl].

"Then it was scoured with coral inside and out; when this was done it was rubbed again with pumice; when the pumice rubbing was done it was rubbed with a polishing stone; and when this was done it was rubbed with charcoal; and when this was done with bamboo leaf; and when this was done with dried banana leaf and kapa; the container may have required that you make a cover and a net; the umeke was for the vegetable food and the ipu kai was for the meat."

The next work to discuss wooden bowls was published in 1908 by the first director of the Bernice Pauahi Bishop Museum, William Brigham. His book, *The Ancient Hawaiian House,* included a chapter titled "House Belongings: The Furniture of a House." Brigham was the first to write of the Hawaiian wooden bowl as an important art form. "In no one thing," he wrote, "has the artistic taste of the old Hawaiian come into closer touch with the best taste of older civilized nations than in the making of wood bowls." Although there is little technical or historic information in his book, Brigham reviewed the different bowl shapes in the museum collection and compiled a list of the entire collection with measurements and comments as to size, type of wood, and shape.

In 1957, the Bishop Museum Press published *The Arts and Crafts of Hawaii.* In a section on wooden bowls, author Sir Peter Buck quoted heavily from an undated, unpublished paper by Henry Kekahuna titled "The Hawaiian Art of Making Wooden Calabashes." Kekahuna's paper, in Hawaiian, gave a very detailed description of the making of wooden bowls. Kekahuna was a Honolulu accountant who made identification and preservation of ancient Hawaiian historical sites his hobby. His knowledge of these sites apparently came from an elder Hawaiian, Naluahine Kaopua, who was born in the Kona district of the Big Island in 1864 and was still living on Hawaii. Kekahuna first met Kaopua in the 1940s and was astounded by Kaopua's memory: "It is his predominant characteristic that is of greatest interest and value — a phenomenal memory . . . a memory that has enabled him, during his roving, care-free life as a sailor and cowboy, to store his mind with hundreds of names, and many of the old stories, of tiny unknown places of interest, not only on his own island of Hawaii, but also on others, especially remote Kauai. Naturally he kindled within my companion and me the ambition to perpetuate all we could of his inexhaustible knowledge."

Kekahuna's paper was almost certainly written in the voice of Naluahine Kaopua. The "author" often mentioned information coming from his grandparents, stating that he saw bowls being made by them: "Perhaps the methods performed by different people in these branches of the art were varied, but those which now I present are as I saw them performed by my grandparents." Kaopua's grandparents would have been old enough to know the art, as wooden bowls were still being made on Hawaii in the middle 1800s.

Kekahuna's paper was divided into six chapters, with an introduction and an index naming bowl types and their uses. All aspects of the making of wooden bowls were covered, from tools used, through carving, curing, polishing, and mending. Kekahuna's paper was certainly the most important written on Hawaiian wooden bowls.

These few sources, along with casual observations written by foreign residents and visitors, are the only primary writings describing this ancient Hawaiian craft. As a result, much of this present study touching upon the early history of the subject is based on fragmentary accounts and observations.

The latter part of this book discusses calabashes made of gourd, coconut, and fiber.

Because of their prevalence, more historical information exists about gourds than about any other Hawaiian container. Gourds were common among Hawaiians well into the nineteenth century. However, they were seldom preserved or collected unless decorated, and even decorated gourds of the chiefs are extremely rare today.

Ancient coconut bowls and cups, once common, are also rare. More modern containers made of coconut became very popular in the nineteenth century when craftsmen added bases and wooden covers to create elegant souvenirs.

Ancient Hawaiian basketry is the rarest and most mysterious form of Hawaiian calabashes. Very little was recorded of these containers in either Hawaiian tradition or by early Western visitors. The few specimens that remain were made with skill and are beautiful. Who made them, how Hawaiians developed the craft, and at what time period, are among the questions for which there seem to be few answers.

The final part of this study discusses the traditional Hawaiian foods and feasts for which calabashes were used. The majority of wooden and gourd containers were made to hold the thick, liquid vegetable staple, poi, and visitors writing of their experiences in Hawaii seldom failed to mention their reaction to first tasting it. The traditional Hawaiian feast, the luau, is also an obligation for all visitors; accounts, which are very often amusing, appeared regularly in their journals, diaries, and publications. In the nineteenth century, special wooden and coconut containers were developed to be used exclusively at these functions.

Although this study attempts to record what is known of Hawaiian calabashes, it also reveals how much has been lost. It is hoped that this work, by furthering an appreciation of these unique and beautiful Hawaiian craft forms, will encourage their continued study and preservation.

Two Hawaiian glossaries, made up of words relating to traditional containers, have been included for comparison at the end of this study. The first is drawn from Lorrin Andrews's *A Dictionary of the Hawaiian Language,* first published in 1865; the second is from Pukui and Elbert's *Hawaiian Dictionary,* first published in 1957. The reader will find variants, omissions, and contradictions between the two, which is further demonstration of the need for continued study in this area.

There has been and there continues to be considerable disagreement and inconsistency concerning orthography, and particularly the use of diacritical marks, in written Hawaiian. To correct all of the variants in the many historical passages quoted here would have meant repeated and cumbersome intrusion of brackets and notes. Therefore, odd spellings are left as they appeared in the original texts unless a confusion of meaning would have resulted. All diacritical marks have been omitted from the text to further simplify it, and to aid the reader. In the glossaries, however, diacritical marks have been retained for reference.

PART I

CALABASHES OF WOOD

LEFT: *These two Hawaiian containers from the British Museum illustrate the range of forms achieved by bowl carvers, from simple and elegant spherical forms to complex sculpture. The smooth, highly polished storage bowl imitates the gourds that were the Hawaiians' earliest containers. The bowl and its cover are of kou. The bowl stands 7 1/2" high and measures 12 1/2" across the rim.*

The small utilitarian sculpture in the foreground is 10 1/2" long. The human figure that connects the two small bowls wears a fiber loin cloth; plugs of white hair and red feathers are inserted as a headdress. A cord is fastened around the figure's hands. The inlaid eyes appear to be pearl shell, as are the ten circular discs inlaid to indicate arm and leg joints. The figure originally seems to have been stained black, while the bowls were left their natural color. The small bowl at the figure's feet is 1 5/8" high and 3 1/8" across the rim. The larger bowl connected to the figure's hands is 2 1/8" high and 3 1/2" across the rim. These bowls may have been intended to hold condiments.

THE "AGE OF WOOD"

Capt. James Cook first touched the Hawaiian Islands in 1778 at the northern island of Kauai. Among the many articles of native manufacture he described during his short stay were wooden bowls: "Their wooden dishes and bowls . . . are of the [kou] tree, or *cordia,* as neat as if made in our turning-lathe, and perhaps better polished."

Hawaiian wooden bowls such as Cook observed are among the most beautiful containers made by any Pacific culture. They are traditionally of rounded form, inspired, perhaps, by the Hawaiians' earliest natural containers: gourds and coconuts. The surface both within and without was worked until very smooth, with the exterior well polished. The external surface decoration of these smooth, rounded forms was limited to the figured grain of the wood itself, and incorporated the dramatic contrast of light sapwood isolated against dark swirling heartwood. They were made to contain both food and dry goods.

Returning later that year, Cook landed on the southern-most island, Hawaii, where again the fine wooden bowls were seen. The expedition physician, twenty-seven-year-old David Samwell, was also impressed with their quality and described them in his journal much as Cook had: "The bowls are of various sizes from two Gallons to a quart, they are made of the red [kou] tree exceedingly neat and well polished & to appearance are as perfect round as if they had been formed in a lathe."

At some early time in their history, Hawaiians had begun making containers out of wood to augment those of gourd and coconut. But unlike those of gourd and coconut, containers of wood required a great deal of labor to make, and it is probable that they were first developed primarily as status symbols.

The 1915 *Bishop Museum Handbook* stated that "the Hawaiians, like their kinsmen throughout Polynesia, did not make pottery but had recourse to the vegetable kingdom, and the large umeke of wood used for poi were wonderfully well made and of good form; by far the best specimens of Hawaiian woodwork."

Henry Kekahuna, in his treatise on Hawaiian calabashes, stated: "There was no chief or chiefess who lacked wooden calabashes or platters, for these things were greatly esteemed and most precious to them. . . . Vessels made from the bitter-gourd were those mostly used by the

LEFT: *These three wooden bowls from the Vienna Museum of Ethnology were collected on Capt. James Cook's visits to Hawaii in 1778 and 1779. The tall bowl in the background is 7 1/8" high, while the low bowl in the middle is 3 1/8" high. The oblong bowl in the foreground, with a figure carved on one end, is 3" high and 8 5/8" long. The bowl itself widens from 1 1/2" near the end with the figure, to 3 1/2" at the other end, forming a kind of scoop. The piece is of highly polished kou. The inlaid eyes of the figure are of pearl shell with polished, black, rounded insets of an unidentified material for pupils. The bowl itself is very thin throughout, tapering to a sharp, crisp edge. The core of the log from which the bowl was carved can be seen at each end of the bowl. Where the figure was not polished, on the chest and the inside of arms, legs, and chin, very small knife-like tool marks can be clearly seen.*

common people, while such trees as kou and others were forbidden to them in that remote period."

William Brigham, writing of wooden bowls in his 1908 publication, *The Ancient Hawaiian House,* stated: "From their material they were more durable than the vessels of gourd; from the labor bestowed upon them they were proportionately valued; and like the precious feather work were preserved in families, and handed down from generation to generation."

Kekahuna wrote of the reverence in which some bowls were held: "Calabashes and wooden platters were highly esteemed, favorite articles to the ancestors of these people. The very best of their favorite calabashes were given various personal names. . . . If the people named their calabashes in honor of their favorite chiefs, or relatives who had performed celebrated deeds, or their ancestors, such calabashes would be cherished as being very sacred. Only a favorite child (keiki punahele) or grandchild would be free to use them. Sometimes a favorite child or grandchild was named after one of these sacred calabashes through family connection, in which case the calabash would become a most precious object, an heirloom for this child to hand down to his posterity.

"The most highly esteemed and favorite calabashes had chants composed for them as though they were human beings, and when they were placed at the table one would hear their owners, with proud countenances, chanting of the celebrated deeds of those for whom they were named."

An article in the *Honolulu Academy of Arts Bulletin* once described such bowls as particularly representative of the Hawaiian character: "The temperament of the Hawaiians is most adequately expressed in woodwork. . . . The Hawaiian bowls were not only appropriate for their uses, but were objects of beauty. They owe their beauty and charm to the dignity of their undecorated surfaces, to the grace of their lines, and to the grains of the well-chosen woods used in their making."

Hawaiian craftsmen traditionally preferred a particular wood, kou, for these containers. William Shaler, visiting in 1804, commented on its beauty: "They make, besides, of a very beautiful species of wood peculiar to these islands, a great variety of table utensils, such as bowls, platters, and vessels of different sizes, in the form of calabashes."

During the late eighteenth century, voyagers who followed Cook continued to be impressed with the elegance of these bowls. Capt. George Dixon, in 1787, wrote: "Another species of ingenuity met with amongst these people is carving. . . . The bowls and dishes are made of a kind of wood resembling ebony and are finished with a proportion and polish equal, if not superior, to any thing made by our turners."

In 1791, Ebenezer Townsend was particularly impressed with bowls belonging to King Kamehameha I: "The King brought his pvoy or puoy and some wooden utensils of very neat workmanship; some dishes to hold three gallons, made of wood as handsome as mahogany, round as if turned on a lathe, as well polished, and the top fitted as well as if done by our country cabinet makers."

In 1792, Kamehameha, who eventually would unite the islands into one kingdom, was given a gift of Western tableware. This was probably the first to be owned by any Hawaiian chief. Thomas Manby recorded the gift of Capt. George Vancouver: "Maiha Maiha had a high respect for the English Nation, and had a great desire to imitate us in many things. . . . The king was supplied with all kinds of culinary utensils, and also furnished with some plates, knives and forks, glasses, etc."

Twenty-six years after Vancouver's civilizing gift, Capt. Vasilii Golovnin, visiting in 1818, found Kamehameha's collection of imported dining utensils impressive: "He has a big collection of European objects, some of which are very costly. For instance, a set of table silverware, crystal of rare workmanship, porcelain objects."

Golovnin also found the high chiefs as a class beginning to acquire Western utensils: "The islanders make their eating vessels out of gourds, coconut shells, and a wood called [kou]. . . . The chiefs, however, are beginning to use European dishes: in the house of any chief one may now find our tea kettles, cups, glasses, wine glasses, bottles, etc."

When Golovnin entertained chiefs on board his ship, he found them surprisingly sophisticated in the use of Western tableware: "At the table our guests used knives and forks as expertly as any European and after each course they would put the spoon, knife, and fork on the plate to have the waiter change them."

The small nation founded by Kamehameha was not only trying to assimilate Western cultural appurtenances and manners, but was also quickly appropriating other aspects of Western civilization as well. By the time of Golovnin's visit, a national flag had been adopted and the small port of Honolulu was protected by a stone fort with a cannon. Golovnin could find nothing to compare with these advancements in either Russian settlements on the Pacific rim of Asia or Spanish outposts along the Pacific coast of North America. He wrote: "What we saw excelled anything that we had seen in the Russian and the Spanish settlements of this area, and when we realized that we were looking at a stone fort, ships, and cannon belonging to a savage people who still go about naked, that these people had a national flag, etc., we could not help but marvel at the degree of their enlightenment, which they owe to their trade with America."

In 1819, French Capt. Louis de Freycinet also noted that although traditional wooden and gourd containers remained in general use, Western tableware was beginning to be used by chiefs: "The poé is served in enormous calabashes; the rest of the food on wooden dishes of various sizes. The chiefs of highest rank, however, are now beginning to use platters of Chinese porcelain, glassware, etc."

Perhaps because Western tableware remained relatively rare and was reserved for special occasions, such as entertaining Western visitors, craftsmanship among Hawaiian bowl makers remained high, and Freycinet was as impressed with the bowls as Capt. Cook had been forty-one years earlier: "As for wooden platters, which are also used for serving food, the skill with which they are finished would not be disdained even by our most able wood carvers."

Kamehameha had died three months before Freycinet's visit in August. He was succeeded by his son Liholiho as Kamehameha II. In return for fealty, the high chiefs demanded to share in the barter of sandalwood which Kamehameha had restricted to government control. The sandalwood tree was plentiful on all the islands and, in 1811, eight years before Kamehameha's death, Western traders had established a market for it in China, where it was valued primarily as incense. Previously, the provisioning of ships had been the chiefs' only means of acquiring foreign goods. Sandalwood thus became Hawaii's first major article of export and, for the first time, traders began importing large selections of goods, primarily from China and some from the United States. Although the common people were largely excluded from the benefits of this trade, the high chiefs began to accumulate Western goods in large quantities.

In 1819, Kamehameha II abolished the ancient religion of the kingdom. Suddenly, the chiefs could no longer forbid commoners to acquire certain possessions, such as kou wood bowls, simply by declaring them kapu, or forbidden by divine right. Nevertheless, the upper classes continued to reserve all valuable possessions for themselves through other sanctions. Taxation and land ownership were still controlled by the king, and the people found their lives generally unchanged. Although a declaration of rights in 1839 gave Hawaiians some right of property, in 1840 Lt. Charles Wilkes found commoners still unable to acquire worldly goods that would have enriched their lives: "Indeed, no valuable article could be held by the lower classes; for if not directly falling under some of the heads of taxation, a mode would be devised by some one of their superiors to enable him to take it, or persuasion was resorted to, until it was given up to satisfy the demands." Danish visitor Capt. Steen Bille noted this class prerogative in 1846: "Everywhere the difference was evident. Houses, dresses, food, baths, everything they kept for themselves; every touch with the people was contamination."

The first example of Western domestic lifestyle that the chiefs were able to study closely was that of the New England missionaries, who first arrived in 1820. These missionaries arrived with the stated goal of not only Christianizing but Westernizing the Hawaiian population. They served as advisors and models for dress, manners, and furnishings, which the chiefs copied.

In 1821, sandalwood trader Charles Bullard recorded the chiefs' growing eagerness to purchase Western household goods: "Some crockery and glassware could do, everything necessary for table use, also table knives and forks — gentlemen who have been here have given them some idea of dinner parties, and they are not backwards in following foreign example. . . . Everyone that comes brings better and better goods and good goods, and such as they have not seen will sell when common ones will not."

Hiram Bingham, leader of the missionary group in Honolulu, wrote the following year of the effect that the mission families were having on the high chiefesses after only two years: "Kamamalu, Kapiolani, Kaahumanu, Kekauluohi, Kinau, Keopuolani, Kalakua, Kekauonohi, Liliha, Keoua, Kapule, Namahana and others, threw around them an air of rising consequence by . . . noticing, and attempting to imitate what, in the mission families, attracted their attention or appeared sufficiently pleasing . . . to induce them to copy."

That same year, 1822, Charles Stewart visiting in Honolulu noted: "Their food was formerly served in wooden dishes and calabashes; but now generally on china brought by the merchants from Canton."

Another visitor that year, Gilbert Mathison, commented on the resulting decline of native crafts: "Their own native arts and manufactures are sinking fast into neglect and disrepute, and no other arts to supply the place have been taught them." Eagerness to Westernize on the part of the high chiefs was so fervent that Capt. Frederick Beechey, a visitor to Honolulu in 1826, was appalled at their spending: "The houses of the chiefs were furnished with tables and chairs, and those belonging to Kahumana with silk and velvet sofas and cushions. Not content with the comforts of life, they latterly sought its luxuries, and even indulged in its extravagances. Kahumana filled chests with the most costly silks of China, and actually expended four thousand dollars upon the cargo of one vessel. Boki paid three thousand dollars for a service of plate as a present for the king, notwithstanding he had other services in his possession; one of which was of expensively cut glass from Pellatt and Green in London."

By 1830, the islands had been denuded of sandalwood and the trade ended. The chiefs had taken so much merchandise in promise of future deliveries that it was not until the 1840s that

ABOVE AND PAGES 12–13: *Kamehameha was the first chief in Hawaiian history to unite the islands into a single kingdom. He achieved that goal in 1810 and ruled the Kingdom of Hawaii until his death in 1819. The Kamehameha dynasty he founded continued to rule until 1874. Historian Ralph Kuykendall wrote: "Kamehameha is universally recognized as the most outstanding of all Hawaiian chiefs of his own and of all other epochs. We can, perhaps, go even farther and say that he was one of the great men of the world." This watercolor portrait of Kamehameha in a black kapa kihei, from the Honolulu Academy of Arts, was sketched from life by Louis Choris in 1816.*

The nine food bowls on pages 12 and 13 belonged to Kamehameha I. They were never used after his death and subsequently lost their polish. They have, however, retained their fine form and grain patterns. These bowls would most certainly have been made by skilled craftsmen and may be considered among the finest surviving examples of their time.

The large dish on the following page, standing on edge in the background, is 2 3/4" high and 14 7/8" in diameter. The wide bowl in front of it is 8" high and 15 1/4" across the rim. The name of this bowl, "Kapea," is printed on a label pasted to the interior. This is the Hawaiian name for the Southern Cross constellation; it can also mean "the boundary" or "the edge." As with most of the few bowl names that have survived, the reason for this name has been lost. The small poi bowl on the right, in front of Kapea, is 6 3/4" high and 7" across the rim. The tall poi bowl on the left is 9 5/8" high and 7" wide at the rim. The low bowl in the foreground is of koaia, **Acacia koaia Hbd.**, *a species of acacia native to Hawaii and found only in the mountains on Molokai, Maui, and Hawaii. This bowl is 3 1/4" high and 9 3/4" across. The large dish on the following right-hand page, standing on edge in the background, measures 2 3/4" high and 15 3/8" across. The wide bowl in front and to the left of the dish is 8 1/4" high and 15 3/4" across the rim. A printed interior label preserves the name of the bowl, "Aia Iluna," which means "up there" or "there above." The reason for this name is not known.*

The wide bowl in front and to the right of Aia Iluna is named "Aloha Kou," which may signify that it was a favorite bowl. Aloha Kou is 6 7/8" high and 13" across the rim. The dish in the foreground is 3" high and 12" in diameter.

the government could pay off the incurred debts. But the king and high chiefs in Honolulu had been Westernized. In 1824, Russian explorer Capt. Otto von Kotzebue had visited Honolulu and declared: "The domestic utensils, formerly in use here, have entirely disappeared even from the poorest huts; and Chinese porcelain has superseded the manufactures from the gourd or the cocoanut."

This was true only in the town of Honolulu, however. Western goods and influence were slow to spread to areas outside the kingdom's principal harbor.

In 1825, one year after Kotzebue declared that traditional food containers had disappeared from use in Honolulu, Robert Dampier, on Hawaii, did not mention Hawaiians in the small port town of Hilo using crockery. On the contrary, he affirmed that Hawaiian craftsmen there continued to "make very beautiful bowls from a fine hard wood of the Country." Rev. Sereno Bishop also recalled that in the 1830s few Western goods were available to chiefs living in the Kona district on the opposite side of the island from Hilo: "Kona district was the residence of quite a number of chiefs of inferior rank, who were supported by the labor of their many serfs from the produce of the rich uplands. Occasionally a chair or a camphor trunk might be seen in the nice thatched cottages of such natives of rank, besides the mats, tapas, calabashes, and wooden bowls and trays which constituted their furniture." Craftsmen on Hawaii apparently maintained their traditions longer than those on the other islands. French visitor Baron de Thierry commented in 1850: "In the great island of Hawaii above all, the people keep their primitive habits." For Hawaiians living in the remote Waimea area, on the island of Hawaii, owning a shallow wooden dish was still a considerable achievement in 1837, as Rev. Lorenzo Lyons remarked in his mission report that year: "The people are already showing very creditable improvement. Not only church members, but others have built them neat and comfortable dwellings, and some have furnished themselves with tables, seats, wooden dishes."

As Western utensils became available to the chiefs, traditional wooden bowls were not discarded, but carefully put away as heirlooms. The importance attached to these bowls was considerable. For example, when Oahu Governor High Chief Mataio Kekuanaoa's ancestors' bowls were destroyed along with a great amount of government property during a political dispute with a French warship in 1843, Consul General William Miller wrote of the incident: "One of the things which they appear most to regret is the destruction by the French, when in possession of the Fort . . . of numerous wooden Calabashes of exquisite and laborious workmanship, and of many other ancient relics, which had been preserved with great care for several generations, & were inherited by the interesting little Princess Victoria, destined to be the future 'Premier.' The articles were broken to pieces and thrown into a well in the Fort."

By the 1840s, Hawaiians even in remote districts were becoming familiar with Western utensils and manners, due to the efforts of American missionaries. In 1846, visitor Gordon Hall attended a feast which was intended as a lesson in manners for Hawaiians at Lahaina, Maui: "The house was filled with people and the whole was conducted with decency and decorum. This is for the purpose of learning the natives to eat off from tables and to use knives and forks. After partaking bountifully of this collation Mr. Baldwin addressed the assembly commending their good behavior and improvement in their mode of living."

In 1848, the discovery of gold in California and the subsequent demand for food for the miners brought a large amount of money to every part of the kingdom. Lyons, in the remote district of Waimea, had complained in 1837: "These people have no money to contribute to the church. Money is very seldom seen." But in 1849 he reported: "A great call for potatoes from California. . . . Some never had so much cash before — never had any before! Many natives growing rich." Similarly, in 1848, Laura Judd had written: "The discovery of gold in California, in fabulous quantities, is reported, and produces a great sensation in our little realm. Provisions are high in California. . . . There are already twenty-seven vessels running between the Islands and the coast. Everyone expects to make his fortune."

Even in outlying areas, money and luxuries became available as never before. In 1850, when Lyons attended religious festivities in remote Waipio Valley on Hawaii, he admired the Western tableware now being used: "In some places there was quite a display of tables, and splendid tablecloths, soup dishes, plates, etc."

Although the economic bubble burst in 1851, fundamental changes in the common use of traditional wooden calabashes had been affected. Unfortunately, during the following decade, the traditional tree from which wooden bowls had been made began dying throughout the kingdom due to the ravages of an introduced insect. By 1870, then, the formal end had come to what William Brigham termed Hawaii's "Age of Wood."

TRADITIONAL SHAPES AND SIZES OF WOODEN CALABASHES

Traditional Hawaiian wooden bowls were fashioned into many different shapes and sizes for various uses. Some were designed with special features and others were carved with figures. The classic Hawaiian bowl, however, was fully rounded and clearly reflected its counterpart in nature, the gourd.

The traditional bowl, while being round and full, nevertheless took several distinct forms: tall bowls, those whose heights and widths are nearly equal; wide bowls, those whose widths moderately exceed their heights; and low bowls, those whose widths far exceed their heights. The Hawaiians also carved plates and platters. All of these forms were fashioned in a range of sizes.

Tall bowls were carved from the trunk or branch of the tree with the heartwood core running vertically through the bottom of the bowl. Typically, the walls of these bowls are thin and often the bottoms are very thick. This may have been, in part, for stability, but the thickness also reinforced the weak endgrain of the bottom. The inspiration for this shape came from the fruit of the hala, or pandanus tree, and the name by which these bowls are known, *pua-hala,* refers to their shape.

Wide bowls were generally made in medium to large sizes. The finest of this type were carved from tree crotches so that three heartwood cores were spaced evenly around the sides of the bowl. This created a rhythmic swirling pattern that makes bowls of this shape most beautiful and dramatic. Much of the surface area of the walls of these bowls consists of the weak endgrain of the heartwood cores, and as a result they are carved with thick walls. The thickness is usually consistent throughout, but thinner areas may be found on the bottom of the bowls, where the

LEFT: *The containers pictured here illustrate the three classic Hawaiian wooden bowl shapes. Their pleasing, rounded forms clearly reflect the gourd, which was their model.*

Distinctive sapwood designs are unique to each shape. The tall kou bowl carved from an upright log displays patterning around its widest circumference.

The wide kou bowl was carved from the crotch of a tree and the three heartwood cores can be seen; the surrounding yellow sapwood dips from the rim three times.

The low kou bowl is carved from half of a log, avoiding the core. The sapwood dips down from the rim on opposite sides or curves up from the bottom on opposing sides, as seen here, depending on how the bowl was cut from the log.

The low bowl in the foreground is 3 3/8" high and 11 1/4" across the rim. The wide bowl is 7" high and 10" across the rim. The tall bowl in the background is 10" tall and 10" wide.

The exterior surfaces of the bowls pictured here have been refinished with shellac. When wooden bowls became popular to collect near the end of the nineteenth century, ancient methods of polishing were no longer practiced. Bowls were therefore treated as any fine piece of contemporary woodwork. They were given glossy shellac, French-polish finishes that enhanced the grain of the wood to finest effect. Visitor Anne Prescott, in her book ***Hawaii****, published in 1891, described the bowls she saw at that time as "very handsome, as highly polished as rosewood, and often 'a thing of beauty.' "*

woodgrain is the strongest. The use of endgrain around the sides also makes this among the most stable of shapes to carve, with little stress to cause warping.

Low bowls, made in all sizes, were generally carved from one half of a block of wood so that the heartwood core just missed either the bottom or rim of the bowls. They are usually of even thickness throughout.

Plates were mostly made in small to medium sizes. Of these Brigham wrote: "They cannot be considered distinctively Hawaiian as the form is found all over the world, and there is hanging before me, as I write, a mahogany platter or dish that my Carib workman carved for me, entirely without my suggestion, quite like the Hawaiian ones . . . except for material."

Hawaiian craftsmen also made a rounded form that looks similar to plates, but which actually is a cover. Wood covers are relatively rare and can be distinguished from dishes by the presence of raised edges that prevent the lids from slipping. Brigham noted: "A cover was a necessary addition. . . . We have noted that large flat gourds were often, indeed generally, used for this purpose, especially among the poorer class, the fine umeke usually had a cover made for them."

Most covers, like low bowls and dishes, were carved from one half of a log, avoiding the heartwood core and incorporating little endgrain. Some covers were made from a section of the tree crotch, avoiding the heartwood centers, and show a dramatic grain.

Traditional wooden bowls and plates were made in a full range of sizes, from small ones for children, holding perhaps two cups, to very large nineteenth-century display pieces holding gallons.

Very small heirloom bowls were sometimes carved after the birth of a favorite child. Often the wood came from a tree that had been planted over the afterbirth of grandparents. The bowl would be used by the child as its personal food bowl. Kekahuna described this pleasant custom: "After being weaned from the breast of the mother such a child would be fed its first hard food, or *mana-ai*, out of this new wooden calabash and platter, which became his personal food-container. It was called a 'mouthful-calabash' (umeke mana-ai), and became a sacred heirloom for this child, to be handed down to his posterity."

The largest wooden bowl in the Bishop Museum is almost twenty inches high and twenty-six inches wide at the rim, with a volume of thirty-three gallons. While small bowls were made before Western contact, it is likely that very large bowls were commonly made by craftsmen only afterwards, and only with the introduction of iron. Very large wooden bowls may have become more common especially after 1795, when Kamehameha I united Oahu, Maui, Lanai, Molokai, and Hawaii under his rule. During this unprecedented period of peace and developing sense of nationhood, all crafts flourished and expanded.

By the middle of the nineteenth century, however, many traditional Hawaiian crafts had disappeared, due to the importation of Western goods and ideas. In 1869, Queen Emma lamented this loss in a letter: "Our beautiful as well as old and original articles of native manufacture such as dress ornaments, tools, impliments of husbandry, warfare, etc. etc. have become so scarce by the universal adoption of foreign habits that nearly all purely Hawaiian things have quite disappeared from disuse."

Nevertheless, there is some indication that demand for large bowls made of kou increased among the wealthy residents in the 1870s, when kou trees began dying throughout the kingdom and it became apparent that traditional kou bowls would soon be made no more. Many residents during this decade had bowls carved or turned from the wood whenever it could be found. In 1871, High Chiefess Kapiolani secured some kou wood and wrote to a relative: "Do not forget about our kou. I have asked Malaihi to remind you to remind Aikake who is the person I have instructed to send it to me. If both, you and Kapule, will assist him, it would be well."

That same month, Queen Emma was also able to find a few pieces of kou, while visiting on Kauai: "Kapo is taking back two pieces of kou wood on this steamer one that has been hewn on the outside but not hollowed out on the inside and one has not been cut at all."

Despite the disappearance of both traditional craftsmen and the favored wood, large and even enormous commemorative display bowls in traditional shapes continued to be made into the twentieth century. These bowls, however, were carved or turned from logs of milo, kamani, or koa.

The vogue for large display pieces, commemorating ancient Hawaiian culture, caused small, intimate heirloom bowls to fall out of fashion and no longer be made.

ABOVE: *Low bowls almost never incorporate heartwood cores. The kou bowls seen here were carved with the log core near the bottom of the bowl. The sapwood decoration on this type of bowl dips from the lip on opposing sides. When low bowls are carved with the core close to the rim, the sapwood wraps around the bottom like a band, usually terminating near the rim on opposing sides.*

Anthropologist Kenneth Emory wrote of this shape: "The Hawaiians had one low bowl with a thick rim.... The Hawaiians probably brought this low bowl with them when they came to these islands, for it is the only Hawaiian bowl closely resembling the bowls used elsewhere in Polynesia. Most of the Hawaiian bowls were probably developed locally."

Low bowls were made in all sizes. Their rim diameter far exceeded their height, as illustrated by the bowl in the foreground, which is 6" high and 13" wide at the rim.

LEFT: *Circular dishes were often carved with a thicker bottom, gradually tapering to a thin edge. The most beautiful of these dishes, like the bowls, are gracefully spherical, with a rounded bottom. These three dramatically grained kou pieces from the Honolulu Academy of Arts display the small to medium sizes in which dishes are usually found.*

The largest plate in this picture stands 3" high and is 15 1/2" across. The smallest plate is 1 1/2" high and 7 3/8" wide.

Bishop Museum ethnologist Roger Rose wrote of Hawaiian dishes: "Wooden plates were probably used by individual chiefs, but persons of lesser rank had to be content with leaves or simple gourd plates and bowls."

ABOVE: *The most dramatic wide bowls were carved from tree crotches. These bowls are characterized by at least three heartwood cores spaced around their circumferences. The contrasting sapwood partially encircles the upper portion of each core. These bowls have thick rims and the wall thickness is even throughout the bowl.*

Repairs are most often found at the three heartwood cores, which tend to be soft. Often, plugs were inserted at the time of carving to reinforce them. These areas were also susceptible to rot and later repairs were often necessary to entirely replace the cores.

Some wide bowls were carved from the log rather than from the tree crotch, as was the bowl in the background. These bowls have the same characteristics as tall bowls, with thin walls and sapwood encircling the widest diameter.

The rim diameter of wide bowls is always moderately larger than the bowl height. The bowl in the back measures 9 1/4" high by 12 7/8" wide, the foreground bowl is 5 1/4" high and 9 1/4" wide.

ABOVE: *This wide bowl from the Honolulu Academy of Arts is a fine example of the combination of impressive size, graceful shape, and dramatic color contrast that Hawaiian craftsmen succeeded in achieving with handcarved forms. It measures 9 1/4" high and 15" wide across the rim.*

The value residents placed on these bowls was indicated in a newspaper article published at the turn of the century, titled "CALABASHES ARE HAWAII'S TREASURE." The article went on to report: "Wooden Bowls, Especially if Old and Patched, Are Very Highly Prized....'They are the gold and diamonds of the Hawaiian people,' an old Hawaiian told the Fire Commissioners who are fixing the value of property destroyed in the Great Fire of 1900. The woman was referring only to the calabashes which she had lost in the fire, and not to any precious jewelry or metals, for there are no minerals to be found in the islands."

ABOVE: *Tall bowls are relatively rare. They are characterized by thin walls with thicker bottoms and were made in all sizes. The most beautiful tall bowls have isolated sapwood designs, like islands, spaced at intervals around their widest diameter.*

It may be that these tall bowls, with thick, heavy bottoms and narrow rim openings, were for chiefs traveling. Kamehameha owned a calabash of similar shape which is now in the Bishop Museum with this accession information: "An umekepoi used by Kamehameha I when in a canoe."

The finest of these bowls are equal to or taller than their rim diameters. The two kou bowls on this page measure 10 1/4" high by 8" wide, and 8 5/8" high by 6 5/8" wide.

Because of the difficulty in hollowing these deep bowls, it is said craftsmen devised a method of carefully burning out the interior without damaging the walls of the calabash.

ABOVE: *This tall kou bowl, 10 1/2" high and 7 1/2" wide at the rim, was once part of King Kalakaua's collection of ancient Hawaiian artifacts. Faint shadows of the netting that once surrounded it may still be seen. Anthropologist Kenneth Emory wrote that "nowhere else in Polynesia were there bowls equal in quality or in variety to the Hawaiian umeke. Nothing but shallow bowls were used in all the rest of Polynesia, and in Samoa and Tonga there were few bowls except the kawa bowl....The most typical Hawaiian bowl is the umeke poi. It is perfectly round in cross-section and is tall and thin-lipped."*

ABOVE AND RIGHT: *Covered wooden storage containers are perhaps the most appealing of Hawaiian bowl forms, for their rounded covers complete the spherical form, best imitating the gourd. Often, these bowls are also impressive for their large size.*

The tall kou storage container stands 16 1/4" high overall and holds seven gallons. The smaller kou container, carved from a tree crotch, is 11 1/2" high with its cover and holds four gallons.

Anthropologist Kenneth Emory wrote that "poi bowls were covered when not in use. The cover was

usually any available wooden plate of suitable size. The finer bowls of the chiefs were fitted with a special cover which might be used as a plate." Covers are differentiated from dishes by a raised lip near the rim which prevents the cover from slipping off the bowl.

The covers for wooden bowls were probably most often made of gourd — those made of wood are rare. The small covered gourd in the foreground was collected by Rev. Elias Bond in the 1840s and sent back to Bangor Theological Seminary in Maine.

RIGHT: *These two bowls illustrate the extreme sizes of Hawaiian wooden containers. The small kou bowl with a kukui oil finish was made for and used by Queen Emma when she was a child. Queen Emma was born in 1836, and this bowl was probably made shortly thereafter. It carries the label: "Own little poi bowl of kou wood when a child." This heirloom bowl is very delicate with especially thin walls. The bowl is 3 3/8" high and 4 1/4" across the rim, with a volume of 2 1/3 cups.*

The large kou bowl is 15 1/2" high and 18" across the rim. With a volume of 12 1/2 gallons, or 200 cups, it is more than 80 times the size of Queen Emma's childhood poi bowl.

This bowl has particularly dramatic grain and thin walls. The bottom is thinner than most bowls of this shape and size, making it somewhat delicate. The making of this bowl may have been a deliberate display of skill by the craftsman carving it, being almost entirely shaped on the outside by adze carving alone with very little stone smoothing. Very small, soft ripples can be seen around the bowl, shallow indents from the adze cuts that shaped it. This bowl was once the property of King Kalakaua and was given by him to his premier and minister of foreign affairs, Walter Murray Gibson. It was subsequently purchased by Mrs. Charles Cooke and given in 1927 to the organization she founded, The Honolulu Academy of Arts. The Academy's accession records state this bowl was "brought by Kalakaua from Hawaii," indicating that it originally came from that island. The record also states that this bowl was made during the reign of Kamehameha I, between the years 1794 and 1819. It is very unusual to find recorded information of this nature. No other bowl in the Academy's collection has any information as to where it was made or at what time period. Unfortunately, no record was kept as to the source of this information.

ABOVE AND RIGHT: *This magnificent wide kou bowl was part of Samuel Damon's collection, now in the Bishop Museum. Damon served as minister of finance under King Kalakaua, the Provisional Government, and the Republic. This bowl is a fine example of the combination of impressive size and graceful shape that Hawaiian craftsmen succeeded in achieving with handcarved forms. It is 14" in height, 18" across the rim, and holds 15 gallons.*

The thatched Hawaiian house was a private museum on the grounds of Damon's estate at Moanalua, Oahu. French consul M. G. Bosserondt d'Anglade, stationed in Hawaii from 1889 to 1893, was enchanted with it and wrote: "The Kamehameha Museum was certainly a necessity for the capital of the Hawaiian Kingdom. I prefer, however, the much more modest effort of Mr. D., who has built a replica of an old-time

Kanaka dwelling-house.... Carefully advised by some elderly natives, Mr. D. has directed the construction of a large native hut. The posts hewn from trees and the limbs or branches which serve as beams are bound together by a cord fashioned of plant fibers, and not a single nail has been employed in the construction.

"The result is a vivid recreation of the recent past. Though the museum is very small, it is nevertheless extremely evocative, for here the dream and the reality converge in a place where one can visualize the way Hawaiians lived when they were still close to a state of nature."

This large bowl was probably seen in the museum by d'Anglade, who observed that "the interior is furnished in the style of the time.... In the corner stands a great calabash, a wooden receptacle shaped like a gourd."

ABOVE AND RIGHT: *Very large bowls like this one were very rare and highly prized. This kou bowl, now in the Kauai Museum, is 14" high and 21 1/4" in diameter at the rim.*

The bowl can be seen on the opposite page prominently displayed in the Honolulu living room of Mr. and Mrs. Paul Isenberg in 1910. In a memorandum dated February 15, 1899, Mary Brazil recorded the history of the bowl: "The history of the Calabash bought by Mr. Paul R. Isenberg. This hansom Calabash next to the largest in Honolulu was owned by the high Chief Moehonua and given in aloha by him to his cousin Keaweawahi and sold by his wife Kalelaina who was in great need of money to Mrs. Mary Brazil at that time acting manager of the Woman's Exchange in Honolulu."

This handcarved kou bowl has a flat bottom and beautifully thin walls, with a slight reverse curve at the base. It has a volume of sixteen gallons.

VARIATIONS ON THE TRADITIONAL FORMS

In addition to making the purely rounded forms, Hawaiian craftsmen also produced containers that were elliptical or marked by special features, such as flat bottoms, ribs, and facets. Elliptical platters were made in all sizes. Kekahuna wrote of these containers: "There were various shapes and patterns of dishes in ancient Hawaii. Some were round, others oblong, or elliptical like a poi-board, except that the ends of some were narrowed, and those of others like those of a poi-board, but all of these platters or plates were smaller. One form was the turtle-back, and greatly resembles the back of a turtle. Of the round platters, some were deep and some shallow."

Flat-bottomed bowls were made in all shapes and sizes. Although this type of bowl was practical in the nineteenth century for use on tables, it may not have been unknown before Western discovery. Often the flattened bottom is slightly convex, indicating this was perhaps sometimes an aesthetic element, and not intended only for stability.

Ribbed bowls were also made in all shapes and sizes, with varying numbers of horizontal flutes or planes. It is not known if there was any intended significance to this other than decoration. Anthropologist Adrienne Kaeppler theorized that there may have been symbolic genealogical implications for this ribbing.

Faceted bowls were generally small, and used for individual servings. Brigham wrote of these: "A more difficult feat than shaping a circular bowl was making a polyhedral bowl. . . . The sides are closely equal and beautifully finished, the flat surfaces fading into the curved ones in a most graceful manner."

Each plane is usually slightly concave, and the bottoms of the great majority are flattened. Many of these bowls have a footed base imitating Western stemware.

Faceted bowls are said to have been made only on Maui. When John Stokes and Kenneth Emory of the Bishop Museum were asked to comment on this type of bowl in the Honolulu

LEFT: *Seen here are six uniquely shaped containers. The two large containers at the top of the picture were for food. The one on the left is actually two connected containers. This seems to have been an experiment in economy, replacing six separate bowls with one utensil. It measures 4 1/2" high and 26 5/8" at its greatest length.*

The oblong platter with connected condiment container on the right is from Queen Emma's collection and is 2 1/2" high, 15 3/8" wide, and 33 1/8" long overall.

The small hourglass-shaped bowl was said to belong to Kamehameha I. This bowl is 4 7/8" high and 13 1/4" long. The lute-shaped bowl beneath that was also Kamehameha's and may have been for washing of hands before meals; it is 4 1/8" high and 9 3/4" long. The container with two connected bowls of the same size, just above the lute-shaped bowl, was also for hand washing. It is 3 1/2" high and 13 7/8" long. Each bowl is 6" in diameter. One side held water, the other held leaves that took the place of napkins. This bowl was also part of Queen Emma's collection. The large washbowl above it also has two circular compartments. This bowl is 5 3/8" high and 14 3/4" wide.

Academy of Arts collection in 1940, each had his own opinion. Stokes said: "Within range of stone working . . . would accept style as pre-missionary Lahaina pattern." Emory, however, disagreed: "Could be old, but not ancient. In any case, pedestal is not ancient form. Made bowls like this in the 1830s and 1840s."

This form is rare and may indicate the lifework of one craftsman or family of craftsmen.

Alternatively, these bowls may have been a briefly popular type of bowl carved solely by Lahaina craftsmen. In the 1830s, Lahaina was the most popular port of call in the islands among whalers. This created a souvenir market for Hawaiian craftsmen. In 1832, Francis Bishop wrote of the wide range of craft items for sale at the Lahaina marketplace: "A great number of minor native merchants frequented the market offering for sale hats made of a kind of brab, shells, native rope, mats, barkcloth, calabashes . . . and various other articles."

Another variant of the traditional form was marked by having a curved waist. These bowls are usually somewhat large and are very rare. They may be the work of one craftsman, although Brigham noted: "We may glance briefly at some unusual forms of umeke . . . two with the upper edge developed into three angles and a marked constriction in the waist, features that I am unable to explain. That it was not a mere freak of one workman is shown by the number of examples in this Museum apparently not all from the same hand, nor of the same age. They are well made, solid at the base, and have a fine surface."

It is doubtful that all bowls of this shape were medicine bowls, although a bowl of similar design, but made of tortoise shell, belonged to Kamehameha I and was reputed to be his personal medicine bowl. Of this Brigham wrote: "We know that this was Kamehameha's medicine bowl, and the legend attaches to it that it measured a dose! Even of sweet water it would be a generous one, for it holds a little more than three quarts; but then the king was a mighty man. Does this suggest to us that the other umeke were the utensils of the native *kahuna lapaau* or medicine men, and used in the preparation of their remedies? We know that the old Hawaiians possessed a considerable knowledge of the healing powers of herbs, and that it was by no means their practice to administer insignificant doses."

There are also a few old handmade containers that are unique in form, each a one-of-a-kind artistic endeavor. Some of these singular bowls may have been carved by craftsmen trying to enhance the beauty or practicality of the utensil. Some may have been carved on the whimsical inspiration of the chiefs or chiefesses commissioning them. The individuality of these containers is perhaps an indication that while traditional bowl forms were routinely manufactured, the craft continued to develop as craftsmen experimented with new shapes and designs. A large number of these distinctive pieces were probably carved after Western contact, when the introduction of new forms and tools certainly must have stimulated Hawaiian woodworkers. Thomas Manby, visiting in 1792, was impressed by Hawaiians' intense curiosity toward Western woodworking tools and techniques, and wrote of "the thirst they have to imitate us in the mechanical arts, the chief of which is carpentry."

ABOVE: *Bowls with horizontal ribbing were made in many shapes and sizes and are relatively rare. All knowledge of the significance of this ribbing has been lost. However, anthropologist Adrienne Kaeppler theorized that the ribbing, notching, and backbones in Hawaiian carving generally "can be said to express metaphorically some of the fundamental principles dealing with the importance of genealogy, the family, and the elevation of individuals by virtue of their descent from specific ancestors."*

The large kou bowl in this illustration was once the property of Charles Kanaina, father of King Lunalilo. It has nine horizontal ribs, stands 17 1/4" high, with a rim diameter of 20" and a volume of 19 gallons. The small bowl of kou in front of it has five ribs, stands 5" high and measures 6" across the rim. The wide, low kou bowl on the right has a single rib near the rim. It is 5 1/8" high and 11" wide at the rim.

***ABOVE:** Footed bowls such as these were probably inspired by Western stemware. They are tenuously associated with the island of Maui, particularly the whaling port of Lahaina. The vertical faceting on the kou bowl in the foreground is known as a "Lahaina pattern." The stemmed and footed kou bowl in the background incorporates horizontal fluting on the body of the bowl — it was the property of a chiefly family on Maui. It is 6 7/8" high and 9 1/8" wide. The bowl in the foreground is from the Kapiolani-Kalanianaole collection and is 5 1/2" high and 8" wide across the rim.*

ABOVE: *Flat-bottomed bowls were made in all sizes and shapes. These bowls have spherical interiors, with no indication of the flat-bottomed exterior. This form may be ancient, for William Brigham noted: "The flat bottoms were not peculiar, but often occur in umeke of undoubted age."*

Often, the bottoms of these bowls are slightly convex, indicating that flattened bottoms were sometimes incorporated into the design more for aesthetic appeal than practical necessity.

Many flat-bottomed bowls were probably made by craftsmen after Western contact, particularly in the early nineteenth century, as some chiefs began to use Western tables. Ethnologist Roger Rose noted: "To be sure, exposure to new kinds of tableware and other items imported from Europe and Asia fostered the development of innovative shapes and styles; besides, flat bottoms and annular or pedestal bases were much more suited to table service than traditional round-bottomed calabashes, which had been intended primarily for use with mats on the ground."

The tall kou bowl with repairs is 7 1/4" high and 7 5/8" wide at the rim. The low kou bowl in the foreground is 4 5/8" high and 8 5/8" wide at the rim.

ABOVE: *These paneled kou bowls from the Kamehameha collection may have originated at the whaling port of Lahaina on Maui in the nineteenth century. Such shapes are often referred to as "Lahaina pattern" bowls. Bishop Museum director William Brigham wrote of these bowls: "A more difficult feat than shaping a circular bowl was making a polyhedral bowl. These are rare, and were evidently valued as they are found only in the possession of chiefs or their descendants. Those shown...belonged to the Kamehameha family and from them came directly to this Museum. The sides are closely equal and beautifully finished, the flat surfaces fading into the curved ones in a most graceful manner." The great majority of these bowls were small and made to hold individual servings. The foreground bowl is 4 1/2" high and 8" wide at the rim. The taller bowl in the background is 6 3/4" high and 9" wide across the rim. Each retains its original surface and finish.*

RIGHT: *William Brigham stated that waisted bowls were for mixing medicine. However, there is little evidence for this theory. Such bowls are extremely rare and may have been the inspiration of a single craftsman. An unusual feature of these bowls is the inside shape. While most bowls of eccentric shape have rounded, spherical interiors which ignore the exterior shape, bowls of this form have interiors which closely follow the outside shape. The rim scalloping seen here is not unique to bowls of this design, but is found on Hawaiian bowls of different shapes and materials.*

This kou bowl, with its original surface and finish, stands 14 3/8" high and is 10 3/8" across the rim. It was purchased in 1877 for the Hawaiian National Museum from the estate of High Chief Charles Kanaina, father of King Lunalilo.

ABOVE: *These two large platters were purchased by Joseph Emerson. They are among the oldest documented containers in the Bishop Museum, originally belonging to an early eighteenth-century ruler of the island of Hawaii. Emerson's notes recorded their history: " 'Na Papa kupalupalu mano o Alapai nui' [the shark-attracting boards of Alapainui], bought of a native woman at Kaupulehu, Kona, Hawaii, April 10, 1883. Koa wood. Alapainui was a great shark hunter. For this purpose, he used human flesh as bait. The victim was cut up and left to decompose for two or three days in the large 'pahu kupalupalu mano' [shark-attracting container]....The putrefying flesh was now placed on these platters and taken out to sea on a double canoe. The 'hinu,' or oil, which was allowed to drip into the water, attracted the sharks which were much sought after for their teeth."*

The platter in the background is 4 3/8" high, 16 5/8" wide, and 23 1/2" long. The foreground platter measures 5 3/4" high, 17" wide, and 24 1/2" long.

ABOVE: *Oblong platters are thought to have been made for meats. Small platters are often identified as fish containers; larger ones, for dog or pig. The large platter in the background belonged to Charles Kanaina, father of King Lunalilo. It is raised on runners and the whole is carved from a single log. The inspiration, or meaning behind this design, is now lost. This platter stands 7 1/2" high, is 11 1/2" wide and 29 1/4" long. The platter in the middle is made of koa and stands 2 1/2" high, is 8 1/8" wide and 20 1/8" long. The kou platter in the foreground is 2 3/8" high, 9 1/8" wide, 12 3/4" long, and is from the Princess Kaiulani collection.*

PERSONALIZED ROYAL CONTAINERS

In addition to the rounded containers and their variations, certain types of royal containers are distinctive because of their unique shapes and personalized features.

Among these types of containers was the spittoon. This small bowl or cup was the most important wood container of the chiefs. It was a personal utensil to contain the saliva, nail parings, and hair cuttings of its owner. These were secretly disposed of to protect the chief against sorcery.

A special attendant cared for the bowl and constantly attended his chief with it, as Charles Stewart observed in 1822: "The chiefs were all under one *ranai,* or rude bower. . . . Behind, or near each one, a servant sat or kneeled, fanning his master or mistress with a fan made of the leaves of the cocoa-nut, and holding in the other a small round bowl of dark polished wood, filled with the leaves of an aromatic vine, for a *spittoon.*"

The position of spittoon bearer was an honored one. Sereno Bishop recalled that in Kona, in the 1830s, "any chief of high rank was attended by one or more fly-brushers, by a spittoon-bearer, and other personal attendants. The spittoon holder was the most honored." The 1915 *Bishop Museum Handbook* stated: "Of the five *Kahu alii* or personal attendants of an Hawaiian moi [king], the *Ipukuha* or spittoon [bearer] was the most trusted."

This attendant was considered literally to hold the life of the chief in his hands. It was believed that if any part of a chief's person fell into the hands of an enemy, that chief could be prayed to death by a particular class of sorcerers, who claimed to have that unique power. This was taken quite seriously. In 1817, Peter Corney noticed that Kamehameha "never spits any where but in the box, the contents of which, together with grosser evacuations, are taken to sea with his cast-off garments, and committed to the deep; it being his firm belief, that if any person got a part of either, they would have the power to pray him to death." Even after the belief in sorcery faded with the introduction of Christianity in the nineteenth century, these utensils

LEFT: *These four kou containers with handles show the complete family of hygienic utensils used by high chiefs and chiefesses. The shallow, oblong bowl in the foreground, with an exterior handle and an interior phalange, was used as a finger washbowl at meals. The three bowls behind it, with flat bottoms, handles, and concave sides, were used to hold refuse and excreta. The smallest container held spittle. The bowl next to it on the right was for food scraps and the wide bowl in the background was called an "ipu mimi," or urine container. The unusual shape of these refuse bowls, carved with concave sides, may have been a design unique to a single craftsman.*

It is sometimes difficult to identify a container's specific function without prior knowledge as to its designated use. The urine containers were usually the largest of the three. This one measures 3 3/4" high and 11 7/8" wide across the rim. The smallest of these waste containers was often the spittoon. The example shown here is 2 1/4" high and 4 3/8" wide at the rim. The refuse container for food scraps in front of it is 4 1/4" high and 8 5/8" across the rim.

The wash container in the foreground is 2 3/4" high, 8 3/4" wide, and 14 1/2" long.

continued to be used as symbols of nobility. Brigham, who first visited Hawaii in 1864, and returned to stay in 1880, remembered at the turn of the century: "I have seen these ipu kuha brought into church a generation ago."

Royal spittoons sometimes served as symbols of office. When Henry Barber, captain of the *Arthur*, was shipwrecked on the southwest coast of Oahu in 1796, natives plundered the ship. Barber went to Hawaii and lodged a complaint with Kamehameha I; he then prepared to return: "On shoving off, a native, bearing a small white bundle, sprang into the boat, where he sat without speaking or sleeping during the trip.

"On arrival at Honolulu this man was the first to leap ashore, when he was lost sight of.

"The next afternoon Barber's things were all brought in, and placed side by side at Pakaka, or Robinson's wharf, even to pieces of rope, bolts, nails, &c. The silent voyager had been one of the King's spittoon-bearers, sent with the royal command to deliver up all belonging to the wreck of the *Arthur*."

Another example of Kamehameha using his spittoon to symbolize his office was noted by visiting artist Louis Choris in 1816: "A very ambitious chief whose mind had become overheated through the use of too much rum, had boasted that he would not obey an order of the King's that had just been published; someone thereupon having made some remonstrance, he declared with some show of dignity; 'Do you think that I am not as much a King in my island as is Tammeamea on Ovaihy?' Tammeamea having been advised of the conversation, he directed

RIGHT: *This large, horizontally fluted refuse container was carved from a block of Northwest American fir. This unique bowl is 5 5/8" high with a 5 5/8" interior rim diameter. It is inlaid with almost 300 human teeth. There is an indication in Bishop Museum records from the Hawaiian National Museum that this container last belonged to Kamehameha I. This bowl is the only old Hawaiian container of fir known. However, this wood had been known to Hawaiians since ancient times. Capt. James Cook commented on fir being seen by his crew on Kauai in 1778: "One of my people actually did see some wood in one of the houses at Wymoa, which he judged to be fir. It was worm-eaten, and the natives gave him to understand, that it had been driven ashore by the waves of the sea."*

In 1793, Capt. George Vancouver also saw fir on Kauai: "The circumstance of fir timber being drifted on the northern sides of these islands is by no means uncommon, especially at Attowai, where there then was a double canoe, of a middling size, made from two small pine-trees, that were driven on shore nearly at the same spot. Some logs of timber, with three or four trees of the pine tribe, were then lying on the island, that had at different times been lodged by the sea, but were too much decayed and worm-eaten to be usefully appropriated. As this kind of timber is the known produce of all the northern part of the west side of America, little doubt can remain of these trees having come from that continent, or its contiguous islands."

Rev. Titus Coan, who arrived in Hawaii in 1835, wrote a humorous anecdote of how highly Hawaiians valued logs of fir: "The things most valued by the natives in old times were the sticks of Oregon pine, which at long intervals came drifting to the islands from the northwest coast, and were eagerly seized to be fashioned into war canoes. It is said that when the translator came to the passage in the Epistles, reading: 'Add to your faith knowledge, and to your knowledge temperance, and to your temperance virtue,' he appealed to his native assistant for the Hawaiian word for virtue, which he described as the most desirable of all possessions. The native was puzzled; neither the conception of virtue, as we understand it, nor any corresponding word, existed in Hawaiian; but at last he said: 'I understand you now,' and gave the missionary a word which made the passage read: 'Add to your faith knowledge, and to your knowledge temperance, and to temperance a stick of Oregon pine.'"

that his spit box which only a King might use, should be carried to the bold one who had done the boasting. When the chief received the unexpected present, he understood the full import of Tammeamea's intention in sending it to him, and with all the respect due from a subject to his sovereign he brought it back to him."

Some of these small, personal wooden bowls were decorated with the teeth of enemies, as an expression of contempt. In 1803, John Turnbull noticed these inlaid bowls on Kauai: "During our stay at Atowaie, one of the Sandwich Islands, we observed the king and his fighting general made use of spitting boxes inlaid with the teeth of their enemies slain in battle."

Choris noticed that Kamehameha I also used a similarly decorated cup: "A man seated behind the King, held in his hand a handkerchief and a spit box made of a very handsome brown wood and decorated with human teeth."

Often, these highly personal containers were placed with their owners in burial, but a number of important ones have survived, for as the 1915 *Bishop Museum Handbook* noted: "The inanimate spittoons were held in great esteem, to which their ignoble use would not entitle them elsewhere, and hence those belonging to Kamehameha I and other renowned chiefs have been preserved."

Like the smaller spittoon, refuse containers were also exclusively owned and personal. They were used at meals to receive their owner's leavings and scraps. Like spittoons they were often highly personalized forms, sometimes inlaid with the teeth of dead enemies as a form of insult and advertisement of triumph.

The 1892 *Bishop Museum Catalogue* states: "These bowls were much thicker and heavier than the Umeke Poi, and those of high chiefs were often inlaid with the teeth and bones of slain enemies. . . . While it was deemed honorable to have one's bones attached to a Kahili or foodbowl, it was a deep disgrace to the unfortunate man whose solid parts decorated what was looked upon as a vessel of dishonor."

While on Oahu in 1818, Peter Corney related an incident that was evidence of the continuation of these practices even after the unification of the kingdom by Kamehameha ended warfare among chiefs. Settler Don Francisco de Paula Marin told Corney of chiefs coming to search his land for royal bones which Marin had hidden from them: "The chief came and searched the island; the man told him that as the island and all that was on it belonged to a white man of whom Tameameah was very fond, he ought not to come there to search for bones, when there was so many on the main island. The chief took no notice, but searched and took several bundles of bones with him, though not those of the king and chiefs."

Chamber pots were also probably used exclusively by their owners. They may have been introduced after Western contact. Brigham described this vessel and wrote of his doubt as to its antiquity: "When the spittoon was of larger size, but of the same general form as the ipu kuha it received the discharges from the distal end of the alimentary canal or from the bladder, and being made of so porous a substance as wood, it was important to cleanse it thoroughly and to expose it to the full sunlight: this custom has been faithfully continued with the crockery successor to the wooden ipu mimi, as may be noticed by the traveler at almost any native house in the country. . . . Fortunately most of these necessary but unpleasant containers were destroyed on the advent of the cheaper foreign crockery pots, and specimens are rarely if ever found in museums.

"I do not believe this to have been an ancient implement, nor was it used by the common people, who were very careless about the natural excretions of the body."

It is often difficult to distinguish between scrap bowls and chamber pots. This may be another indication that chamber pots were a relatively recent introduction which craftsmen had not yet developed into a distinctive form.

Hawaiians ate with their fingers, and the upper classes in Hawaii ordinarily washed their hands before, after, and sometimes during meals. Although gourds filled with water were commonly used for washbowls, specialized wooden bowls were also carved for this purpose.

Many of these containers were made with a narrow wood projection extending from the rim of the bowl into the bowl cavity. Some were made with a projection rising from the center of the bowl. These may have been meant for washing between fingers. Although Capt. Cook's lieutenant, James King, wrote in 1779 of the Hawaiians' cleanliness at meals, no mention was made of washing before or after meals. King wrote: "They are exceedingly clean at their meals."

However, John Ledyard, seaman on the same voyage, described a feast at Kealakekua Bay for the captain's officers where the washing of hands was a part of the meal: "There was no ceremony, except that of washing the mouth and hands both before and after dinner with clean water." Neither Ledyard nor King mentioned special washbowls.

In 1816, visitor Adelbert von Chamisso attended a Hawaiian religious feast and noted this practice: "The courses are served on banana leaves; one eats with one's fingers, and the sticky taro mush which takes the place of bread is removed from the fingers by licking. Water, for the purpose of washing, is served before and after the meal."

One of the earliest mentions of wooden washing bowls was in 1823. Rev. William Ellis, visiting High Chief Kuakini in Kailua-Kona, noticed: "Neat wooden dishes of water were handed to the governor and his friends, both before and after eating, in which they washed their hands. Uncivilized nations are seldom distinguished by habits of cleanliness; but this practice, we believe, is an ancient custom, generally observed by the chiefs, and all the higher orders of the people, throughout the islands."

Brigham described these washbowls as finger bowls: "An article of elegance doubtless confined to the Hawaiian aristocracy, — the Alii, were the finger bowls so comfortable to the guest at a meal of greasy dog or pig, where fingers were the only forks, and not less where the food was sticky poi. It was usual after eating the meat to dip the fingers into the poi umeke and finish with the *ipu holoi lima.* In many cases the hands were also washed before meals, but this was not the case with the common people, who were, according to the missionaries who first had to suffer from their filth, dirty in the extreme."

Visiting in 1850, Henry Coke described the custom of washing between the handling of meat and poi: "Generally they eat raw fish at their meals; when this is the case, each person has a small pan of fresh water by his side, wherein he carefully washes his fingers after each mouthful of fish, before he sticks them into the poe-jar."

In Kekahuna's paper on Hawaiian bowls, he also wrote of washbowls: "There were many shapes and sizes of this kind of calabash, from small to fairly large, and the way in which the insides were carved were various. Some were carved with handles and inside of them was carved a ridge on which poi was rubbed off from their fingers. In them, the Hawaiians washed their hands before and after meals. Those who lacked wooden finger-bowls used bitter-gourd bowls (pohue) in which to wash their fingers, and these were made in different shapes. But most were shallow like the wash-basin of this new era."

RIGHT: *These two chiefly refuse containers decorated with the protruding teeth of dead enemies are from the British Museum. William Brigham described the decorative effect of inlaid teeth in Hawaiian bowls as "a device well known to the mediæval jewelers in their gem-studded chalices."*

The container in the foreground is 4 3/4" high with an outer diameter of 6 3/8" across the rim. The museum accession record states that this bowl is "said to have been in the possession of Kamehameha I." Forty-nine teeth are inlaid in it. The rim is 1 1/8" thick. The bowl walls become 1 1/2" thick at the bottom.

The larger refuse container in the background stands 6 1/2" high. The mouth of the bowl is 4 1/8" across. The rim itself is 3/4" thick, increasing to 1" thick at the bottom of the bowl. Thirty-nine teeth decorate this bowl. Each bowl is pierced by a drilled hole, which secured a thick rope handle. Also, both bowls were carved from tree crotches, which is unusual for this form of container.

The food scraps these bowls held would be carefully destroyed by trusted servants to avoid sorcery. The Hawaiian National Museum descriptive catalogue records state: "The old natives believed that the leavings of anything eaten by anyone constituted the means of a powerful charm for evil to that one, if passed into the hands of any enemy. The leavings or refuse of high chiefs are therefore always gathered, and dried, and burnt by their servants. The servants of a high chief were not commoners, but particularly trusted lesser chiefs."

ABOVE: *These four kou spittoons display a diversity of shapes. The container in the background was part of the Kapiolani-Kalanianaole collection and is the largest of those pictured. It stands 3 5/8" high and measures 6 1/4" wide at the rim. The other three spittoons are approximately 3" high and 4" across the rim.*

The bowl in the foreground was purchased by Joseph Emerson and may have belonged to Kamehameha I. Emerson wrote of it: "Ipu kuha, kou wood, bought of Kaumuloa of Honolulu, Sept. 15, 1886, $2.00. It has belonged to Kamehameha I, II, III, and V. Kamamalu. Kalai Heana K., kahu of Liholiho, etc., had the charge of it. At his death, it passed to his wife Kalama who again married Kaumuloa from whom I obtained it." When in use these containers would have flowers or leaves in them. Charles Stewart in 1822 described chiefs' attendants at a gathering each holding "a small, round bowl of dark polished wood, filled with the leaves of an aromatic vine, for a spittoon."

ABOVE: *This small spittoon is 3 1/4" high with an opening 2 7/8" wide and is decorated with eighteen adult molars and premolars. Although the exterior is well polished, the interior was not smoothed at all and still displays the raw marks of the blade used to roughly hollow it. This spittoon is identified as belonging to Kamehameha I, but he may have simply been one of the last high chiefs to own it. Archibald Campbell may have seen this spittoon, or one like it, during his visit in 1809. Describing the three attendants with Kamehameha, he wrote: "A third carried his spit-box, which was set round with human teeth, and had belonged, as I was told, to several of his predecessors."*

*William Brigham commented on the custom of inlaying teeth in these containers: "This disposition of the bones was insulting to the dead and the insult was intentional. This is also shown in the insertion of teeth and bones in vessels of dishonor, such as spittoons (**ipu kuha**), slop basins (**ipu aina**), and the like. Hence the care taken to hide from the enemy the bones of a chief or important person."*

This spittoon came to the Bishop Museum from the Hawaiian National Museum in 1891. About the inlaid teeth the descriptive catalogue states: "The teeth were those of persons of consequence who had been killed or had died a natural death, and whose memories the King or Queen wanted to desecrate. They were generally rivals who had been guilty of some low, mean, and despicable acts, and fastening the teeth of such to a spittoon bowl was an illustration to posterity in what estimation such persons should be and were held."

ABOVE: *Three of the refuse containers shown here have human teeth inlays. The bowl in the foreground has only one inlaid tooth, a premolar from an upper jaw, and is of a unique form. The bottom of this refuse bowl has been carved in a graceful concave form, with four softly rounded support points. The unique plasticity of form gives the impression more of clay than of wood. The hole directly above the inlaid tooth was for a carrying cord. This bowl is 4 1/4" high with an opening 4 1/8" wide. The fully rounded undecorated refuse container in back of it has a pierced wooden projection for a carrying cord. This bowl was part of Queen Emma's collection, has an interior rim diameter of 5", and stands 4 1/2" high.*

The bowl on the left in the rear has forty-four teeth inlaid in a random pattern so that they project significantly from the surface of the bowl. This bowl is 5" high with an opening 3 1/4" wide.

The bowl next to it has sixty-three human teeth inlaid in eighteen vertical rows around its circumference and ground down flush to bowl level. Nine rows begin with teeth inlaid into the thick rim and alternating rows begin just beneath the rim. Also inlaid into this bowl are five strips of mammal bone. All five bone inlays were identified by William Brigham as one or more harpoon barbs brought from the northwest coast of North America. This refuse container is 5 5/8" high and is 5 7/8" across the interior of the rim.

Scrap bowls are characteristically thick and heavy, with the heaviest scrap bowl in the Bishop Museum weighing seven pounds.

ABOVE: *This beautifully polished and inlaid refuse container has forty-four insets which may be human bone. If so, then this is the only refuse bowl in the Bishop Museum collection decorated with human bone inlay. Unlike many refuse bowls with inlaid teeth, the bone inlay of this bowl appears to have been carefully designed and inset with all the material previously gathered, perhaps from one skeleton. If these carefully shaped and polished inlays were meant to insult, it is curious that the tasteful design and careful craftsmanship should be so aesthetically pleasing. There is only one other refuse container with bone inlay in the Bishop Museum. This container, seen on the opposite page, obviously used bones as decorative elements, for they have been identified as being trade items, perhaps from Alaska. The bowl here was part of Queen Emma's collection and stands 4 3/8" high with a 4" opening.*

The container in the background has been tentatively identified as a refuse container, but its size and simple plug repairs indicate it may have been a urine container. It stands 6 1/2" high and is 9" across the thick rim.

ABOVE AND RIGHT: *These wooden washbasins were used before, after, and sometimes during meals. They were probably personal items, intended for the use of their owner only. Wooden washbasins may have developed as specialized utensils after Western contact, for no mention of them is recorded by early voyagers, and the curious interior projections which characterize them would seem to have been worthy of comment. Like spittoons, many of these washbasins were carved into unique shapes.*

Containers of gourd were probably more commonly used for washing at meals. As late as 1832, gourd washbasins were observed in use by surgeon Francis Bishop while dining with the governor of Maui: "A small calabash of water was presented to each guest to wash his hands previous to the dire attack meditated on the smoking mullet, that reclined before us, for our fingers were to supply the place of knives and forks. The meal being concluded calabashes of water were again introduced to wash the adhering fragments of poe, fish and sour sauce from our fingers." Despite this and other similar descriptions, no surviving gourd containers have been identified as reserved for the washing of hands.

The large circular washbasin in the background on the opposite page is 3 3/4" high and 13 7/8" across the rim. The two smaller bowls seem more like Western finger bowls. The eccentrically shaped bowl in the middle is 2 3/4" high and 9 7/8" long. The bowl in the foreground is 3 3/8" high and 9 5/8" long.

The circular bowl above has two thick interior phalanges, stands 3" high and is 11 1/4" wide at the rim.

FIGURED BOWLS

Among the most dramatic wooden bowls made by Hawaiian craftsmen were those that incorporated carvings of human figures. In fact, some of the finest examples of Hawaiian carving occur on these bowls.

Eighteenth-century descriptions of these containers state that they were used for serving awa. However, the shapes of some of the few bowls of this type that have survived indicate that they may have not been limited to that use. Of the fourteen old, figured bowls known to exist, four are in the shape of platters, two have been identified as refuse bowls, and one may have held condiments. Little is known about what the figures symbolized or the exact circumstances under which the bowls were used. It is possible that bowls with carved human figures began to be crafted for uses other than awa ceremonies only after Western contact. Hawaiian oral history and legends never mentioned any of these carved works, and surgeon David Samwell found them to be rare in 1779: "These Ava bowls are very scarce being only in the Possession of their Kings."

Capt. Cook's second-in-command, Lt. James King, wrote of them: "The most curious specimens of [carving], which we saw during our second visit, are the bowls, in which the Chiefs drink *ava.* These are usually about eight or ten inches in diameter, perfectly round, and beautifully polished. They are supported by three, and sometimes four, small human figures, in various attitudes. Some of them rest on the hands of their supporters, extended over the head; others on the head and hands; and some on the shoulders. The figures, I am told, are accurately proportioned, and neatly finished, and even the anatomy of the muscles, in supporting the weight, well expressed."

Samwell described the bowls further: "Some of them are made with images to them & these are their Ava bowls, the feet of the Images are made to support the bowl & a hole is made for the Liquor to flow out of their Mouths, and in some of them out of their back sides."

Awa, *Piper methysticum,* is a shrub related to pepper. Marie Neal, in *In Gardens of Hawaii,* described its origin and use: " 'Awa is a native of Pacific islands, and in early times it was distributed eastward through tropical islands by migrating people, who valued the root as the source of a drink and of medicine. In Hawaii more than 15 varieties were known. In many islands of the Pacific, 'awa has long played an important part in the life of the people, being used in ceremonies, festivals, and as a sign of good will."

Capt. George Dixon described the preparation of awa in 1786: "The Ava is a root, somewhat resembling our liquorice in shape and colour, but totally different in taste. None but the Arees,

LEFT: *This patterned water gourd from the Saffron Walden Museum in England, and the figured awa bowl from Cambridge University Museum were collected by members of Capt. James Cook's crew in 1778 or 1779. The bowl is of a dark polished wood, perhaps milo, with inlaid pearlshell eyes. It stands 3 1/4" high, with an overall length of 7" and a diameter of 6" across the rim. Although the hands and feet extend equally to form a level support, the bowl rests on its spherical bottom, which extends approximately 1/8" below the hands and feet. A pouring hole exits through the figure's mouth.*

or Chiefs, are permitted to use it, and they never prepare it themselves, but always keep a servant, whose sole business is (Ganymede like) to prepare and administer this delicious potation to his master. He first begins by chewing a sufficient quantity, till it is well masticated; this is put into a neat wooden bowl, made for the purpose, and a small quantity of water being poured over, it is well squeezed, and the liquor afterwards strained through a piece of cloth. The delicious beverage is now compleat, and is drank with the highest relish."

The ceremonial significance of awa in ancient Hawaiian society was soon forgotten, as a result of the overthrow of the religion in 1819. Lt. King, however, witnessed and recorded the ceremony that always attended the drinking of awa by the priests and chiefs: "Amongst their religious ceremonies, may be reckoned the prayers and offerings made by the priests before their meals. Whilst the *ava* is chewing, of which they always drink before they begin their repast, the person of the highest rank takes the lead in a sort of hymn, in which he is presently joined by one, two, or more of the company; the rest moving their bodies, and striking their hands gently together, in concert with the fingers. When the *ava* is ready, cups of it are handed about to those who do not join in the song, which they keep in their hands till it is ended; when, uniting in one loud response, they drink off their cup. The performers of the hymn are then served with *ava*, who drink it after a repetition of the same ceremony; and, if there be present one of a very superior rank, a cup is, last of all, presented to him, which, after chanting some time alone, and being answered by the rest, and pouring a little out on the ground, he drinks off. A piece of the flesh that is dressed, is next cut off, without any selection of the part of the animal; which, together with some vegetables, being deposited at the foot of the image of the *Eatooa,* and a hymn chanted, their meal commences. A ceremony of much the same kind is also performed by the Chiefs, whenever they drink *ava,* between their meals."

Only fourteen bowls with figures are known to have survived. Anthropologist Adrienne Kaeppler, in 1978, published documentation proving at least four of these bowls were collected on Capt. Cook's visits in 1778 and 1779. During the ship's short stay off Kauai in 1778, the first of these bowls was given as a gift from the king of the island to Capt. Charles Clerke, commander of the *Discovery.* Capt. Cook wrote of the gift: "Captain Clerke made him some suitable presents; and received from him, in return, a large bowl, supported by two figures of men, the carving of which, both as to the design and the execution, shewed some degree of skill. This bowl, as our people were told, used to be filled with the *kava,* or *ava* (as it is called in Otaheite), which liquor they prepare and drink here, as at the other islands in this ocean."

On the expedition's return to Kauai the following year, 1779, surgeon David Samwell recorded another awa dish given as a gift: "King Teeave came on board the ship in a small double Canoe attended by about thirty people, he is a fine Boy about ten years of age. When he came on deck a priest attending him presented a small pig to the Captain but made no Speech as they used to do at Ouwaihee, then Teeave himself made him a present of a very curious Ava Bowl, after which he was taken into the Cabin with the Chiefs who attended."

The only other eighteenth-century visitor to comment on these bowls was Capt. George Dixon, who provisioned in the islands three times between 1786 and 1787, while engaged in fur trading between China and North America. Dixon described the bowls as masterpieces of carving: "Sometimes their ava dishes are supported by three of these little wooden images, and this I reckon a master-piece in their carving." Little mention of these bowls was made by later visitors despite steadily increasing contact by Western fur traders and explorers.

ABOVE: *The small, shallow oblong container is suspended between two figures. It is 5 1/8" high and 14 3/4" long overall. The two support figures face each other, mouths open, heads thrown back, and arms raised and flexed as if lifting a great weight. Each is connected to the platter at the chest. One figure has inlaid eyes of mother-of-pearl. The container they support is 2 1/2" high, 4 1/2" wide, and 10 1/4" long. This piece retains its highly polished dark finish, with only the interior of the container itself not stained black. Plain oblong bowls of this form traditionally held meats.*

This treasure was last owned by King Lunalilo, who ruled from 1873 to 1874. William Brigham identified this bowl as "a sauce or gravy dish, belonged to King Lunalilo, and was used during his reign as a card receiver."

ABOVE AND OPPOSITE: *These two large figured awa bowls were very probably carved by the same craftsman and are considered among the finest examples of Hawaiian carving. They came from the island of Kauai and belonged to that island's highest chiefs. One of the bowls was presented to Captain Charles Clerke at Waimea in 1778 by the sacred high chief Kaneoneo. The second bowl was given to Clerke on his return the following year by young chief Keawe, son of Kamakahelei, then ruling chiefess of Kauai.*

Kamakahelei and Kaneoneo had been husband and wife, and both were grandchildren of Peleioholani, high chief and ruler of the island of Oahu.

The bowl on this page is the property of a private collector. Two partial figures opposing each other support the bowl. Each figure consists only of head, bust, and extended arms which elevate the bowl. Pouring holes on opposing sides of the bowl exit through the mouth of each figure. Pearl-shell eyes are secured with dark wood pegs as pupils. The carving is 9 1/2" high and is 17 1/2" long. The bowl itself is 4" high, 10" across the rim, and is 5/8" thick throughout.

ABOVE: *This figured awa bowl from the British Museum is a companion piece to the one on the opposite page. Each was carved from a single block of kou. The eyes of both are inlaid pearl shell, and the inset teeth appear to be sections of pig tusk. The figures were stained black, with the bowls left their natural color.*

Two pouring holes pierce opposing sides of both bowls. On this bowl one hole emerges from the figure's mouth, the other exits from the rear figure's buttocks. The inlaid pearl-shell eyes of this bowl have drilled holes for pupils. The rear figure was carved as a complete body, while the front figure consists only of head, bust and arms. This carving stands 9 3/4" high and 19 3/4" long. The bowl itself is 4 5/8" high, 10 7/8" across the rim and is 3/4" thick throughout.

The crescent-shaped awa dish in the foreground was collected during Capt. George Vancouver's visits to Hawaii in 1792 and 1794, and is now in the British Museum. This uniquely shaped container is of kou and stands 1 7/8" high and measures 8 5/8" across its widest diameter.

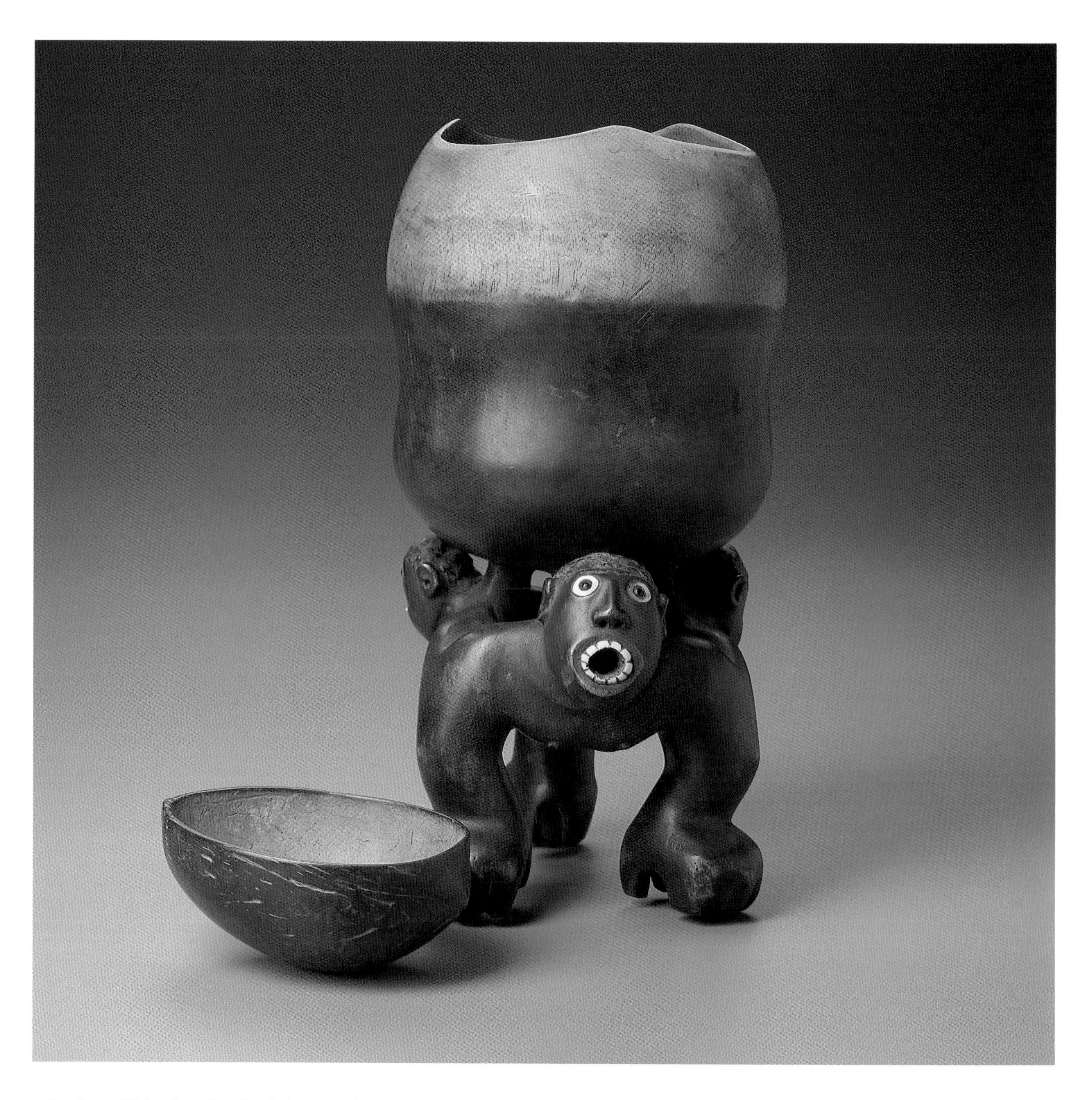

ABOVE: *This deep bowl with constricted waist and scalloped rim is supported by three figures. It is from the British Museum and stands 11 3/4" high overall. The bowl itself is 6 3/4" high and 4 3/4" at its widest rim diameter. It is joined to the supporting figures by three vertical shafts, each hidden by a head. The figures themselves consist of only head, bust, and arms. They are joined at the shoulders to form a circle under the bowl. The joined shoulders form three extended arms descending to stylized hands, again divided into three elements. Each point in the scalloped rim lines up vertically with a head, and each dip lines up with an arm support.*

The inlaid eyes are pearl shell with polished pupil insets of an unidentified material. The teeth of each figure were formed from a solid piece of bone inset deep into the mouth cavity and carved with notches on one end to resemble teeth. The figures have been stained entirely black but the bowl's upper part has been left unstained. The entire work was carved from a single piece of kou. Although the carving gives the illusion of large size, the priest's coconut awa cup in the foreground gives an idea of how small this bowl actually is.

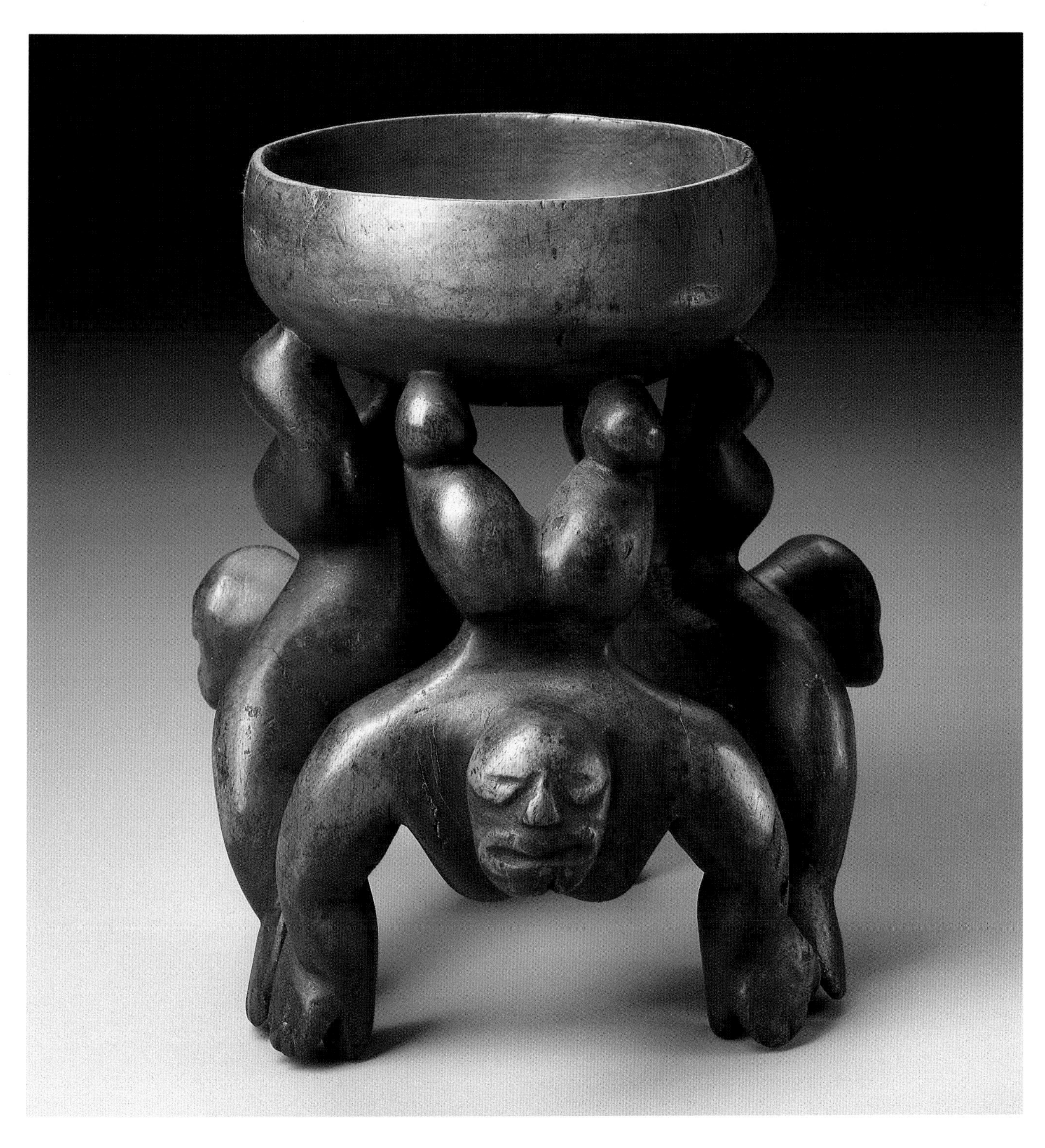

ABOVE: *The three powerfully carved figures supporting this bowl or cup appear to be large. However, the entire piece is only 7 7/8" high. The container the figures support is just 2 3/8" high and 4 7/8" across the rim. The three figures support the bowl with their feet at six equally spaced points while standing on their hands, which are joined to form a triangular base of three points. The figures and part of the bowl were originally stained black. The bowl itself was stained only on the bottom, leaving an inch of exterior rim and the whole of the interior plain polished wood. The faces of the figures carry the only detailed carving and they appear worn, perhaps indicating long use before the piece was carried to England. This bowl was purchased there by the British Museum in 1854.*

RIGHT: *Both of these bowls with figures have been previously identified as refuse containers. The bowl in the background closely resembles a Western spittoon. It was found in a small cave at Waimalu, Oahu, in 1953. Both back legs and one of the arms on which it stood have been broken off. The carving stands 10 3/8" high and is 17 1/2" long.*

The container itself is 5 5/8" high and 9 1/2" across the outside rim. The flared rim slopes inward to an opening 3 3/8" wide. The eyes of the figure are inlaid mother-of-pearl, and originally the entire carving had a dark polished finish. J. Halley Cox described similar support figures in **Hawaiian Sculpture**: *"A great number of practical objects such as food bowls, carrying poles, drums, and spear and pole racks for fitting to canoes were enhanced with carvings of human figures. These support figures have an ingenuity of composition, charm, and informal treatment that is completely lacking in the better-known religious images....The support figures are informal, suggesting the buffoon, the acrobat, or the playful imp."*

Despite a missing arm and both back legs, which played no small part in the overall composition, this carving is one of the most obviously playful of all known containers with figures and best fits Cox's description: "The images are carved as acrobats and tumblers, standing on hands, playing strange games, and twisting into unlikely positions."

In contrast to the playful figure in the background, at least one of the figures on the foreground container may have been intended as an insulting portrait caricature. The figure in the extreme foreground is typically playful, with both legs arched over its head as if tumbling. However, this figure is unusual in that two human bicuspids have been inlaid to indicate breast nipples and one tooth has been inlaid between the legs to indicate the anus or vagina.

The opposing figure has been carved as a mature woman with fully developed breasts. The arms spread the legs into a distended position, displaying a carved vagina. In no other sculptured container is the sex of the figure made so obvious. Inlaid molars decorate a nostril, navel, forehead hairline, and perhaps anus.

This may be a unique example of Hawaiian ribaldry in wood. However, of all existing figured bowls, this figure may best illustrate the theory that many of these figures represent real people and were depicted in order to denigrate their memories. Viewed as a portrait, the large female figure has been carved in a most demeaning and insulting position. William Brigham examined the bowl when it came to the Bishop Museum and wrote a detailed description and evaluation: "The present example surpasses any Hawaiian carved bowl known in the grotesque originality of the design.

"The figure in an inverted position has her ankles connected by a round bar which serves as a point of suspension, the other end of the suspending cord (aha or coconut braid) being knotted around the neck of the opposite figure which is also female. The holes made in the head of this last figure are very neatly cut; the hair and many of the pegs have disappeared. A good bushy wig must have added character to the rather insignificant head. Why so much labor should have been expended on a mere ipu aina, a dish to contain the refuse of a feast, such as fish bones or banana peels, is hard to explain."

Although it is difficult to determine due to damage, just over twenty teeth may have originally been inlaid in this sculpture in an organized decorative pattern.

While this utensil has always been presumed to be for refuse, the shape of the bowl is that of a food container. Furthermore, the interior surface of the bowl has been worked until very smooth, a refinement usually reserved for food containers.

The bowl itself is 4 1/2" high and 9 1/2" wide across to the rim, which is 1" thick.

ABOVE: *This large utilitarian sculpture is 45 1/4" long and 12" high. Originally, it was given a polished, glossy black finish, much of which still remains. The platter the figures support is 5 1/2" high, 10 3/4" wide, and 32 1/2" long. The oblong shape of the shallow platter indicates that it was intended to hold meat, and the open mouth of each supporting figure may possibly have been intended to hold condiments. William Brigham identified the figures as being High Chief Kahahana and his wife, Kekuapoi.*

This carving may have been done for Chief Kahekili of Maui to commemorate his victory over his nephew Kahahana, Chief of Oahu. Kahahana was the ruling chief on Oahu when Capt. James Cook first landed on Kauai. He was decisively defeated in a battle on Oahu in 1783 and driven into hiding with his wife and friend Alapai. Two and a half years later they were discovered and Kahekili ordered Kahahana and Alapai killed.

This heirloom last belonged to members of the Kamehameha dynasty. It may have come into their possession in 1795 as spoils of war when Kamehameha I conquered Kahekili's son Kalanikupule, on Oahu, to gain control of Oahu, Maui, Lanai, and Molokai. However, the history of ownership can be traced only as far back as Princess Ruth Keelikolani, who died in 1883 and willed her collections to Princess Bernice

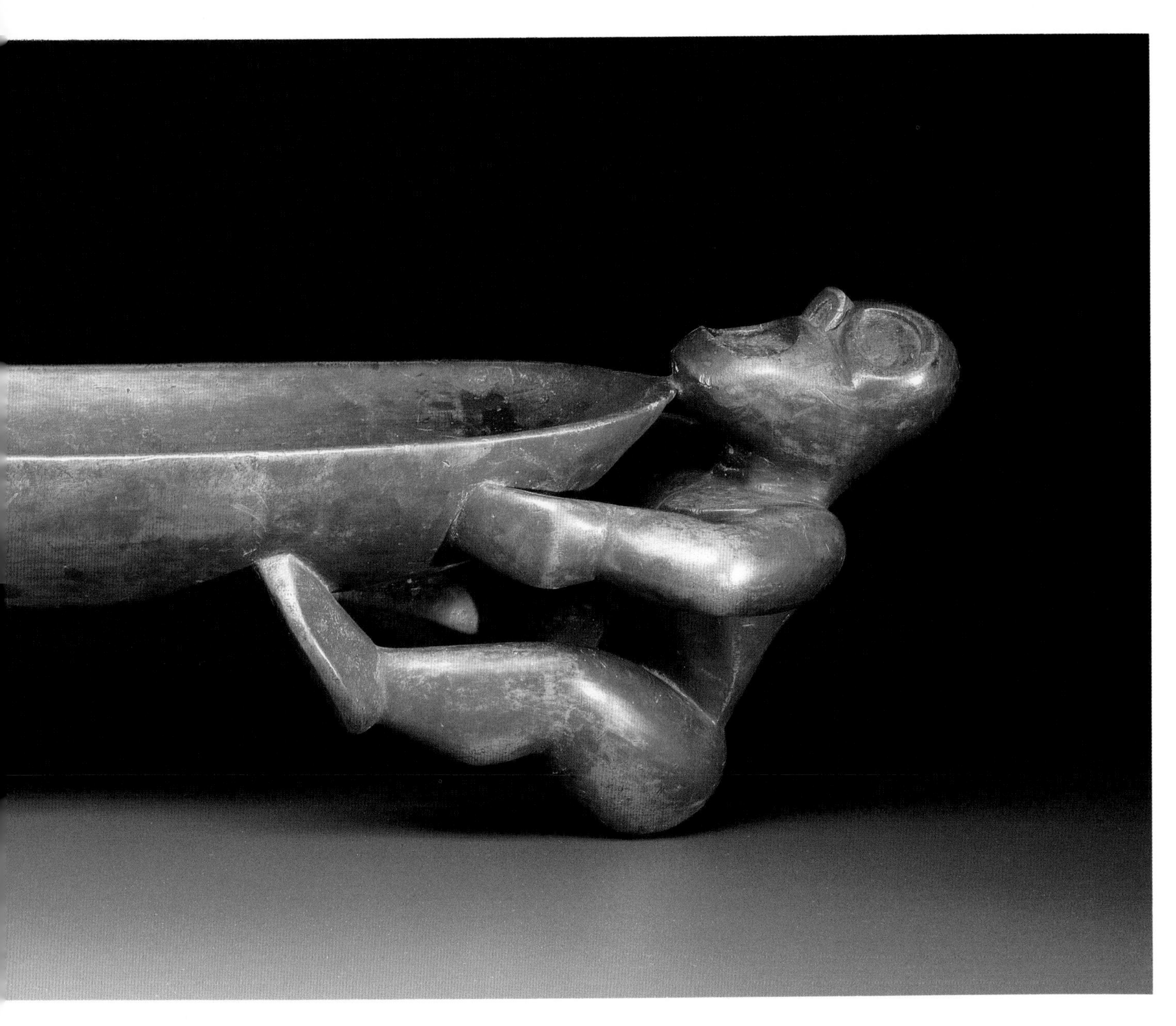

Pauahi Bishop; it came from her estate to the Bishop Museum. In 1875, a visitor to Ruth's home in Kailua, on the island of Hawaii, published an article describing various articles seen in the house, one of which was this figured platter:

"The next relic is a long shallow dish for cooked pig or dog, supported at each end by a figure carved like an idol, both figures and bowl being of one piece of dark polished kou wood. The dish is about 3 feet long and the figures a foot high. The latter do not point in opposite directions, but face the same way, so that the arms and legs of one bend backwards while supporting the dish, while those of the other point forward. The whole shows evidence of considerable skill, and taking into consideration that it was made before metal implements were known in Hawaii, the design and finish of both figures and bowl are remarkable. Efforts should be made to procure the relic as a loan for the proposed National Museum. It belongs to H.R.H. Luka Keelikolani and is stowed away at her country seat (Hulihee) at this place."

It has not been determined what tools were used in carving this piece. However, it is very likely that High Chief Kahekili would have had access to some of the iron left by Capt. Cook's ships, which may have been made into adzes for craftsmen in his employ.

THE TRADITIONAL WOODS USED FOR CALABASHES

Hawaiian craftsmen carved the majority of their bowls from three woods: kou, milo, and kamani. Bowls from other native woods may have been carved either as a challenge to the craftsman or because a particular wood or tree held special meaning for the eventual owner. In the Bishop Museum collection, the great majority of wooden bowls are of kou. However, there are also bowls made of nenelaau, monkeypod, rosewood, coconut, loulu palm, koaia, koa, breadfruit, and other woods. While it is unusual to find bowls of these woods in private collections, it is not unusual to find a few bowls of kamani and milo.

It is not completely understood why certain woods were chosen over others. It is only recognized that the ancient craftsmen had intimate knowledge of the woods available to them and each wood's particular strengths and weaknesses; much of this practical knowledge is now, for the most part, lost. The spiritual or cultural reasons for selecting certain woods have also been lost. Charles Judd, in "The Woodcraft of The Early Hawaiians," wrote of this considerable practical knowledge: "Hawaiians developed into expert wood technologists and possessed intimate knowledge of the qualities of various woods, gained by long usage and experience and doubtless handed down from father to son for generations.

"Dr. W. T. Brigham records that up to fifty years ago he seldom met a mature native who could not give him the Hawaiian name of any tree he found in the mountain forests. The younger generation of today, from my personal observations, knows only the most obvious trees, such as the *Koa* and *Kukui.* A few years ago, when I discovered the existence of the *Mamani* tree on Oahu, at Keaau in the Waianae Range, I showed the yellow pea-like blossoms and the foliage to an aged Hawaiian with me and he called the tree 'Ohai'. This was symbolic of the fast-disappearing woodcraft of the natives, for the red-flowered *Ohai,* once so abundant on the larger islands of this group, had been almost entirely wiped out by the depredations of live stock."

Henry Kekahuna, in his treatise on Hawaiian wooden bowls, could state that the ancients had great knowledge of woods, but he could not repeat what they knew: "There are a great many kinds of large trees which can be easily used for calabashes and other articles, but there were reasons why the ancestors of this race did not use them. It was due to their knowledge and

LEFT: *These blocks of kou show the thickness of the sapwood surrounding the dark, rich heartwood. The bowl in the foreground illustrates how Hawaiian artisans carefully incorporated only a thin portion of the sapwood next to the heartwood as a decorative design on the outside of bowls.*

Kou trees with particularly beautiful wood grain were highly prized. One such grove, called Ulukou, was located in Waikiki on Oahu. Ethnologist John Stokes wrote in 1940: "Ulukou, namely, 'kou grove,' is still a land name, a subdivision of Waikiki, so given when a magnificent stand of kou was there. The site is at or near the Royal Hawaiian Hotel." An unpublished, descriptive catalogue from the Hawaiian National Museum identified a bowl in the collection made of wood from the Ulukou grove and went on to comment: "Wood from this celebrated grove was much sought after for making dishes, as it was remarkable for the beauty of its markings, in curly or wavy lines."

ABOVE: *Seen here are kou leaves, flowers, and seed pods. Ethnologist John Stokes wrote of the flowers: "In Hawaiian poems and chants, references are found to stringing the kou blossoms into lei. The blossoms, with a texture like crepe, and shading in color from gold to mahogany, are very beautiful." About the seed pods he wrote: "The spherical pod is composed of a cork-like substance, which floats very readily, and no doubt this is nature's way of disseminating the kou. Encased in the cork are three or four seeds, in size and shape like apple pips." Joseph Clark, visiting the islands in 1840, described the tree itself as similar in appearance to apple, stating the kou was "an ornamental tree, resembling, at a distance, a large and flourishing full-topped apple tree." These trees grew plentifully on all the islands, and Stokes stated that "in earlier days, it was common in the Hawaiian Islands. Honolulu Harbor itself, so 'tis said, was named Kou on account of the many kou trees lining its shores."*

awareness of their defects, for they were trained until they became expert in the different departments of work which pertained to the life of those remote days.

"This was a rule that was taught till expert in selecting the woods which they desired for the making of objects of benefit to them. They knew the hardness, the color, the nature of the grain, the scent, and the durability of the various trees that grew about them."

Judd lamented this lost knowledge and its long-dead craftsmen: "The Hawaiians of today are still good fishermen and superior seamen, excellent swimmers and athletes, but they have lost the art of woodcraft.

"The ancient Hawaiians had considerable additional knowledge of trees and plants and of their qualities, both economic and therapeutic, but many of the old Hawaiian processes have been lost to the world by the passing away of the old masters of woodcraft.

"But let us not forget that there once were masters of woodcraft in these islands, expert woodmen, who knew the forests and what they produced."

KOU

Kou, *Cordia subcordata,* is an evergreen tree that grows along shorelines throughout Polynesia and the southern Pacific, and as far west as the coast of East Africa. William Brigham, in *The Ancient Hawaiian House,* describes kou as being "of large growth and spreading habit, found as far south of the equator as Madagascar, and formerly planted near native houses along the beach for its greatful shade, but seldom seen now, owing to the ravages of a small moth, *Azinis hilarella = Ethmia colorella W.* It is almost extinct on this group."

At one time, kou was a dominant tree along the shorelines of all the islands, particularly the warm western coasts with their large native populations. They were the first trees noticed by Capt. James Cook as he approached the island of Kauai in 1778: "We saw no wood, but what was up in the interior part of the island, except a few trees about the villages." Upon landing to examine a religious enclosure at the village of Waimea, he recognized the trees he had seen as kou: "In several parts, within the inclosure of this burying-ground, were planted trees of the *cordia sebestina.* . . . In general, the trees round this village, and which were seen at many of those which we passed before we anchored, are the *cordia sebestina;* . . . but of a more diminutive size than the product of the Southern isles."

It is generally believed that this tree was brought to Hawaii by colonizing Polynesian voyagers. Brigham was somewhat cautious about this assumption: "The opinion of some botanists is that it has been introduced, but if so it must have been in very early time in the history of the people, as the ancient songs often mention the kou. . . . Some of the oldest umeke in existence, which have been found in long ago closed burial caves are of this rather soft but durable wood."

Although the kou apparently had some medicinal qualities, and its bright yellow-orange flowers, available most of the year, were popular as leis, it was the wood that gave this tree its great worth. It was from the wood of this tree that the great majority of traditional Hawaiian wooden bowls were carved.

Historian David Malo, in his important nineteenth-century work, *Moolelo Hawaii,* identified kou as "a tree of considerable size, the wood of which is specially used in making all sorts of platters, bowls and dishes, and a variety of other utensils.

"Those who were skilled in the art carved bowls and dishes out of different woods; but the *kou* was the wood generally used for this purpose."

Kou has a rich, dark brown heartwood with darker streaks and no discernible annual growth rings. Bowls were carved from the heartwood closest to the sapwood, and as an added design element the yellow sapwood was carefully incorporated as decoration against the dark heartwood for dramatic contrast.

Hawaiian royalty particularly enjoyed this yellow against dark drama, for not only did their wooden containers reflect this aesthetic, but also their canoes, with painted black hulls contrasted against light yellow woods used on gunnels, bow, and stern pieces.

While being a very beautiful wood, kou may have also been favored for bowls for practical reasons. *Scientific American of New York,* discussing the Hawaiian woods displayed at the Philadelphia Centennial Exhibition of 1876, described kou as "similar in appearance and character to black walnut, but has a grain and is not so heavy. It can be turned into all shapes, and never cracks or checks, as is the case with most woods."

There is an indication that ancient Hawaiians held bowls of kou in special esteem. In 1779, Lt. James King spent much time on shore with the Hawaiians and became a great favorite among them. He acquired knowledge of their culture and compiled a modest phonetic vocabulary which was later published in the official account of the voyage. The vocabulary listed two different words for wooden bowls. One was a general term to designate any wooden bowl: *Paraoo,* a wooden bowl." A separate word designated bowls made of kou: *Epaee,* wooden bowls made from the [kou]."

In 1871, the *Hawaiian Gazette,* wrote of the esteem in which bowls of kou were held in an article that stated: "The kou is the luxurious wood of the islands, and dishes made from it hold the same relation to ordinary dishes that China-ware does to wedge-wood."

As late as 1891, thirty years after kou had all but vanished from the kingdom, the *Hawaiian Gazette,* in an article on Hawaiian woods described kou as a royal wood: "It has been a favorite wood of the Aliis, or Chiefs, as far back as can be ascertained, and was worked up for calabashes, trays and sundry containers."

The Hawaiian newspaper *Hoku o Hawaii* stated that kou trees themselves were associated with nobility: "The trees that grew in the yard of the house of the chief and beautified it were the kou. It was customary to have such trees growing in the yard of chiefs."

Historian Samuel Kamakau also stated that the kou trees were reserved by nobility: "Kou trees were another thing planted in the old days to be used for wooden calabashes and dishes, and the farmer took pride in these things. But the planting of kou trees was discouraged because they were stolen and taken away by the chiefs."

Kekahuna's twentieth-century treatise on Hawaiian wooden bowls stated: "Vessels made from the bitter-gourd were those mostly used by the common people, while such trees as kou and others were forbidden to them in that remote period. Only if the landlord (konohiki) permitted it could the commoner hew them down and carve them. They were valued possessions of the landlords and great chiefs."

The government enforced its rights to kou trees well into the nineteenth century. A dispute over harvesting rights between a minor chief and the government, in 1848, caused the governor of Hawaii to write of it to the minister of the interior in Honolulu: "I wish to inform you, that the kou trees standing at Onouli, Kawaihae, have been cut down by the children and descendants of the ones who planted them. The cutting down came about in this way, it was Kauwe,

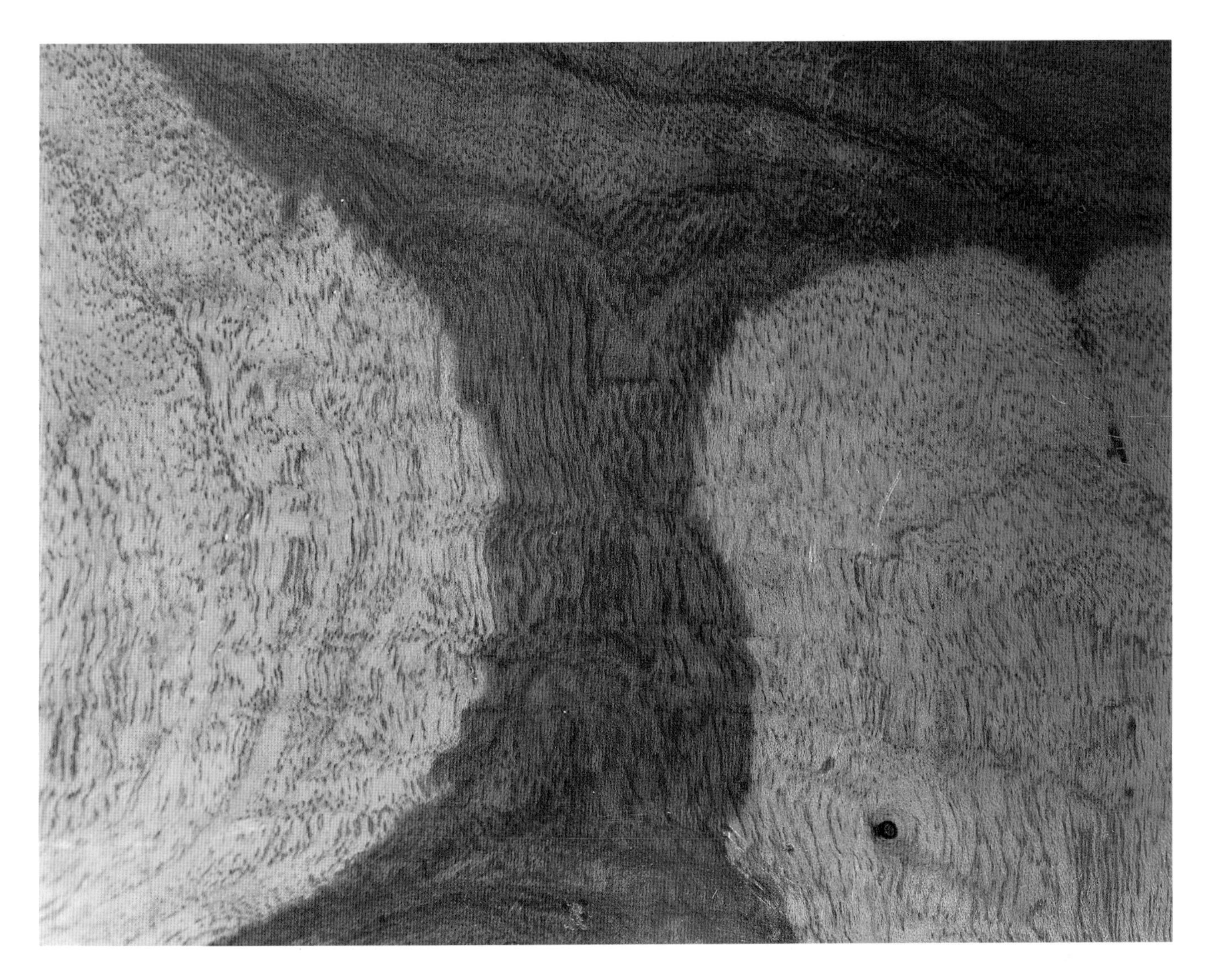

ABOVE: *This close-up of the surface of a shellac-finished kou bowl illustrates the dramatic contrast of golden sapwood against rich, dark heartwood. Not only was the wood beautiful, but the tree itself was admired wherever it grew. In 1823, William Ellis wrote of how the trees enhanced the village of Lahaina on Maui: "The appearance of Lahaina from the anchorage is singularly romantic and beautiful. A fine sandy beach stretches along the margin of the sea, lined for a considerable distance with houses, and adorned with shady clumps of kou trees, or waving groves of cocoa-nuts." Going ashore to preach, he again admired the trees: "Most of the chiefs, and about three hundred people, assembled under the pleasant shade of a beautiful clump of kou trees, in front of Keopuolani's house."*

one of the military officers of our king, who ordered his relatives to cut them down.

"Their right to the trees were all right, but they gave up taking care of this right long ago, nearly twenty years have those trees been standing without any care, the government was the only one who looked after them.

"I did not hear about the cutting of the trees, I heard later on that they had been cut down and when I did hear it, I thought if the government has any right to said trees, then, these descendants have no right to cut them without my being told.

"And therefore, I placed a restriction on these trees, instructed officers near Kawaihae, to forbid that man from cutting the kou, that the pieces were not to be taken away, little by little, until I have heard they have been cut down.

"This is what I truly believe, I think the right of these persons who did the cutting has expired, and that only the government and the Konohiki are the remaining ones who have an interest therein, because the abandonment has been very long, some of them, however, are living at Kawaihae, but not at the place where said trees are growing, it was somewhere else. I am going to put a stop to their secret cutting and without my knowledge, and without the Konohiki having been told, and therefore, I am setting aside their right to said trees. G. L. Kapeau, Governor of Hawaii."

In 1856, the governor of Maui challenged the rights of High Chief Charles Kanaina, father of King Lunalilo, to cut kou trees on that island. The Interior Department ruled against Kanaina: "Dear Sir: The District Attorney has made a complaint to this office, against Charles Kanaina, in relation to the cutting down by him of the kou trees outside of Peter's place. I hereby instruct you to inform Kanaina, that he must not do so, unless he can produce his title to this land, because, the government owns the ground, and everything upon that ground belongs to the government. I furthermore direct you, that if Kanaina should cut down the remaining trees, order the government officers to oppose him.

"If he cannot produce his title to the kou trees, then, the District Attorney could bring legal action against him for the trees."

In the 1860s, an accidentally imported insect began killing kou trees throughout the island chain. Rev. Sereno Bishop, born in Kailua-Kona, Hawaii, in 1827, remembered their beauty and their disappearance: "There were two or three young kou trees, perhaps ten or fifteen feet high which we children would climb. The bright orange-hued flowers held a trace of honey, and their rather fleshy texture was not unpalatable to chew. The large, glossy cordate leaves formed a thick and beautiful foliage. The small nuts contained sweet kernels which repaid some effort to extract by pounding between stones. The kou tree used to be the most beautiful tree in the Hawaiian Islands, as well as supplying the choicest of ornamental wood. Lahaina was once fringed with these massive spreading trees. One of the finest was in the yard of Mr. Richards, on whose great low boughs we boys loved to climb. About 1860, a minute insect called 'red spider' came to infest the under-side of the leaves to such an extent as in the course of a year to destroy every kou tree, not only in Lahaina, but throughout the group."

In 1823, Rev. William Ellis toured the island of Hawaii preaching. His journal, describing a journey from the western to the southeastern coastline, constantly mentioned kou. It gave a good picture of how much the tree was a part of Hawaiian life. Landing at Kailua, in the district of Kona, Ellis noted: "The houses, which are neat, are generally built on the sea-shore, shaded with cocoa-nut and kou trees, which greatly enliven the scene." Returning to Kailua a month later, in July, to begin the tour, he wrote: "This morning, the 17th, we perceived Keoua, the governor's wife, and her female attendants, with about forty other women, under the pleasant shade of a beautiful clump of *cordia* or kou trees, employed in stripping off the bark from bundles of wauti sticks, for the purpose of making it into cloth."

Beginning his southward walk, he wrote: "Our road now lay through a pleasant part of the district, thickly inhabited, and ornamented occasionally with clumps of kou trees." At Waiohinu, in the district of Kau, he continued: "Our path . . . suddenly turned to the east, and presented to our view a most enchanting valley, clothed in verdure, and ornamented with clumps of kukui and kou trees.

"When we had passed Punau, Leapuki, and Kamomoa, the country began to wear a more agreeable aspect. Groves of cocoa-nuts ornamented the projecting points of land, clumps of kou-trees appeared in various directions, and the habitations of the natives were also thickly scattered over the coast."

At Kaimu, he observed: "Between three and four hundred assembled, under a clump of shady cordia trees, in front of the house, and I preached to them.

"Kaimu is pleasantly situated near the sea shore, on the S. E. side of the island, standing on a bed of lava considerably decomposed, and covered over with a light and fertile soil. It is adorned with plantations, groves of cocoa-nuts, and clumps of kou-trees.

"About half-past one, we arrived at Opihikao, another populous village, situated within a short distance of the sea. The head man, Karaikoa, brought out a mat, spread it under the umbrageous shade of a kou-tree in front of his door, and invited us to sit down and rest, as the sun was vertical, and travelling laborious."

By 1864, when botanist Horace Mann toured the same country collecting and noting plant specimens, disease had apparently totally eradicated kou, for not once did he mention the tree: "The shore is nearly barren, mostly composed of bare lava, with a few sandy beaches on which grows the coconut and it continues to retain the same character around the southern and eastern coasts of the island, through Kau and Puna, until we reach the southern border of the District of Hilo." Interestingly, the disappearance of the kou was not mentioned in Honolulu newspapers until 1875, when the *Pacific Commercial Advertiser* noted: "The beautiful kou, which furnished a remarkably rich grained furniture wood, and which old residents remember as growing abundantly as a shade tree on the sea coasts all over the islands, has quite disappeared within the past ten or fifteen years, having been destroyed by a new insect enemy."

A few trees continued to grow, but with such rarity that the *Advertiser* found it newsworthy when one was discovered: "A few days since, a gentleman whose occupation called him to the extreme low point of land seaward from Moanalua, discovered a sturdy young kou tree growing in front of a native dwelling, on which were a number of the bright yellow blossoms." The *Hawaiian Annual* of 1875 also took note of kou's rarity: "The *kou,* one of the handsomest of woods for cabinet work, has been almost eradicated from the Islands."

Rev. Sereno Bishop also noted that "young trees of the species exist here and there. The trees have always succumbed to the insect pest before attaining any considerable size. . . . The chiefs' great calabash bowls of kou are now rare and choice."

What became of the wood from these trees is unclear. The majority was probably cut and sold as firewood. In 1868, Dowager Queen Emma wrote from Hawaii mentioning kou firewood: "On this boat I will forward the barrel of arrowroot, barrel of coffee and sections of kou wood given me by Kimona for firewood."

As large groves of trees throughout the islands became infected and died, little other use could be made of so much wood other than for fuel. In 1869, the Interior Department in Honolulu wrote to Henry Greenwell on Hawaii instructing him to sell a grove of dead standing kou trees on government land: "I am directed by his excellency the Minister of Interior to authorize you to sell at auction the dead kou trees (said to number about thirty) on the land . . . in Kona. It is left entirely to your judgment to put them up for sale singly or in lots."

Although there is no record of who purchased this wood, or to what use it was put, by 1871 some residents were avidly seeking out surviving trees to have them carved or turned into bowls. In that year, Queen Emma wrote to her mother from Kauai: "If you have twenty-five dollars now send it to buy a kou log to be made into calabashes. It is growing up at Wailua, a big tree and Waikani intends to go and look at it and if it is any good, to cut it for me. It may not be good because of growing in the mountains."

By 1883, the kou had been a rare tree for so long a time that it was forgotten how plentiful it had once been throughout the islands. The *Hawaiian Annual* reported: "Another valuable tree that is about extinct, as far as the Islands go, at least, is the *kou* (*cordia*), which indeed is hardly to be seen at all. There are a few small, carefully cherished trees remaining, but it can never have been very plentiful nor in any sense a common forest tree."

Some chiefs and wealthy residents had stored quantities of kou to make containers or furniture. When Princess Bernice Pauahi Bishop died in 1884, many of her possessions were put up for auction. The *Pacific Commercial Advertiser*, in an article titled "Important Sale of Hawaiian Curiosities, Etc.," listed kou logs among the princess's possessions: "There are also some huge old logs of the valuable kou wood, that is when properly worked, so dark and rich." These logs were believed to have been purchased by cabinetmaker Johann Wicke and used by his son John to produce curios in Honolulu up to 1904. These logs were the last of the ancient kou.

RIGHT: *The wood sample in the center is kou. The other woods are, clockwise from top left; koa, milo, kamani, and monkeypod. Milo and kamani, though very dark and rich when first cut, fade relatively quickly with exposure to sunlight. In* ***The Ancient Hawaiian House****, William Brigham described old umeke of milo in the Bishop Museum collection as being a "peach color." He wrote of milo: "Its distinguishing feature is a rich peach color and under polish a translucent agate-like appearance."*

MILO

Brigham wrote of milo, *Thespesia populnea,* as having "the same geographical range as the kou, the same habitat, and like the former tree is passing away and is seldom seen out of gardens, while a century ago it was planted about the houses of the alii, as is well remembered around that of Kamehameha the Great at Waikiki. Even the name is the same on the southeastern groups, where it was almost a sacred tree. It is a smaller tree than the kou, hence we have no large umekes [bowls] from its wood, but there are very choice small bowls or cups."

Kekahuna identified milo as "the wood of second choice, which, like *kou,* was much used for the carving of wooden calabashes and platters. . . . Kou was more desirable because its grain was softer, and therefore easier to carve, while *milo* grain is harder."

Bowls made of milo look similar to kou, the heartwood also being a dark, rich, reddish brown, with perhaps a more even character, having less dark streaking than kou. The milo tree also yielded dye and medicine, and is in flower most of the year. Before kou trees began dying out throughout Hawaii in the 1860s, milo was probably the rarer tree, and this may be one reason why there are fewer old handmade milo bowls still in existence.

In 1891, the *Hawaiian Gazette* commented on milo's rarity: "This was another favorite wood of the chiefs, and was held in somewhat sacred esteem, as it is referred to occasionally at this day as 'kapu' wood. This, as is the Kou, is found only at low elevations and near habitations, or where dwellings formerly existed. They are also to be had only in limited quantity and now it is becoming scarce its beauty and value as a furniture wood is better appreciated."

KAMANI

The *Hawaiian Gazette,* in an 1891 article on Hawaiian woods, listed kamani, after kou and milo, as the most valued tree for woodworking: "The Kamani ranks next, probably, in the Hawaiians estimation, particularly the red variety, and is used as a furniture wood, for calabashes, and was used also for spears."

Brigham also noted its use: "Another beautiful and durable wood is the *Kamani Calophylluminophyllum,* a tree found all through tropical Asia and the Polynesian islands and used in Hawaii to some extent for umekes."

True kamani is an indigenous tree, not to be confused with false kamani, *Terminalia catappa,* which was introduced to the islands in the nineteenth century. True kamani is a large tree, larger than kou, with a hardwood of suitable strength for furniture making. In *In Gardens of Hawaii,* Marie Neal stated that "the hard, tough wood is valued in tropical Asia for cabinet wood and boats."

Hawaiian wooden bowls of kamani are of an even color and grain, showing only the heartwood, which is lighter than kou or milo. They are less dramatic than bowls of kou or milo when finished and were more difficult to carve because the wood is harder. Perhaps bowls were carved of kamani primarily for the wood's traditional significance. According to Neal: "The kamani is mentioned in old chants of Hawaii, and a grove of it was noted on Molokai by early navigators. In many parts of Polynesia the kamani was a sacred tree, corresponding to the oaks of the Druids, and it was much planted around temples."

Brigham also noted the reverence in which it was held in Hawaii and elsewhere in Polynesia:

"The tree itself is even more beautiful than its wood, and its glossy leaves and sweet-scented flowers caused the old Hawaiians to plant it near their houses while other Polynesians attached a semi-sacred character to groves of the tree, of which we find a trace in the sacred grove near the Puhonua or place of refuge at Halawa at the east end of Molokai."

KOA

Acacia koa is a large evergreen hardwood tree endemic to Hawaii. Although it was a common wood for canoes, very few containers were carved from koa. When kou started dying out in the 1860s, Western turners looked to koa as a replacement wood, primarily because of its beauty and commercial availability.

Henry Kekahuna, in his paper on Hawaiian calabashes, commented on the continuing popularity of koa in the twentieth century: "The calabashes and boards most desired at the present time are those with curly grain. This is because of the natural beauty of the grain, and the fact that when you apply the present day polish (the white man's polish), you have beauty indeed."

In 1900, William Castle wrote of the particular attractiveness of turned koa bowls: "Many of the modern calabashes, less expensive because not laboriously chipped out by hand, but turned by machinery, are beautiful because of the colour of the koa . . . from which they are made." Ancient Hawaiian bowl makers had found koa a difficult wood to work, so Kekahuna also had reason to comment on the ease with which modern lathes could produce bowls of the hard, beautiful koa: "There is no obstacle in this period of progress and great knowledge, when there is superior equipment, and machines that turn with great speed, revolving whistlingly."

MONKEYPOD

Monkeypod, *Samanea saman*, the tree called ohai by Hawaiians, was introduced to the islands in the mid-1800s. Native to South America, this large tree reaches a height of eighty feet or more with a beautiful, thin, spreading, symmetrical crown. The most prized of this wood is light yellow with swirling dramatic grain.

The earliest commercial use of this wood in Honolulu was by carver Frederick Otremba, who in 1883 began turning monkeypod covers and bases for his coconut curios.

When the first interior decorators in Hawaii popularized light-colored furniture woods in the 1930s, monkeypod was the popular choice because of its beauty and availability.

This wood also began to be widely used for leaf-shaped bowls, an art form developed by Swiss craftsman Fritz Abplanalp, whose favorite wood for carving was monkeypod.

Unlike koa, which grew in remote upland areas and was logged commercially, monkeypod grew well at all elevations and could be procured by craftsmen inexpensively and in relatively large quantities. This wood remained popular in the islands until cheap and inferior craft items made of monkeypod began to be imported from the Philippines in the 1950s.

THE INTRODUCTION OF IRON FOR TOOLS

In ancient Hawaii, wooden bowls were shaped with stone and coral tools. Among the most important of these tools were the stone blades made for cutting, shaping, and hollowing. The 1915 *Bishop Museum Handbook* stated: "Of all the Hawaiian tools the stone adze is the chief." By the time Cook arrived, the Hawaiians had acquired some iron in the random arrival of flotsam, and understood its value as a much more suitable material for woodworking tools. When they saw that they could acquire iron through barter with Western ships arriving in the late 1700s, they avidly traded for it. By 1790, iron had probably entirely replaced stone tools among Hawaiian woodworking craftsmen for carving.

In 1778, when Capt. James Cook anchored off the northwest coast of Kauai, he noted that the Hawaiians who came on board were surprised with everything except iron, "the wildness of their looks and gestures fully expressing their entire ignorance about every thing they saw, and strongly marking to us, that, till now, they had never been visited by Europeans, nor been acquainted with any of our commodities, except iron." Cook was careful to determine that the Hawaiians did not know anything of iron except it was harder than any material they had: "They seemed only to understand, that it was a substance, much better adapted to the purposes of cutting, or of boring of holes, than any thing their own country produced."

The Hawaiians were well aware of the commercial implications of this material, as were other South Sea islanders. In Tahiti, Cook recalled: "They held it in such estimation, before Captain Wallis's arrival, that a Chief of Otaheite, who had got two nails into his possession, received no small emolument, by letting out the use of these to his neighbours, for the purpose of boring holes, when their own methods failed, or were thought too tedious."

Capt. Clerke, with Cook, surmised that the few small pieces of iron on Kauai had washed ashore as flotsam, and when his expedition returned to the islands the following year, that very thing had happened in their absence: "At this time, an Indian brought a piece of iron on board

LEFT: *These two iron-hafted adzes and the small wooden adze handle between them illustrate the range of sizes in which these tools were made. An adze handle was carefully crafted from the branch of a tree, incorporating a section of the trunk to hold the blade. The binding was protected from abrading against the sides of the blade by adding a thick, dried leaf or pad of tapa cloth between them. In 1819, visitor Jacques Arago admired the woodwork produced by Hawaiian craftsmen using these tools: "They are made by means of an instrument called in this country* ***toë****, which may be compared to a carpenter's adze, though much smaller, and fit to be used by one hand."*

Sereno Bishop, growing up in Kailua-Kona, Hawaii, in the 1830s, remembered that "with these sharp edged adzes they would deftly dub away and carve out almost any desired smoothing of timber."

Bowl carvers would have worked with adzes while seated on the ground, securing with their feet the piece being carved. This technique was observed by French voyager Louis de Freycinet in 1819: "These workmen, just like the Chinese, hold the pieces on which they are working with their feet, especially all those parts that our artisans would place on a bench."

the Discovery to be fashioned into the shape of a *pahooah* [dagger]. It was carefully examined both by the officers and men, and appeared to be the bolt of some large ship timbers. They were not able to discover to what nation it belonged; but from the pale colour of the iron, and its not corresponding in shape to our bolts, they concluded that it certainly was not English. This led them to make a strict inquiry of the native, when and where he got it; and, if they comprehended him right, it had been taken out of a piece of timber, larger than the cable bit, to which he pointed. This piece of wood, they farther understood from him to have been driven upon their island, since we were here in January 1778."

As soon as Cook landed on Kauai, in 1778, he began trading for provisions: "We were surrounded by a great [number] of Canoes which brought us Hogs, Fowls, sweet potatoes and Plantains for which we gave them small nails and adzes."

Capt. Charles Clerke described iron's initial purchasing power: "This is the cheapest Market I ever saw; a moderate sized Nail, will supply my Ships Company very plentifully with excellent Pork for the day, and as to the Potatoes and Tarrow, they are attained upon still easier Terms, such is these People's avidity for Iron." If Clerke was right, he could feed the crew of seventy men on the *Discovery* for one day for a sixpenny nail, which was less than two inches long.

The expedition sailed away after two weeks, planning to return the following winter.

In October of 1778, while in Alaska, Cook began preparing iron stock for the return to Hawaii. Cook's surgeon, David Samwell, described a very large amount of iron being made into flat planes for trade: "The two Forges were erected & the Armourers set to work to make them, at which they continued from this Time till we left the Islands in March 1779. These Tois [koi; adze-like, sharp] which were made in shape like Plane irons & of different Sizes answered our purpose very well, the Indians being very fond of them, the largest Size were about 12 or 14 inches long & two or three broad. We generally gave three or four of these for a Hog of 100 lb weight or more & there was nothing went so well as these Tois."

These first rectangular pieces of iron, sharpened on one end, immediately replaced the stone blades that had served Hawaiians for centuries. Surgeon David Samwell wrote: "Their own Adzes were made of blue Stone like those of Otaheite but these soon gave way to our iron ones which came into universal use in a very short time."

A large number of iron blades were probably thus acquired by the Hawaiians from Cook, for the expedition spent almost a month anchored in Kealakekua Bay and well over a month sailing along the coast of various islands trading with Hawaiians for provisions. A significant amount of these iron blades probably ended up in the hands of the chiefs' favored craftsmen. On the third of February, just before the expedition prepared to sail from Kealakekua, Cook and his officers witnessed the display of annual taxes to the king, among which was a large part of the traded iron: "On our arrival, we found the ground covered with parcels of cloth; a vast quantity of red and yellow feathers . . . and a great number of hatchets, and other pieces of iron-ware, that had been got in barter from us."

As with much of the annual tribute to the king, the majority of this iron was probably redistributed to lesser chiefs in his retinue for their own use and for craftsmen in their employ.

The Hawaiians apparently also learned the basics of blacksmithing from Cook's men. Clerke wrote: "The eager curiosity, with which they attended the armourer's forge, and the many expedients they had invented, even before we left the islands, for working the iron they had procured from us, into such forms as were best adapted to their purposes, were strong proofs of docility and ingenuity." As Clerke implied, Hawaiians were not interested in Western tools. Rather, they simply wanted what they correctly understood to be a superior material, iron, from which to fashion their own traditional tools. Capt. George Vancouver, in giving a set of blacksmith's tools to a Kauai chief in 1793, commented on this preference: "These people are fond of forming iron for their several purposes after their own fashion." Rev. William Ellis also noted in 1823: "The fishermen would rather receive a wrought nail, to make of it a fish-hook according to their own taste, than the best English-made fish-hook we could give them." One of the few Western woodworking tools that was initially accepted was the axe, for it was recognized as a form of adze.

After Cook's ships sailed away in 1779, it was seven years before Hawaiians had an opportunity to again acquire any iron through trade. Capt. Nathaniel Portlock, in bartering for provisions off Oahu in 1786, traded "some cloaks considerably better than that of captain Clarke's, for a small piece of iron worked into the form of a carpenter's plane-bit: these the Sandwich islanders make use of as adzes, and call them *towees;* and to them they answer every purpose wherever an edge-tool is required."

John Nicol was with Portlock and described the avidity with which iron was sought after: "I was as busy and fatigued as I could be cutting iron hoops into lengths of eight and nine inches, which the carpenter ground sharp. These were our most valuable commodity in the eyes of the natives."

This expedition started a commerce between Western traders and Chinese merchants for otter furs. Furs were bartered for on the northwest coast of North America, then sold in Canton. Hawaii, midway between the two destinations, was used for obtaining provisions, and these provisions were purchased primarily with iron. Thus, fur traders supplied Hawaiians with the majority of the iron they acquired from 1786 to the turn of the century.

In 1789, fur trader John Cox recorded a typical visit: "A great number of canoes now came off to us, and we commenced a brisk trade with the natives for hogs, salt, cabbage, cloth, spears, ornaments of feathers, etc.; all of which they exchanged with us for different-sized spike nails, which they preferred to every thing else that we offered them."

French voyager Etienne Marchand, investigating the fur trade in 1791, found that in Hawaii "iron is almost the only article which the natives chose to accept in exchange for their provisions. They set a great value on large spikes."

There were enough fur traders stopping to acquire provisions or spend winters in the islands to have introduced a large amount of iron into Hawaii before 1800. Spanish Navy Lt. Manuel Quimper described it as common in Hawaii in 1791: "They make . . . canoes . . . spears, plates, trays and pots of wood admirably worked, adzes which they form from the pipe barrel hoops left by ships and which they exchange for fruits and use to carve their woods." And Thomas Manby, with Vancouver's voyage in 1792, agreed with Quimper: "They are now so well acquainted with the great superiority of our metal implements and working tools as not to be able to do without them, for at this time, a Stone Hatchet or a shark's tooth knife is as rare a thing among them, as an iron axe, or a pair of scissors was twenty years ago."

Around the turn of the century, Hawaiians on every island apparently had enough iron to meet their needs, since by this year iron was no longer a valuable article of trade. Russian Capt. Urey Lisianski discovered this during his visit to Hawaii in 1804, reporting: "Though the islanders took knives and small looking glasses in exchange for their goods, they always gave the preference to our printed and common coarse linens, while pieces of iron hoop, of which we had a great number, were held by them in no estimation."

Probably the great majority of early wooden bowls that have survived into the twentieth century were made with iron tools. Iron made woodworking easier, and a greater number of wooden products could be produced with less effort. Larger bowls could also be made much more easily, and after the introduction of iron, bigger and bigger bowls began to be described by visitors.

For example, in 1779 David Samwell wrote of Hawaiian wooden bowls as being "of various sizes from two Gallons to a quart." Twelve years later, in 1791, when iron had become somewhat plentiful, Ebenezer Townsend observed wooden dishes capable of holding three gallons, and by 1809 Archibald Campbell observed bowls twice as large, "to five or six gallons." A 1893 article in the *Hawaiian Gazette* stated: "Some of these wooden calabashes were very large, and would hold close on fifteen gallons."

An article in the *Islander* described the extreme size of later containers as being limited only by the size of the tree: "I was shown a poi calabash of one piece of Kou, which is probably the largest one in existence, as I found it to measure 25 1/2 inches in diameter at the mouth, 18 inches in depth and 7 1/2 feet in circumference. It is only used by royalty, being *kapu* to common natives. The cover is made of wood, as there cannot be found a calabash large enough to close it." This calabash, now in the Bishop Museum, holds thirty-three gallons.

The Hawaiian craftsmen's preference for the traditional adze, which they now fashioned from iron, is understandable in part because of its great versatility. Rev. William Ellis described Hawaiians interchanging the adze for Western tools in 1823: "Though they now use an axe in felling the trees, the adze is still their favourite tool, and many of them use no other. The stone adze is, however, exchanged for one made with a plane iron, bent, and tied securely to a handle of light wood. This they prefer to the European adze, which they say is too heavy. Sometimes they use a saw, chisel, and gimlet, in framing their houses, but they are not yet adept in the use of these tools; we have often seen them throw down the saw, and take up the adze to finish that which they had commenced cutting with a saw."

Western tools were not only rare throughout Hawaii in the early 1820s, they were also nearly useless if they could not be sharpened. As late as 1844, Rev. Elias Bond, writing from the remote Kohala district on Hawaii, stated: "Axes are rare among the people and when possessed, no means are had wherewith to keep them sharp, save as the owner is able to round off the edge a little, on any common rock he finds. I have accordingly known the people to fell large trees and get out timber as hard as oak 12 to 15 inches square and 40 to 50 feet long, all with two or three axes whose edges were no sharper than the back of one's razor. These poor creatures often must exhibit an almost incredible amount of patience and perseverance."

In the late 1840s, however, Western tools slowly became more readily available, and by 1848, when the California gold rush brought unprecedented money and goods to the islands, the Hawaiian adze had dropped from sight.

ABOVE: *Shown here are two traditional stone adzes, a carpenter's plane blade bent to convert it into an adze, and a small piece of iron made into an adze blade. Peter Corney, visiting Hawaii in 1815 and twice in 1818, described the iron blades then in use: "The tool in most general use is a kind of tomahawk, or adz, called toe; it was formerly made of hard polished stone, but is now universally made of iron. To form it, they lash a thin plate of iron, from one to four inches broad, and five or six inches long, to a branch which has a piece of the stem attached to it. Plane irons are much in request for this purpose; but the toe is frequently made of an iron hoop."*

THE CRAFTING OF WOODEN CALABASHES

After the Hawaiian craftsman had chosen the type of wood to be used, he next had to select a particular tree, which was in itself an art. Milo, and particularly the softer kou, have a tendency toward pithy or hollow centers, even in the limbs. It is not known whether the limbs of the chosen tree were cut as needed, or the whole tree was cut down and stored. Concerning the cutting, Kekahuna recorded: "One of the most important features in this profession of calabash-making was this. The portions of the trunks of the *kou* and *milo* trees that adjoined the earth, including the tap-roots and large side-roots, were never used, as was the case with those of all other trees in that period. . . . The principal reasons were these:

"*First,* there was the great amount of toil required to excavate the stumps and roots.

"*Secondly,* the grain of this part of the tree-trunk was known by the ancients to be wave-like or curly (nalu), very brittle, and exceedingly difficult to carve and hollow. Besides, if such wood were continually wet and dried in the sun, it would very soon crack. Therefore the ancients did not at all like the kind of wood with the grain called nalu [wavy]. 'It causes fatigue of the body to no purpose,' said they.

"No calabashes in ancient times were ever made from the parts of the tree named, for the reasons stated above. Therefore it was not because the ancients did not know the beauty of the wood, but because it was so brittle that the effort of working it would be wasted. The calabashes that show a slightly curly grain were made from the wood at the junction of a branch above the main part of the trunk."

Rev. Lorenzo Lyons, stationed in Waimea, Hawaii, for fifty-four years, noted Hawaiian craftsmen burning trees instead of cutting trees down. In 1833, a year after arriving, he wrote: "The native when destitute of axe uses fire as substitute. Hence a tree instead of being cut down is burned down. The tree is set afire in such a way as to burn only at the bottom — after awhile the man goes to see whether it has fallen or not. Then if he wishes to make a tray the only tool he uses for the purpose is an adz wh.[ich] is generally made of an old plane iron bent up in a proper shape and attached to a sort of a handle — this answers for a saw, axe, auger, chisel, gauge, plane, and what not."

Although Lyons's observation is the only written account of such a method, it may very well have been a common way for bowl makers to fell their trees.

Once the tree was felled, the craftsman probably marked out sections of trunk and limb suitable for particular bowl shapes and sizes. The usable parts of the tree would have to be

LEFT: *Three flat-bottomed scrap bowls made of kou are seen here, two roughly hewn and one completely finished and polished.*

The unfinished blocks were part of a cache of five dug from the sands of Waikiki in 1890. The completed bowl in the foreground is from Queen Emma's collection. The finished container is 3 5/8" high and 8 1/2" wide across the rim. The unfinished block directly behind it is 3" high and 11 1/4" long overall, while the tipped block is 4 1/8" high and 10 1/4" long.

immediately cut into bowl blanks or at least into sizes that one man could carry.

Brigham, in his 1906 publication, *The Ancient Hawaiian House,* writes of the bowl maker "cutting it into suitable blocks and then sinking it in some pool where it might soak for months." This storage for freshly cut wood preserved the wood indefinitely and kept the green blanks from drying out and curing into hard blocks before being worked. This was important, for one medium-sized kou tree, if sound throughout, would yield a large number of blanks.

From the blanks, tall, medium or shallow bowls were carved. Each was carved in a particular way. Tall, deep bowls were carved so that the grain ran vertically and the heartwood core ran through the bottom of the bowl. In low bowls, the grain ran horizontally; these bowls were cut from half of a log, avoiding the heartwood core. Particularly beautiful bowls of medium height were cut from the trunk of the tree where it branched. These bowls showed three heartwood cores spaced evenly around the sides of the bowl.

After leveling a flat plane, which, after shaping and hollowing, would become the rim, the outside shape of the bowl was carved. Once the form of the bowl was determined, the hard work of hollowing the interior was begun. Bowls were probably carved in much the same manner as canoes, the shaping of which began immediately after the tree was cut down. After the log was roughly hollowed out, the thick walls were gradually thinned as the wood cured. Similarly, the bulk of the interior of a wooden bowl would be removed when the wood was soft and green. It would then be set aside to cure for a time. When the wood had dried to the extent that the thickness could be reduced without causing the walls to crack or warp, the bowl was again worked on. This process of gradually thinning the walls and setting the bowl aside would be repeated over an extended period of time. As the carving of the bowl neared completion, the wood would have cured completely. Because each bowl could thus only be worked on for a relatively short time, craftsmen probably carved several bowls at once.

In 1890, five wooden bowls, in various stages of completion were found buried in the sand on the Waikiki estate of Charles Bishop. It was assumed at the time they had been hidden. However, burying the wood in sand would also slow the curing process while bowls were being carved. Craftsmen may have routinely buried partially completed bowls as they worked them.

Brigham mentions that Hawaiian craftsmen sometimes also soaked wooden blanks in mud to darken the wood: "When a dark tone was desired, the block was sunk in the mud of a kalo patch where the ferruginous mud soon produced the appearance of age even on light colored wood fresh from the maker's hand." Whether this was done routinely or only on particular woods is not known. In fact, no additional information remains either orally or in writing about this technique.

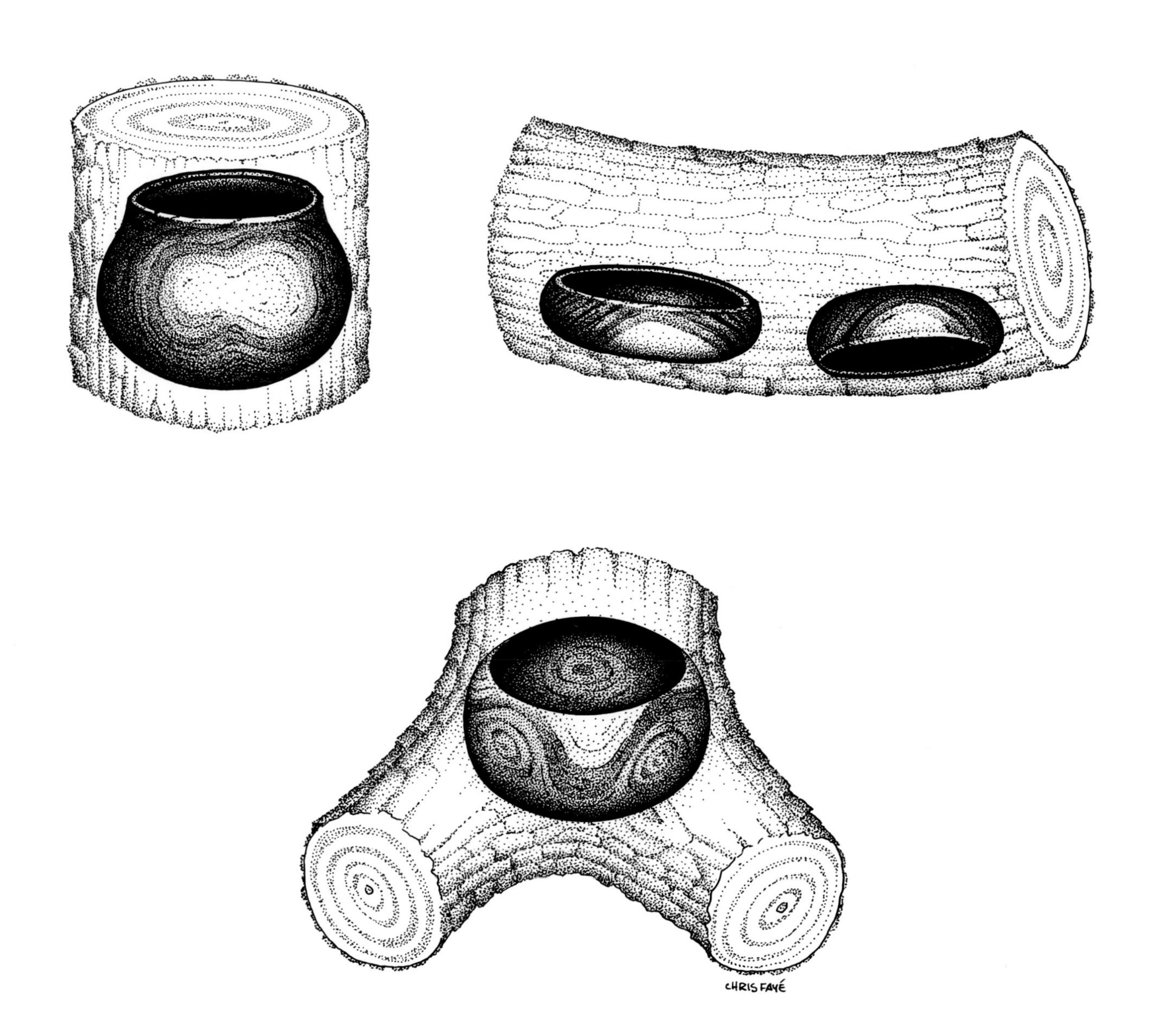

ABOVE: *Illustrated here are the different parts of the log from which the three basic bowl shapes were commonly hewn. Tall bowls, like those shown top left, were carved with the core running through the bottom of the bowl. Low bowls were carved from the outer part of the log, avoiding the core. Wide bowls were often carved from tree crotches, as in the bottom drawing.*

ABOVE: *The two bowls pictured here illustrate different stages in carving. The low bowl in the foreground shows how hollowing was begun by carving a rim around the bowl, then excavating an inch or so of wood across the inner diameter. This hollowing was repeated in concentric circles until the desired depth was reached. The result was a series of descending steps leading down to the bottom. These steps or ledges were finally ground down with stones.*

The tall bowl in the back has been completely shaped and hollowed and is ready for smoothing with stone. The depth of this bowl indicates initial hollowing may have been done with fire, after carefully shielding the walls with stones.

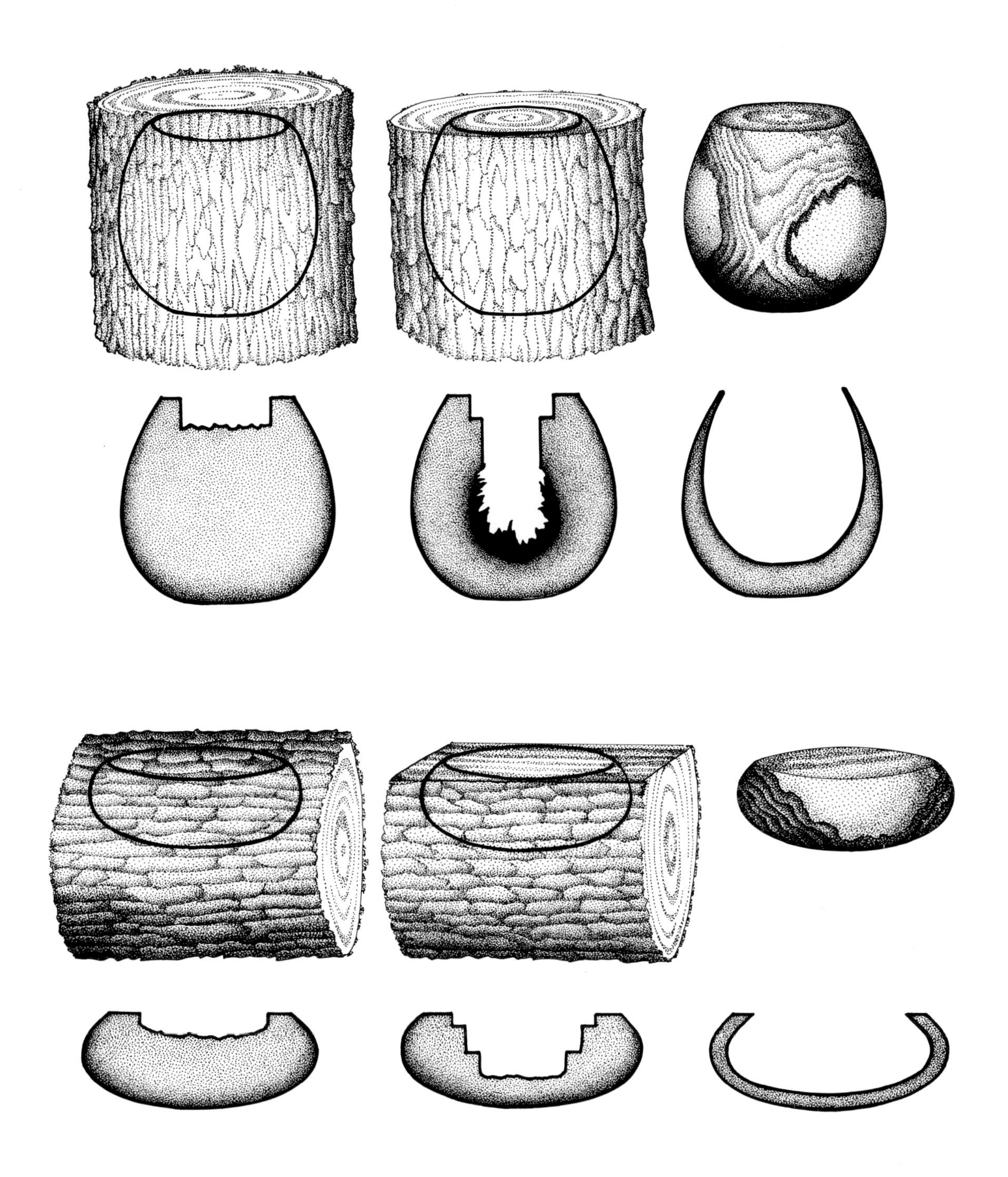

ABOVE: *This illustration shows how tall bowls were carved. The first step was selection of a log appropriate to the bowl form being made. The next step was to level the rim. After this, the outside shape of the bowl was established. Next, the hollowing of the bowl began. Possibly, fire was used on tall, deep bowls to hollow them. Flat stones were placed around the walls so the fire burned straight down. Once the interior was roughly hollowed, the wood both inside and out was smoothed and polished.*

BELOW: *Low bowls were carved from the side of the log, avoiding the heartwood core. A large amount of excess wood may have been carved away, as there is little evidence that Hawaiian bowl makers split the logs. Once the outside form was carved, the bowls were hollowed a few inches at a time, creating a series of ledges. The carved ledges leading down to the bottom were ground down with stone abraders.*

FINISHING AND POLISHING

After the bowls had been shaped and hollowed by adze, Hawaiian craftsmen turned to other traditional tools and materials to finish and polish them.

Brigham described the finishing process: "Where we should saw, bore or chisel, he patiently abrades, first with rough stone, and certain varieties of the Hawaiian cellular basaltic lava had great abrading power, then with stones of smoother grain until both the shape and surface are to his satisfaction.

"While it is true that the outside is first finished, that does not mean that the polish is complete, but only that the form is determined and a smooth surface that is to be the final one before polishing, for from this the artisan determines the extent to which the interior is to be dug out. The interior was made beautifully smooth for cleanliness in use rather than for appearance, and when this was satisfactory the finer polish of the outside was taken in hand. The order has been often stated in which the stones of various kinds were used, but there was no rule in practice that was generally followed: each man had his own way of doing his work and it would vary with the wood he was polishing. . . . The patient application of whatever medium was the secret of the beautiful finish of the best of the old umeke."

According to Kekahuna's paper, after bowls had been carved to the desired shape and thickness, but before final finishing, those that were intended to hold food were specially treated. These bowls were put through a series of soakings to draw out any aftertaste or bitterness the wood might impart to food put in them.

Kekahuna gave a detailed account of the process: "Before finishing and polishing their wooden containers the ancestors would soak them in the sea for perhaps a week, weighting them down in places where they would not be harmed by the breaking or receding waves, after which they would remove and bleach them in the sun.

"When they were thoroughly dried, waste parts of taro or potato (kele ai) were placed in them. These were left to ferment for about a week, when they were thrown out and replaced by a fresh supply until the bitterness of the wood had been somewhat reduced.

"Ordinary fermented taro-poi or potato-poi was then put into the calabashes. The purpose of this was to hasten their sweetening, for to accomplish this with fresh poi of taro or potato would require a much longer period.

"The fermented poi was allowed to remain in the calabashes for about a week, when it was thrown away. The vessels were then filled with plain water and allowed to stand for about two days, after which the water was thrown out. This process was continued until the bitterness was

LEFT: *Two bowls, carved with an adze and ready for smoothing, are shown here with the stone abraders Hawaiian craftsmen used for finishing. By the beginning of the nineteenth century, iron had completely replaced stone for cutting wood; nevertheless, the only abrading tools continued to be made of stone and coral. Not only were Western smoothing implements simply not available, but these stone smoothers — from the very rough square stone lying in the low bowl, to the highly polished circular stone in front of the bowl — were very effective and efficient tools.*

In 1819, visitor Jacques Arago wrote: "Our cabinet-makers do not polish the most costly furniture better; and without planes or any of the tools employed by our workmen, those of Owhyhee are capable of competing with the best artisans of Europe."

completely removed. If after the first treatment the bitterness was still somewhat strong, the putting in of fermented taro-poi or potato-poi was resumed, and the vessels then filled with plain water.

"As a final test for bitterness, ordinary taro-poi or potato-poi was put into these calabashes and left for perhaps a day and a night, after which the food adhering to the sides was tasted to see whether it was bitter or sweet. If any bitterness remained slightly the process was continued as above mentioned. This method was generally performed after the plain water process."

In describing the final smoothing, historian David Malo wrote that the bowl was first rubbed with coral, then rough lava, and finally pumice. Malo also described the order in which the polishing materials were used: charcoal, bamboo-leaf, breadfruit leaf, and finally tapa. However, he did not mention the polish itself.

Kekahuna's paper also described a similar process, but followed by describing the polish and how it was applied: "When the smoothing had been done with the kinds of pumice-stone mentioned and perhaps with the skins of shark or sting-ray, polishing was begun with dry or green bamboo-leaves. During this process, kukui-nut oil was rubbed in, not in an excess amount that would smear the calabash, but only just enough.

"They worked cautiously, using the bamboo-leaves with a few drops of oil till the beauty of the grain was greatly enhanced. Work with yellowed breadfruit-leaves was then commenced, and continued until a polish was attained, and the surface dried with a tapa-cloth wet with a few drops of kukui-nut oil. This part of the process was done vigorously till perspiration appeared. The principal reason was this. In performing this process, rubbing had to be performed with celerity until the palm of the hand became very warm, when you would see the wood attaining a brilliant polish."

The kukui, *Aleurites moluccana,* are large trees found throughout Polynesia and in Southern Asia. In Hawaii, they grow in abundance on the wet, lower-mountain regions of all the islands. The nut of the tree was eaten as medicine, worn as jewelry, burned as candles, and used to polish and seal wood products.

The kernel of the kukui nut is about fifty percent oil and is of the same class of drying oils as linseed oil. Kukui is botanically related to trees which produce tung oil, which is a drying oil developed in China and used in the West as a substitute for linseed oil in making varnishes, lacquers, and enamels.

Although the oil application appears like an oil finish, leaving little gloss on the surface, a sheen can be produced with repeated applications.

Raw kukui nuts are a strong purgative, and craftsmen cooked them before use on the interior surfaces of bowls. Kekahuna wrote: "When the insides of the calabashes were treated with kukui-oil, the method of preparation was this. Dry kukui-nuts were roasted until thoroughly cooked, when their kernels turned yellowish. They were then pounded soft, placed in a piece of tapa-cloth, and rubbed onto the insides of the calabashes." With the final application of oil, the bowl was finished.

Hawaiians apparently had developed techniques for attaining a high gloss, for Capt. James Cook, on Kauai in 1778, wrote that "some of these stained gourd-shells are covered with a kind of lacker." Several eighteenth-century visitors commented on the high polish of the bowls. Capt. George Dixon's description in 1787 is typical: "Another species of ingenuity met with amongst these people is carving.... The bowls and dishes are made of a kind of wood resembling ebony, and are finished with a proportion and polish equal, if not superior, to anything made by our turners." Knowledge of any techniques or compounds that may have been used, other than repeated applications of kukui oil, is now lost.

RIGHT: *Kukui nuts range in size from 1/2" to 1" in diameter. The oil extracted from the thick-husked, hard-shelled nuts was the primary ingredient in compounds used to seal and polish canoe hulls; kukui oil was also the principal substance used to polish bowls of wood in ancient Hawaii. It probably remained in use by Hawaiian bowl makers into the 1860s. As the craft of hand carving wooden bowls died out, kukui was supplanted by shellac and varnish by Western turners. However, there were several attempts by Western businessmen to find other commercial applications for the oil.*

Some early missionaries had used kukui oil to paint their houses, and in 1840 the **Polynesian** *reported the establishment of a business in Honolulu to extract and sell the oil commercially: "An enterprising German has established a copper foundry and a press for the extraction of oil from the Kukui nut, which is used largely in painting."*

That same year, visitor Lt. Charles Wilkes commented on the new business and also noted one of the kukui's major drawbacks, its slowness in drying: "These nut-trees grow with great luxuriance on this island; and an excellent oil is expressed from the nut, which already forms an export from these islands. We heard here, that at New York, it was pronounced superior to linseed-oil for painting. There is a manufactory of it at Honolulu; but I understand that it dried with difficulty. It is said to bring one dollar per gallon on the coast of South America."

The following year, visitor Sir George Simpson also commented indirectly on this drawback: "The oil, though inferior to linseed, is yet so much cheaper, that it finds a market at Lima to the annual amount of upwards of a thousand gallons." The **Pacific Commercial Advertiser** *stated that between 1840 and 1850 the industry produced up to 10,000 barrels a year. By 1851, however, the cheapness of whale oil and the quicker drying linseed oil drove kukui oil from the market. David Frick reported in the* **Pacific Commercial Advertiser***: "The late intelligent and industrious William French was the first to erect a mill for the production of kukui oil, and his produce was used for paint and light — but the cheapness of the whaler's oil, and the quicker drying properties of linseed oil have reduced that business to a less than profitable condition than many other undertakings, and it was already abandoned when I reached these shores, in 1851."*

Several other attempts were made to find commercial application for kukui oil, the last in 1929. That year, the Archer Daniels Midland Company of Minneapolis ordered five tons of kukui kernels to be shipped to their Portland, Oregon, mill for experimentation. The **Advertiser** *reported: "Definite Commerce in Kukui Nuts Seems Established With World's Largest Linseed Concern.*

"Kukui nuts appear definitely established as a new island commercial product. Yesterday, the chamber of commerce received by cable an order for five tons of the kernels from the Archer Daniels Midland Company, world's largest producer of linseed oil which has been interested in kukui oil since last February, when the Archer family were spending their yearly vacation as guests at the Moana Hotel." With the New York Stock Market crash that year, nothing came of the venture.

ABOVE: *The wood inserts seen in these bowls are known among Western craftsmen as "butterflies." Hawaiians termed them "fishtails" or pewa. It is not known whether this was an ancient repair method or was introduced after Western contact. Pewa are considered traditional and are the most dramatic of Hawaiian bowl repairs. The small bowl in the foreground belonged to Queen Liliuokalani.*

REPAIRING

The Hawaiian craftsmen were as adept at repairing wooden bowls as they were at making them. As Kekahuna's paper on wooden bowls stated: "The mending of various kinds of wood and gourd containers, and other objects of the wood carver's art, was a branch of skilled practice that the ancestors of this race did not lack."

That previous owners cared enough about preserving a bowl to have it repaired when damaged is thought to be evidence of how highly it was valued. Repairs on old wooden bowls are considered, therefore, marks of beauty and worth.

However, many ancient wooden bowls show few repairs other than those inserted during the process of making them; weak areas and faults were reinforced and patched at that time. Once the containers were in use, weaknesses would have been noticed and repaired quickly. Extensive repairs on ancient wooden bowls, therefore, may indicate long abandonment or abuse before refurbishing. Many of these have histories of being found in country areas, abandoned under houses, being used to feed livestock, or of being discovered in closed burial caves.

In 1900, a United States newspaper reported of Hawaiian wood bowls: "The demand for the wooden utensils has increased so rapidly that there are now natives who spend their entire time in searching for old caves in which these calabashes might be hidden." In 1902, the *Hawaiian Annual* noted: "The growing demand for them has given a regular calling to several native Hawaiians for the hunting up in out-of-the-way places throughout the islands of all old and damaged wooden utensils for the repairing and polishing of the same for order customers or for the market. And a well repaired calabash loses nothing in estimation or value from the fact that it is patched, for this is to be regarded as another evidence of antiquity and, if anything, should command a premium."

In writing of repairs, Kekahuna stated: "There are six methods used in this part of the work that are known to me, with their individual names, and the practice followed by those skilled in this branch of the work." Five of the repairs Kekahuna referred to were used on wooden bowls; the sixth was a sewing technique used on gourds. These repair techniques for wood included large and small wooden plugs to fill holes and cracks, pegs to secure repairs, and two repairs designed to prevent existing cracks from enlarging. The only nontraditional technique that became accepted in the nineteenth century was the use of orange shellac or hide glue to fill holes and depressions, particularly on the unfinished interior of bowls. Otherwise, the traditional methods of repairing wooden bowls were adhered to by craftsmen into the twentieth century.

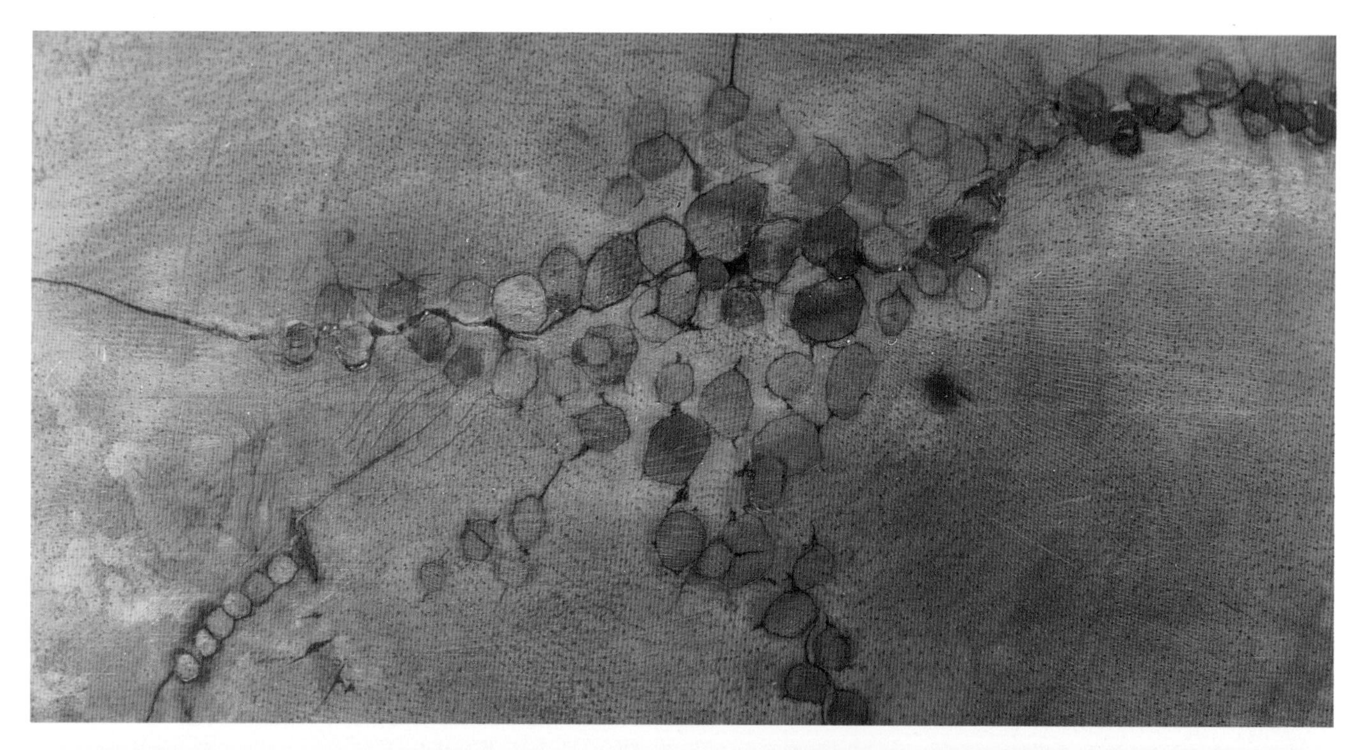

ABOVE: *Round pegs were often inserted into holes drilled into heartwood core areas. When this part of the log was incorporated in a bowl, pegs would be driven into these areas while it was being cured and the wood was still green. The wood dried and shrank around the dry wood pegs holding them firmly in place and strengthening the soft endgrain.*

BELOW: *This repair is termed kepa, or kepakepa, which means, in this case, "to turn back upon itself." These wedges were inserted at alternating angles across the length of a crack. Kekahuna described the completed repair: "When this method had been used the place mended looked like an ascending road."*

ABOVE: *Large wooden patches were called poho, and the hardwood pegs used to secure them were called huini. To secure these pieces, holes were drilled at an angle piercing both the bowl and the patch. The pegs were tapped in until a tight fit was assured.*

In the repair illustrated here, smaller pieces of wood were tapped in at one end to fill a gap before the securing pegs were fitted.

BELOW: *Here pieces of wood are driven into cracks to fill them. Sometimes pegs were used, but more often these repairs were wedges termed kiki. Kekahuna wrote: "In the places where the crack was narrow, or where it was slightly open, these pieces of wood would be inserted and hammered till they fitted perfectly."*

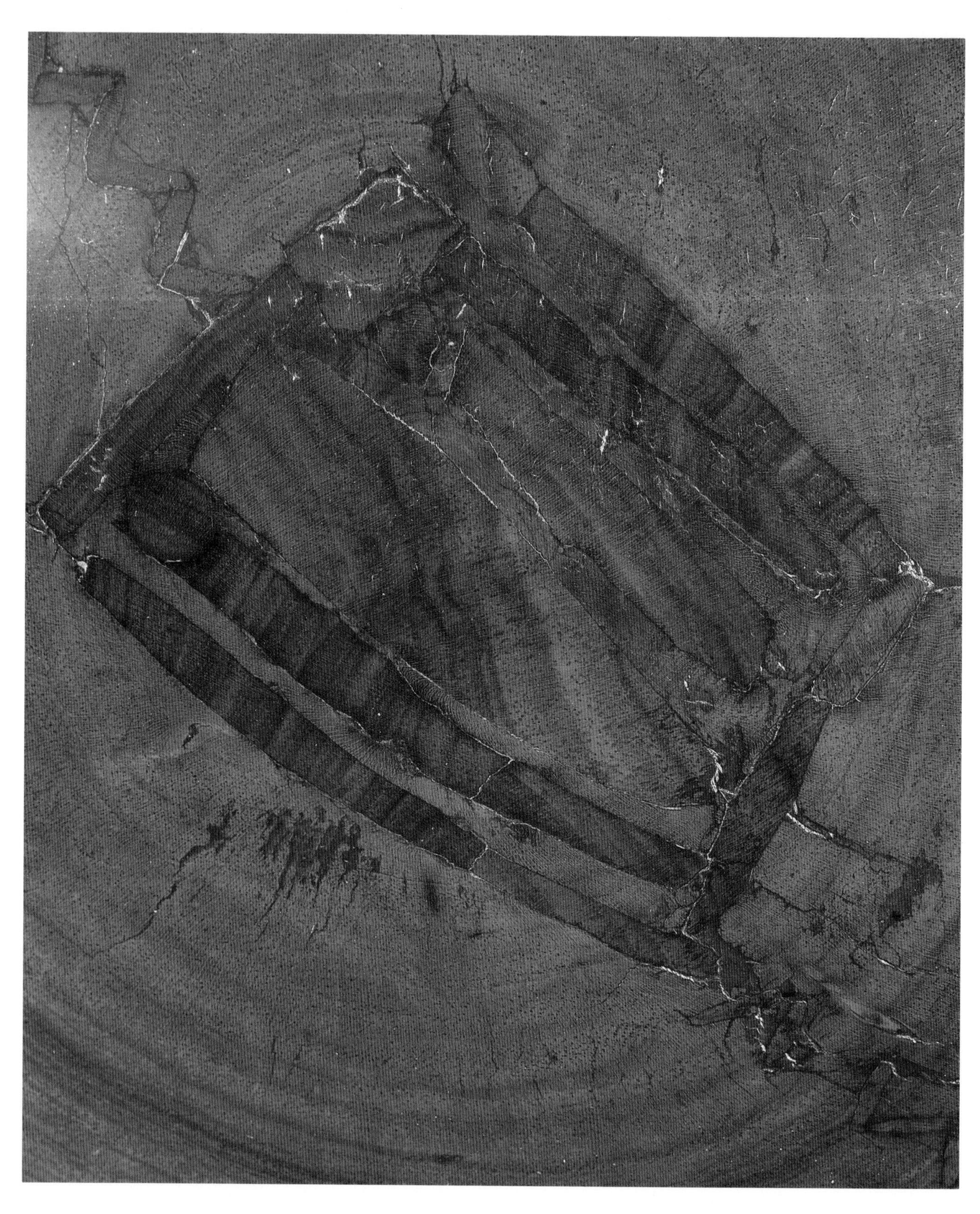

ABOVE: *Several types of repairs can be seen here. A large plug was inserted and smaller wedges surround it. Radiating cracks were checked with kepa repairs.*

ABOVE: *Careful repairs often enhance a bowl's beauty. In this bowl, a deep rim insert is held firmly in place with hardwood pegs. The decorative "butterfly," or pewa, may have been a later addition to further strengthen a repair weakened with age.*

TRADITIONAL CRAFTSMEN

As beautiful and well crafted as Hawaiian bowls were, almost nothing is known of the old Hawaiian craftsmen who made them. The carving of wooden bowls may have been a craft in which the chiefly class participated, for in 1840 Charles Pickering, zoologist with the United States Exploring Expedition, was very impressed with bowls being carved by a village chief in Waianae on Oahu: "Reached Waianai in the afternoon. . . . Mr. Bishop visits it occasionally, and in his absence our host, the Chief, preaches — who is also the school master — but his chief occupation during our stay was the making of wooden bowls, at which he seems particularly expert."

Hawaiian oral tradition is entirely silent about all those men, chief or commoner, whose products so impressed early Western explorers. William Brigham, writing *The Ancient Hawaiian House* in 1908, commented on the anonymity of Hawaiian bowl makers: "Unlike the Maori, who carefully kept and honored the memory of the artists among them whose carving was good, the Hawaiian has not preserved a single name of those who patiently with stone tools fashioned the umeke, plain or grotesquely carved, that have come down to us."

One of the few woodworkers whose identity had been preserved carved wooden bowls as well as canoes. Homer Hayes, a descendant of this nineteenth-century Hawaiian craftsman, stated that his great-great-grandfather's skills caused him to be remembered at least among his neighbors: "I have a few calabashes from my great grandfather's father, whose name was Puakoa. He made canoes and calabashes. He was born about 1790 and died in 1867. A neighbor of his, Puapo Hale, was a very young boy when Puakoa died. Puapo had been present at his burial and one day he took me to the cave where my great-great-grandfather was interred and reminisced about him. Puapo remembered as a child awakening mornings to the sound of Puakoa's adze next door. He recalled that my great-great-grandfather was renowned in the community for the thin walls of his wood bowls and the thin light shells of his canoes."

The Hawaiian society in general, however, did not preserve the identity of its craftsmen; moreover, relatively little is preserved of their traditions, methods, or knowledge. This loss was largely the result of the sudden termination of the traditional Hawaiian socio-religious system in

LEFT: *Next to two adze-hewed bowls are seen an iron-hafted adze and a large smoothing stone with a knob for gripping. To the left of the smoothing stone is a very smooth polishing stone, probably the final stone implement used in polishing.*

Archibald Campbell, visiting Hawaii in 1809, was impressed with the quality of the products which craftsmen made with these few tools: "In every article of their manufacture these Islanders display an extraordinary degree of neatness and ingenuity, considering the simplicity of the tools with which they work.

"The tool in most general use is a kind of tomahawk, or adze, called toe . . . this, with a piece of coral for a file, is almost the only tool used in the construction of their houses, canoes, and implements of wood.

"The circular wooden dishes, containing from half a pint to five or six gallons, are formed with these simple tools, and are as neatly made as if they had been turned in a lathe."

1819. When the ancient system was abolished by royal decree, the strict laws that had governed every aspect of Hawaiian work and family life were slowly and permanently forgotten. After 1819, the specialized traditions of bowl makers vanished, in part then, because the craftsman's work lost ritual significance. The prayers and ceremonies that had given importance to the different steps in turning a product of nature into an object serving society became meaningless and were forgotten. Kekahuna's paper on the making of wooden bowls could only state that such ceremonies had existed: "According to what I understand from my grandparents, they performed this part of the work with religious ceremonies, and with the aid of wood-hewing deities, which was similar to the practice when carving canoes. Religious observance extended from the time of cutting down the tree, through the periods of hewing and of removing the bitterness from the calabash, to the time of the ceremony of initiating the calabash into service."

Although craftsmen continued to carve bowls well into the nineteenth century, by the end of it they had quietly disappeared. There were many changes in the lifestyle of the Hawaiians during this period which affected these craftsmen. Perhaps one of the earliest was the sudden ending of ancient religious practices in 1819. Under this system men and women ate apart, each with their own utensils, as Peter Corney observed in 1817: "They [women] are not even allowed to touch anything that goes inside of the men's eating house; they have their own vessels to eat and drink out of." After 1819, men and women ate together communally, and households no longer needed the duplication of utensils as previously.

Perhaps a more fundamental reason for the decline in bowl carvers was the precipitous decline of the Hawaiian population. At the time of Capt. Cook's arrival on Kauai in 1778, the population numbered perhaps 250,000. By 1850 the population had dropped to less than 100,000.

Further, the 1848 discovery of gold in California, and the subsequent establishment of towns and cities there, increased the general availability of Western utensils throughout the islands.

In addition, changing tax laws had a small but significant impact on craftsmen. Previously, taxes to the government could be paid in produce and craft products, among them wooden bowls. After 1850, the government no longer recognized these products as tax payments, and accepted only money.

Some wooden bowls continued to be made, however, for the staple food, poi, was always eaten from containers of wood or gourd. Visitor Isobel Field found the sophisticated King Kalakaua still adhering to this tradition in 1883: "Wondering what Royalty ate for breakfast, I glanced at the table and saw to my surprise the remains of a roast suckling pig and a large calabash of *poi.*"

A few professional bowl makers continued to be employed by chiefs in some districts at least until the middle of the nineteenth century. Rev. Oliver Emerson, born in 1845, remembered the ending of that position in the Waialua district on Oahu when he was a young boy: "One day, when I was a child, a native boy about fourteen years old came to our house. His father had been a calabash maker for the chief, but had lost his job, for crockery was coming into use. So the son had to a seek a new employment, and though rude in manner and speech, the boy showed good spirit."

The occurrence that finally ended the ancient craft of bowl carving was the disappearance of the traditional trees from which containers were made. As kou trees began dying throughout the kingdom from an introduced insect in the 1860s, skilled bowl makers were rarely to be found. One of the few indications that the art was still practiced appeared in an article in the

Hawaiian newspaper *Ke Au Okoa* in 1867. Unfortunately, legal action had been brought against the craftsmen and the purpose of the article was to report a pun that had circulated due to one man's name, Paakai, which in Hawaiian means "rock salt": "On Wednesday of this week, Pupule and Paakai appeared before the court regarding a matter of the handling of several pieces of kou wood from which several wooden containers were to be made. During the trial Pupule was dismissed and Paakai was sentenced to 1 year at hard labor in addition to a $10.00 fine. The foolish among the people remarked: 'It is certainly stiff (as stiff and as old as salted fish), for it is a thing seasoned by Paakai.' "

By 1870, bowl carvers were very difficult to find. In 1871, Queen Emma in Honolulu wrote her mother, visiting Lahaina on Maui, inquiring after craftsmen. Her mother wrote back: "I have seen your letter. There is no one who knows the fundamentals of making containers. There is some knowledge but not much."

With the gradual disappearance of traditional bowl makers, Western turners and cabinet-makers began turning wooden bowls on lathes out of koa in significant·numbers. By the 1880s, these craftsmen had replaced Hawaiians as the bowl makers of the kingdom.

WALERY
PHOTOGRAPHER TO THE QUEEN
V R
164 REGENT STREET
LONDON

MODERN WOODEN CALABASHES

The era of the traditional, hand-carved Hawaiian wooden bowl symbolically ended with the arrival of the first lathes in the islands in the 1830s. As early as 1834, a noncommercial lathe was in operation at the missionary station in Lahaina, on Maui; and the Rev. Jonathan Green was given a lathe for the Wailuku station on Maui, in 1835, by a sea captain. The missionaries, however, had little interest in fashioning wooden bowls in traditional forms; their lathes were intended for making furniture for themselves and their families.

The kingdom's first commercial lathe was probably imported by merchant William French and sold to Honolulu's earliest cabinetmaker, Louis Morstein, in 1837 for the price of twenty dollars. The first commercial lathe on Maui was perhaps the one owned by American cabinetmaker John Halstead, in operation at his shop in Lahaina by at least January 1842. And on the island of Hawaii, Hilo sawmill owner Daniel Castle was recorded as possessing a lathe in an 1843 inventory, although he may have been using it much earlier.

The kingdom's first advertisement for lathe-turning appeared in the Honolulu newspaper the *Polynesian,* in 1844. It was placed by German cabinetmaker Christian LaFrenz: "Sofas, Chairs, Bureaus, and all kinds of furniture, made and repaired at the shortest notice, and on the lowest terms. TURNING, of all kinds."

The perfection of machine-made bowls would have been attractive to Hawaiians, and the number of bowls that survived indicates they were prized. There is, however, very little information concerning lathe-turned bowls until the 1870s, when the kou tree had become scarce in the kingdom and Hawaiian bowl makers had disappeared.

That lathe-turned calabashes were in some demand can be inferred from the 1874 billhead of the Hawaiian Keg Factory in Honolulu, which advertised that wooden bowls were always part of its cash and carry inventory: "Turned bed posts, table legs, calabashes, etc., and sawed fire wood, always on hand."

These bowls may have been stock items in many shops, for the 1887 *Honolulu Almanac and Directory* recorded lathe-turned bowls still in common use as food containers: "Of late years,

LEFT: *This 12 1/2" tall cabinet photograph is of a large royal covered presentation bowl on an elaborately designed stand believed to have been a gift to Queen Victoria from Queen Kapiolani or one of her party when visiting England to attend the British Monarch's Golden Jubilee celebrations in 1887. The metal band that encircles the bowl is decorated with a fern and taro leaf motif. Four evenly spaced ovals placed over the band carry Queen Victoria's Coat of Arms.*

American cabinetmaker William Miller was commissioned to design and create the wood work. Miller worked in Honolulu for sixteen years, from 1883 to 1899 and was commissioned by Kalakaua to make a series of presentation bowls of similar design.

What may have been the earliest of these bowls were reported in the **Daily Bulletin** *of November 4, 1886: "Mr. Wm. Miller is making two enormous calabashes for His Majesty's birthday. The bodies of these calabashes are made of cocoanut wood, the covers of kou, and the stands of koa."*

notwithstanding the introduction of all kinds and qualities of foreign ware, the natives use vessels made from [koa and kou], and by the aid of machinery all articles included under the general name of 'calabashes' are carefully turned and finished."

As collecting of ancient, handmade wooden bowls came into vogue in the 1880s, the turning of wooden bowls as curios became quite popular. Lathe-turned bowls continued to be popular into the twentieth century, particularly as trophies and commemorative mementoes.

Shortly after commercial lathes were introduced into Hawaii, a new variation on the traditional Hawaiian bowl was developed. Although Hawaiian craftsmen may have pioneered the new form in carving, Western craftsmen were to refine and popularize it on lathes.

The new design was a sophisticated synthesis of Western and Hawaiian forms, and consisted of lathe-turning the traditional bowl shape with a footed pedestal. The design was further formalized by adding a Western-style knobbed cover. These covered pedestal bowls were made primarily for display and as presentation pieces.

One of the earliest recorded presentation bowls was given by Kamehameha IV in 1859 to visiting English Capt. Montressor of HMS *Calypso.* This large piece stood fourteen inches tall with an ivory-knobbed cover. The body of the bowl incorporated the traditional design element of light sapwood against dark heartwood. It was probably turned in Honolulu by a German cabinetmaker then favored by Hawaiian royalty.

By 1876, lathe-turned pedestal bowls with covers were routinely made by Honolulu woodworkers along with traditional forms. In that year, a number of these bowls were included in the Hawaiian exhibit at the Philadelphia Centennial Exhibition. The exhibit catalogue listed them as turned by J. A. Hopper, who owned the Hawaiian Keg Factory, where calabashes were advertised as being always in stock. In 1885, the *Hawaiian Gazette* reported that lathe-turned pedestal bowls from the Honolulu Planing Mill, the city's largest construction company, were included in the Hawaiian exhibit at the New Orleans Exposition: "The Honolulu Planing Mill Co. sends turned calabashes and cups, mouldings and other specimens of the fine island woods used for ornamental purposes." Listed in the exhibition catalogue were "four calabashes of coconut and koa. A centre piece (turned) of koa."

The popularity of Hawaiian covered pedestal bowls reached its apogee in 1886, with the extraordinary celebration of King Kalakaua's fiftieth birthday. Having ruled the kingdom for twelve years of unprecedented economic stability, Kalakaua decided to celebrate his golden jubilee birthday with a week-long series of festivities. During this time, the king was given hundreds of presentation bowls of all sizes and designs in an outpouring of craftsmanship that was never again equalled in quality or quantity in the kingdom. Never before and never again was this bowl form so celebrated.

The celebration committee recommended its program to the president of the legislative assembly in September 1886: "Sir: the undersigned, your special committee appointed to prepare a programme of events for the celebration of the fiftieth anniversary of the birthday of His Majesty the King, have had this matter under consideration, and after due deliberation recommend that a series of events; a reception at the Palace, illumination and fireworks, historical panoramic procession, regatta, baseball tournament, grand ball, grand luau, historical drama and tableaux, horse races, parade tournament and state dinner, commencing November 16 and to conclude on the 29th of the same month, be provided for by the Honorable Assembly as an expression of loyal feeling of nobles and representatives toward the Sovereign, on the occasion of his jubilee birthday; and to recommend that the sum of ten thousand dollars ($10,000) be voted and inserted in the Appropriation Bill, to defray the expenses of the celebration."

This was all to the chagrin of at least one member of the legislature, Sanford Dole, who was later instrumental in overthrowing the monarchy. Concerned with the kingdom's finances, Dole remonstrated before the assembly: "If there is anything more melancholy than a funeral, it is an official celebration of this kind." He was ignored. The legislature appropriated $15,000, $5,000 more than was recommended by the celebration committee.

Part of the celebration was to be set aside for the presentation of gifts. This was to be in the form of an ancient Hawaiian presentation ceremony, similar to those reinstated by King Lunalilo in 1873. Kalakaua had continued the tradition, having already declared two gift-giving occasions during his reign prior to his fiftieth birthday. The first had been declared in honor of the king's election to the throne in 1874. The *Advertiser* at that time explained the tradition: "Hookupu. – This native word signified originally to pay tribute, but in these times it means to bring presents of provisions to a chief or the King. It is an old native custom that was notedly revived in the reign of the last King, and to-day we learn, the people of this district are intending to bring their *Hookupu* to King Kalakaua."

The second hookupu was held in 1883 in honor of the king's coronation and the completion of his new palace. Minnie Grant was visiting Honolulu at the time and described the event: "Another feature of the homage paid to King Kalakaua was the 'Hukoopu,' a very ancient custom, but to the performance of which none but natives were admitted; this was the laying at the King's feet presents of every description by every native who could possibly do so, and the majority of the presents were mainly of eatables, alive and dead, cooked and uncooked. Pigs, chickens, fish, notably the squid or cuttle fish, delight of the Hawaiian appetite, pink taro (grown for and eaten only by high chiefs), poi of many kinds, bread fruit, water melons, sweet potatoes, native fruits, such as mangoes, cocoa nuts, alligator pears, limes, etc., leis of feathers and shells, calabashes, rolls of *tapa* cloth, mats of every degree of fineness, all those were taken in such quantities, that the courtyard of the palace was heaped with the gifts offered."

Kalakaua's third hookupu differed from tradition. All residents were invited to participate, not just Hawaiians, as had been the custom previously. The gifts presented on this occasion were not only foodstuffs, but furnishings of plate, crystal, silver, and hundreds of lathe-turned covered pedestal bowls. How and why these turned bowls came to be given in such large numbers is unclear. There was no precedent for these unique gifts.

They may have been the solution to an awkward problem. Traditionally, hookupu gifts were either food or products of native manufacture. There was nothing uniquely Hawaiian and yet modern for affluent Hawaiians to give. The problem had first arisen in 1873 during the reign of Lunalilo, when some subjects wished to give their king something more than traditional offerings: "They presented money to the King. This his Majesty declined at first, saying that he had no need of it. Thereupon there was a Hui or meeting of the natives, and resolutions passed and presented to the King, setting forth that whereas he received a great deal of money, his revenue from the foreigners, they, his native people, would feel that he did not love them if he would not receive from their own hands a contribution of cash for his support and so he, fearing to offend his artless people, kindly accepted their little cash donations."

Kalakaua was a collector of Hawaiian artifacts and had a great interest in ancient culture.

ABOVE: *The two handcarved kou goblets in the background were very probably carved in imitation of Western stemware. The taller goblet is 6 1/4" high and was part of Queen Emma's collection. The smaller belonged to Princess Ruth Keelikolani and stands 5 1/2" high. It cannot be determined whether these were forerunners or copies of the elegant wooden goblets turned by Western craftsmen in Hawaii in the nineteenth century. The bowl in the foreground, which stands 6 3/8" high and is 6 3/4" wide across the rim, is of a form that may pre-date Western contact. The pestle-shaped base closely resembles that of a small wooden religious figure thought to have been brought to England from Hawaii in the eighteenth century, perhaps collected on Capt. Cook's third voyage.*

ABOVE: *These two bowls display interesting combinations of carving and turning, and may be considered transition pieces. The koa vessel in the background is completely lathe turned, except for the faceting on the bowl itself. There are three bands of facets, with eight facets each. The bowl stands 11 1/4" high. In contrast, the bowl in the foreground is completely handcarved except for the base, which was turned on a lathe. It stands 11 3/8" high and has four levels of faceting, each row containing eleven facets. The knobbed cover of this bowl was also completely handcarved.*

These lathe-turned pedestal bowls, which combined ancient and modern elements, were perfectly suited gifts for a progressive monarch with a respect for ancient customs and beliefs. These bowls were given primarily by members of the Hawaiian community, and a large number were presented by Hawaiian societies that were sponsored and supported by the royal family. Others were presented primarily by nobles and dignitaries in the court circle. The idea of commissioning these bowls as presents for Kalakaua may have originated with the royal family itself, perhaps with Kalakaua's acquiescence or even under his direction. The Educational Society, sponsored by the royal family, seems to have been the first to commission these unique gifts. On October 15, the *Bulletin* reported: "Mr. Wicke is making about 200 calabashes of fine woods for the Educational societies, to be presented to His Majesty on his birthday."

Earlier in the year, Kalakaua's sister and heir apparent, Princess Liliuokalani, had organized the society to arrange for the education of poor Hawaiian girls. On the king's birthday, the queen and the royal princesses, Likelike and Liliuokalani, along with Kaiulani, Kalakaua's niece, and Poomaikelani, the queen's sister, led the various divisions of the Educational Society to the palace. Not only did the princesses and queen each give Kalakaua wooden bowls, each member of the society also presented the king with a lathe-turned kou goblet with knobbed cover.

The *Honolulu Almanac and Directory* described the presentation procession: "Each division was preceded by a beautiful silk banner and kahili bearers. The Princesses rode in carriages, preceded or accompanied by attendants carrying the insignia of their rank. The members were very elegantly attired, and each one carried a calabash as a hookupu to His Majesty."

Other Hawaiian societies presented the king with these bowls also. The *Almanac* recorded their picturesque processions: "One of them was led by nineteen little children, neatly dressed, followed by over one hundred native women costumed in white, each one waving a kahili, the rear being brought up by boys and men. Another society was preceded by twenty-four kahilis of various colors, each of the women and girls comprising it bearing a gift, or hookupu, in their right hand."

Very probably, the idea for giving the gifts of wooden bowls had been discussed beforehand

RIGHT: *This kou presentation bowl, 14" high, is one of the earliest turned goblet forms yet identified. In 1858, an English naval captain, C. M. Montressor, visited the Hawaiian Islands. While visiting the island of Hawaii, he met Kamehameha IV and his wife, Queen Emma. Montressor invited the king aboard his ship to sail around the island, the king accepted, and a warm friendship developed. Before Montressor left the islands, the king gifted him with this bowl. Montressor wrote of it in his memoirs: "On parting, he presented me with a vase wrought...in the native wood, most beautifully polished and rounded; the wood is of a rich brown and takes the polish well. It will be a pleasant memento to me of he whom I have learnt to regard as a friend."*

The bowl is composed of three turned pieces of kou; base, bowl, and ivory-knobbed lid. The base is fastened to the bowl with screws. The bowl itself incorporates the traditional Hawaiian use of yellow sapwood for decoration.

If this bowl was commissioned by Kamehameha IV while Montressor was visiting, the commission would have been awarded to Wilhelm Fischer. Fischer was a German-trained cabinetmaker who came to Hawaii in 1855, and for twenty years enjoyed commissions from four Hawaiian kings. He retired and left the islands in 1876. However, if this bowl was in the king's possession before Montressor's visit, it was probably turned by Fischer's predecessor, Christian LaFrenz, who worked in Honolulu from 1844 to 1855.

in the Hawaiian community, for three of the most impressive presentation bowls given by Hawaiian societies were matching in pattern and size. These matching gifts may have been commissioned by members of the royal family in the names of the societies, for these organizations were associated with the royal family through sponsorship, membership or financial support.

The gift given by the Seven Kings' Society was overshadowed by its presentation. The *Honolulu Almanac and Directory* simply reported: "This society exhibited emblems symbolical of the reigning dynasty, and attracted much attention." The *Almanac* did record the two bowls given by a military elite guard known as the King's Own: "The military companies came last. The King's Own led, and their commander, Captain Clark, delivered a suitable address and presented two handsome calabashes."

Some organizations, like the King's Own, probably relied on membership contributions toward commissioning a gift. Some Hawaiian societies may have been able to give bowls through the generosity of sponsors other than the royal family. The *Daily Bulletin* indicated that the Minister of Finance commissioned a large number of bowls, probably for a Hawaiian society or association: "The Enterprise Mill has made some three or four hundred calabashes for the 16th. They have turned 50 for P. P. Konoa, Minister of Finance, besides scores of fine molded Kou calabashes for various parties."

That so many of these hundreds of bowls were made from the traditional wood used for ancient containers, kou, is significant. The trees began disappearing in the 1860s and by the 1880s kou was very rare in the kingdom. The wood used for the hundreds of bowls made for the king on this special occasion constituted the last of the ancient kou. Much of it was very likely donated by members of the Hawaiian community who had saved this wood out of sentiment. The *Daily Bulletin* reported that a government official from Waimea, Kauai, had brought a particularly fine kou log to Honolulu to be made into presentation pieces, probably to be given by Hawaiian organizations: "A SPLENDID piece of kou wood, property of E. L. Kauai, is being cut into calabashes by Geo. Lucas, for His Majesty's birthday." The source of much of the kou may have been the large kou logs that had belonged to Princess Bernice Pauahi Bishop, and which had been auctioned off the year before, in 1885.

All of the turners in Honolulu were involved in making articles for Kalakaua's jubilee. The *Hawaiian Gazette* wrote of the extraordinary preparations: "There is no wonder that abroad these islands are called by many 'The Empire of the Calabash'. In looking into the various workshops, and noticing the number of calabashes in the various stages of completion, a stranger would readily come to the conclusion that the above quotation is correct. What will ultimately be the fate of all these calabashes, after they have been donated at the Jubilee, is hard to say. The amount of money now being spent for this class of royal presents is something wonderful."

The Hawaiian newspaper *Kuokoa* described the event itself: "From the morning to the evening hours of that day, people visited the king. The gates of the Palace grounds were opened wide to admit the Educational Society, the Industrial Society, the Society for the Increase of the Native Population, the Nihoa Association, and many more, as well as government officials, laborers, companies of soldiers, and government officers of foreign lands. In the afternoon, a great number of people came. The Fire Department, Company 4, was led by the Keone'ula Band and the visits to the king continued all day. Many gifts were given."

ABOVE: *The smaller turned kou goblet in the foreground may have been commissioned by the king's sister, Liliuokalani, for members of the educational society she sponsored. Over ninety identical bowls in this pattern were presented as gifts to Kalakaua on his birthday. They may have been turned by Johann Wicke, a prominent German-trained cabinetmaker who worked in Honolulu from 1864 to 1886. It is 8" high.*

The larger ribbed kou goblet stands 12 7/8" high and is one of at least four of this pattern given to Kalakaua.

PAGES 120–121: *Displayed here are the presents received by King Kalakaua on his fiftieth birthday, November 16, 1886. Displayed in the Iolani Palace throne room were over 250 bowls, goblets, and platters. The majority of the containers were of wood, with a few coconut goblets, at least one gourd, and one covered tortoiseshell presentation container.*

HUI
Hookuonoono
Nov.16,
1886.
ALOHA

ALOHA
HALE NAUA

The following day, the *Advertiser* published a description of the gifts that were displayed in the palace dining room: "His Majesty was the recipient during the day of countless gifts, presented by all classes of his loyal subjects and foreign residents of the Kingdom. So numerous were they that the space at our disposal would be utterly inadequate even to catalogue the rich and costly array, much less to attempt anything in the way of a detailed description. The dining hall was devoted to their exhibition, and the spacious apartment was none too large for the purpose. The following are some of the more prominent: handsome calabashes by Their Royal Highnesses the Princess Liliuokalani, Likelike, and Kaiulani; ancient calabashes and dishes by H.R.H. Princess Poomaikelani . . . Ipu calabash, J. S. Emerson . . . Tortoise Shell calabash, gold riveted, with silver trimmings, Hon. A. N. Tripp . . . Large calabash, Hon. S. G. Wilder . . . Nalanaihiku calabash, Fisherman's Society . . . A handsome calabash, Kaumakapili Church Society. . . . In addition to the foregoing list, there were about one hundred and fifty calabashes of all sizes."

The *Hawaiian Almanac* found the highly polished wooden bowls the most memorable of Kalakaua's gifts: "Among the many beautiful and costly presents of that day those that possessed the most interest were the calabashes, vases, cups and bowls of Hawaiian design and workmanship."

These bowls were later placed throughout the palace as ornamental furnishings. That the king had anticipated this use was perhaps evident in his acknowledgement published in the *Daily Bulletin*: "ROYAL ACKNOWLEDGEMENTS. The King's Chamberlain, in the name of His Majesty, tenders thanks to all loyal subjects and friends for their most hearty greeting on the occasion of His Majesty's jubilee birthday. Also for the numerous and valuable gifts and tokens of affection, which will be long preserved to adorn the Palace and serve as a pleasant memento of the happy event."

Three years later visitor Helen Mather commented on the bowls she saw displayed at the palace: "Our presentation was to take place at eleven o'clock. At a few moments before the hour we drove to the palace and were received by the vice-chamberlain in the grand hall. There we registered our names in the visitors' book, and were shown into the 'blue room. . . .'

"The royal arms, embroidered on white satin with gold thread, hung as a standard in one corner, but was less interesting than several calabashes, unique in shape, carved out of koa wood, and which were polished and decorated very curiously."

The popularity of the lathe-turned pedestal presentation bowls faded quickly in the last years of the century as ancient Hawaiian bowls became the rage among collectors. Presentation bowls were now commissioned in the traditional shapes. The *Hawaiian Annual* of 1902, commenting on the popularity of wooden bowls as souvenirs and mementoes, noted the reversion to older, traditional shapes: "Of late years numbers of calabashes have been turned out on the lathe by

RIGHT: *This turned kou bowl with a carved crown on the lid was one of three identical gifts given to Kalakaua on his fiftieth birthday by Hawaiian organizations. Each of the three large bowls had the name of the society presenting it carved into the bowl. This one has the name Kaumakapili carved into it, referring to Kaumakapili Church congregation whose gift it was. Three identical kou and koa stands raised these bowls to an impressive four-foot height.*

All of these bowls were commissioned from German cabinetmaker Johann Wicke. They were his last commissions, and stand among his finest work. Wicke died in December 1886, a month after completing them. The bowl itself is 12 1/8" across the rim and, with its cover, stands 19 1/4" high.

KAUMAKAPILI

foreign as also Hawaiian mechanics.

"Calabash turning is done to order by various turners and cabinet makers; more particularly as souvenirs in the medium and smaller sizes, and it is noted the shapes of the ancient type are better observed than was the case twelve years or more ago. Many of these souvenirs are produced . . . for the preservation of some sentiment attached, as in the case of those made from rafters and beams taken out of Kawaiahao church in its recent renovation."

The golden jubilee birthday of King Kalakaua was a unique event, and the pedestal presentation bowls turned out by all the community's craftsmen remain some of the finest work of its kind ever done in the kingdom.

It was a supreme moment for this nineteenth-century art form and also its denouement.

RIGHT: *These two very large turned presentation bowls were given to Kalakaua's sister, Queen Liliuokalani, on her birthday in 1891. They are made of milo and were commissioned from John Daniel Wicke, the older son of German cabinetmaker Johann Wicke. These bowls were closely patterned after three large kou presentation bowls the elder Wicke was commissioned to turn for Kalakaua in 1886. The taller bowl in the background stands 27 1/4" high. The legend carved into the body of the bowl in Hawaiian reads: "A gift from the people honoring Liliuokalani Sept. 2, 1891." The bowl in the foreground is 23 1/4" high. The brass plaque engraved in Hawaiian translates: "Liliuokalani, 1838-1891. An offering from the group of native children of Hawaii at her birthday." These were among the last royal presentation bowls made.*

HE MAKANA
NA KA POE HOANO
IA LILIUOKALANI
SEPT 2 1891

WESTERN CRAFTSMEN

There were several lathe craftsmen who distinguished themselves in the islands. The names and records of many of them have been lost. Those few that can be identified include individual Western, Chinese, and Japanese craftsmen, all of whom made wooden calabashes in Hawaii in the late nineteenth and early twentieth centuries.

The only Western craftsman in nineteenth-century Honolulu to specialize in turning and repairing wooden bowls was William Everett Herrick.

Herrick was twenty-three years old when he arrived in Honolulu from New York in 1857. There he met Massachusetts cabinetmaker Charles Williams, who had returned from the Australian gold fields that same year. In 1859, Williams opened the first furniture store in the kingdom and hired Herrick as the company turner. The firm of C. E. Williams offered imported furniture, custom-made furniture, and coffins. It quickly grew, and for thirty-five years it was one of the largest furniture stores in Honolulu.

Herrick remained with Williams until 1878. In that year, after nineteen years with the company, forty-four-year-old Herrick went into business for himself. He opened his own, modest, one-man "Turning Establishment" and advertised that he was "prepared to do TURNING IN WOOD, IVORY, &c., in all branches of the business. Special attention given to turning Billiard Balls, and all fine work." This was the first and only specialized turning shop to succeed in the kingdom.

Herrick probably went through a traditional apprenticeship in the United States beginning

LEFT: *Many of the bowls turned by foreign craftsmen in the nineteenth century were either commemorative or presented as trophies or awards.*

The bowl in the foreground is 7 1/8" high by 12 3/4" wide and was turned for the wife of Koloa Plantation manager William Wright on Kauai in 1871. It was made from the stump of Hawaii's only native palm, loulu, discovered while draining a swamp. Mrs. Wright wrote of the bowl: "Some of the stumps of the loulu palms were quite large; the natives called 'Hawana', they cut away the fibrous roots, and made poi calabashes out of the hard wood in the center of the stump. John Hobbs, one of the lunas, gave me a very large one which Mr. J. D. Neal our carpenter turned out for me; I took it to Honolulu a few months later and had it polished, it made a beautiful calabash."

The very large covered bowl in the background was turned of koa at the Honolulu Planing Mill, the largest construction firm in the city in the 1880s and 1890s. It is 25 1/2" tall. The large hand carved kou bowl in the center displays graceful and subtle shaping that Western turners often found difficult to reproduce. This bowl was awarded to Emelie Wedeman Macfarlane in 1897 in recognition of her work in behalf of Kapiolani Maternity Hospital. It was given by a society organized by the queen, and the size and quality of this ancient bowl indicates it may have come from the queen's own collection. This bowl is 14" high and 18" across the rim.

In the twentieth century smaller lathe-turned wooden bowls with attached engraved plaques became a common form of trophy in Hawaii.

ABOVE: *This faceted kou goblet with a fine shellac finish may have been made by professional turner William Everett Herrick. It is decorated with twelve circular inlays under the rim, each centered over one of the twelve vertical facets that surround the body of the bowl. The faceting is an exceptional design element requiring a high degree of skill to execute so precisely. The quality of the design, turning, and finish indicate this piece was made solely for display. This goblet is 5 1/4" high and 6 1/2" wide. It is part of the Kapiolani-Kalanianaole collection.*

RIGHT: *This covered, lathe-turned kou bowl stands 9 1/2" high and is part of the Kapiolani-Kalanianaole collection in the Bishop Museum. Ethnologist Roger Rose wrote of this collection: "Many fine examples were amassed as showpieces by 19th-century royalty, not least King Kalākaua in the 1880's, whose family collection was deposited partly in the Bishop Museum in 1923 by Princess Elizabeth Kalaniana'ole Woods in memory of her late husband, Prince Jonah Kūhio Kalaniana'ole, and his aunt, Queen Kapi'olani."*

This turned presentation bowl illustrates a new specialized form that was developed by Western craftsmen. While Hawaiian craftsmen carved commemorative bowls, they were still intended to be functional. Western turners in the nineteenth century, however, began turning commemorative pieces solely to be admired. Rose wrote of this piece: "Machine turned and provided with a domed lid to accentuate its globular form, this late 19th-century 'calabash' once belonged to Queen Kapi'olani, consort of King Kalākaua. Never intended for food, it epitomizes the evolution of the traditional **poi** *bowl into a work of Victorian decorative art."*

when he was fourteen years of age, for in one of his first advertisements for the shop he stated he had "an experience of thirty years in this business."

One of Herrick's prized possessions was his turning lathe, which he had purchased second hand. The lathe had been one of the earliest in operation in Honolulu, brought there by William Cooper Parke in 1843. New Hampshire cabinetmaker Parke and his partner were the first American cabinetmakers in Honolulu, and Parke later served as marshal of the kingdom for thirty-four years. In 1889, the *Daily Bulletin* wrote of this historic piece of machinery: "Mr. W. E. Herrick has now in use in his workshop the first turning lathe introduced here, which was imported by Mr. Parke and is still in first-class condition."

King Kalakaua had been elected to the throne in 1874. His interest in Hawaiian culture was partly responsible for generating a regional pride in cultural objects, particularly those made of local woods. Wooden canes and turned bowls became standard items offered by many independent cabinetmakers.

Although most cabinetmakers and companies in town who had lathes may have regularly turned wooden bowls, Herrick cornered a large share of this business, for he not only turned new bowls, he also began repairing and repolishing old, handmade wooden bowls, which were becoming fashionable to collect.

Eight years after starting his business, he began to attract mention in the papers. In 1886, the *Daily Bulletin* took notice of a bowl of traditional Hawaiian form which he had recently completed: "Mr. W. E. Herrick has turned out a beautiful piece of work, in the shape of a kou calabash. It is without a flaw, and bears a mirror-like polish." Later that year, the newspaper praised a bowl of contemporary design: "Mr. Herrick has just finished, and has on exhibition, an artistically made and splendidly polished calabash of Koa and kou woods."

Although he continued to turn bowls throughout his career, his work in repairing ancient calabashes, brought to him by island residents and collectors, was probably a substantial part of his business in later years. Residents began avidly to acquire bowls to form collections, including previously discarded and abandoned ones. A particularly large bowl was noticed by the *Daily Bulletin*: "Mr. Herrick has now for repair an old time, hand-made calabash, probably fifty or sixty years old, which is 7 inches deep and 20 inches in diameter."

Herrick's business apparently became synonymous with anything concerning Hawaiian bowls. In 1886, he was commissioned to design and create a unique bowl made of tortoiseshell as a gift to King Kalakaua on his fiftieth birthday. It was a tour de force of craftsmanship and design. Five days before it was to be presented, the gift was not finished. The *Daily Bulletin*, however, could not resist publishing a description of it: "A NOVEL CALABASH. Mr. W. E. Herrick is engaged on the manufacture of a very fine calabash, put together in sections composed of plates of tortoise shell. The pieces are fastened with gold rivets. . . . When finished, it will have a cover of the same material, and be surmounted by a gold crown. It is intended for a birthday present,

RIGHT: *These two tortoiseshell bowls are unique. The tortoiseshell bowl from Iolani Palace in the foreground, with its cover resting next to it, was commissioned from turner William Herrick and given to King Kalakaua on his birthday in 1886.*

The engraved plaque fastened by two chains to the top reads: "His Majesty King Kalakaua, Presented by Haku o ka Poni anai Moi, Nov. 16th 1886, 50th Anniversary Jubilee, Hon. A. N. Tripp." The top is made up of fourteen pieces of tortoise and thirteen pieces of silver metal fastened around the rim, all secured by ninety-three rivets. The bowl height and rim diameter are both 6 1/4" and it stands 9 1/4" covered. The body is made up of eight pieces of tortoise with a turned kou base covered on the outside bottom with tortoise and fastened with eleven screws. Eighty-six rivets fasten the tortoise pieces together.

The bowl in the background is from the Bishop Museum and was the property of Kamehameha I. It is 7 3/8" high, 7 5/8" wide, and is made up of two large pieces of tortoise with one small tortoise rim fill. Thirteen stitches sewn with two thin strips of tortoise bind the two sides. The base is made of a slightly convex piece of kamani, sealed with red wax, and nailed to the tortoise body.

Ethnologist Roger Rose observed that "this was on display in the Hawaiian National Museum since 1877 and may have inspired the gift commissioned by Tripp for Kalakaua."

on the 16th, by the gentleman ordering it."

One of Herrick's last important commissions again involved the king, this time commemorating his death. In 1891, Kalakaua died in San Francisco. His body was returned to the islands by Rear Adm. George Brown, commander of the North Pacific Squadron of the United States Navy. The admiral had also been host to the king's sailing to California, and the Catholic church of Honolulu sponsored a traditional Hawaiian gift-giving ceremony to honor the admiral's "attentions to our Sovereign while living and dying." For this ceremony, a Hawaiian civil organization, The Native Sons of Hawaii, commissioned Herrick to create a suitable present. Herrick combined both the old and the new, turning a contemporary stemmed base for an ancient Hawaiian bowl. The *Daily Bulletin* reported the event and described Herrick's commissioned work: "Besides the large gifts of fruits, vegetables, pigs and fowls laid at the Admiral's feet, many rare and valuable Hawaiian relics and curios were presented to him.

"The Native Sons of Hawaii gave an ancient calabash of kou on a stand of milo wood. They had a gold plate inserted in it by Wenner and Co., containing the following inscription: 'To Rear-Admiral George Brown, from the Native Sons of Hawaii, February 17th, 1891.'

"The Native Sons' calabash to Admiral Brown had been beautifully renovated by Mr. W. E. Herrick before presentation, several pieces of other woods than its original composition being skillfully inserted."

A year after Kalakaua's death, Herrick closed his shop. He died five months later, in February 1893, at fifty-nine years of age. He was remembered as "an old and respected resident of this city. . . . He was very skillful in his craft and did a large business once in turning and repairing calabashes and other Hawaiian articles."

RIGHT: *These covered, lathe-turned kou containers once belonged to members of a Hawaiian society, Hale Naua, founded by King Kalakaua in 1886. With over 75 founding members, primarily from the elite of Honolulu Hawaiian society, membership quickly grew to over 200 by the following year. The semi-secret society remained active until Kalakaua's death in 1891.*

In 1889, the ***Pacific Commercial Advertiser****, in an article titled "Annual Meeting and Celebration of the Royal Scientific Society," described the society and its elegant yearly ball: "His Majesty formed the Hale Naua Society — in plain English, 'The House of Wisdom' — on the model of the Psychical Society of London, only on somewhat broader lines. The London Association devotes itself almost exclusively to researches in spiritual phenomena, while the Hawaiian seeks to establish amicable relations between the material and the spiritual economics of nature....*

"After business and intellectual exercises dancing began and was gaily sustained until about 11 o'clock, when a sumptuous dinner was served in the State Dining Room. Afterwards, dancing was resumed with zest and maintained until after midnight....The whole event constituted a grand entertainment."

The taller bowl has an oversized cover with netting, which derives from the chiefly fishline container covers made of gourd, even to the dimple on top where the plant stem joined the gourd. Many of these containers held paraphernalia related to the society, some of which may be seen in the foreground. Members may have been presented a bowl upon attaining one of the nine degrees awarded by the society. However, little is known about what these bowls symbolized, or the meaning of the articles stored in them. The name of the craftsman who was commissioned to design and turn these bowls was never recorded. However, the covers of the smaller bowls are similar to a cover designed for Kalakaua by American cabinetmaker William Miller. The tall Hale Naua container is 13 5/8" high; the two smaller ones are just over 7" high.

RIGHT: *The bases and covers of these two ancient, handcarved kou bowls were designed and made by American cabinetmaker William Miller. The smaller bowl may have belonged to Keopuolani, a wife of Kamehameha I. There is almost nothing known about the circumstances that created the turned cover, base, and engraved brass banding of the smaller bowl. The work that Miller and perhaps jewelers at Wenner & Co. did probably served as a model for the larger bowl, for this bowl was quietly completed first, and was presented to Kalakaua on his birthday in November 1886. The widest band is engraved with decorative foliage interspersed with eight scenic vignettes. The original base given with this piece was a simple stand with four bandsawed legs. The shorter, more ornate base it now rests on was a later design commissioned by Kalakaua and executed by Miller. The complementary design of this base with that of the taller bowl may indicate that Miller made both at about the same time. This smaller bowl is 12 3/8" high, 16 1/2" across the rim, and with base and cover measures 23 1/2" high.*

Originally, the tall storage container probably had a gourd or handcarved wood cover which, with the bowl itself, was at one time covered with basketry. The contemporary cover, engraved banding, and ornate base, now considered integral parts of the piece, evolved into this final composition over a period of time. Kalakaua was given this container in 1883. In 1886, he commissioned Miller to refinish it and to design and turn a cover for the piece. The following year, the engraved brass banding was added, and sometime later the ornate and elegant base was designed and also added.

Kalakaua's intent may have been to elevate this unique container to the status of sculpture. Never before in Hawaii had contemporary Victorian design been applied to such a degree for the purpose of turning artifact into art. The container itself created a small sensation in Honolulu. The **Daily Bulletin** *reported in November 1886: "Mr. Miller is also polishing several ancient hand-made kou calabashes, and a 500-year old kou jar. This jar is said to have been used centuries ago by chiefs, who, while fighting, spoke in it to the gods. After this cylindrical piece of kou wood is polished by Mr. Miller, it will receive three ornamental gold bands."*

Eight months later, in July 1887, the newspaper again reported the work still in progress: "AN IMMENSE CALABASH. A large calabash, the largest in the Kingdom, is on view at Wenner's jewelry store. It has been decorated and ornamented with gold bands and gold plate by Mr. Wenner. The plate bears an historical motto while the lower gold band bears engravings of places of interest throughout the group."

The widest of the brass bands had twelve engraved vignettes from published illustrations of Hawaii by early visitors, primarily copying the illustrations of James Webber, who was with Capt. Cook.

The engraved brass plate fastened to the cover recorded the container's provenance in Hawaiian, stating that it was the property of Lonoikamakahiki, a sixteenth-century high chief who ruled Kau and Puna, two of the six districts on Hawaii: "The wind container of Laamaomao that was in keeping of Hauna, personal attendant of Lonoikamakahiki I. It was passed on to Pakaa, a personal attendant of Keawenuiaumi. It was placed in the royal burial cave of Hoaiku, on the sacred cliffs of Keoua, at Kaawaloa, island of Hawaii, and received by King Kalakaua I on January 1, 1883, from Kaapana, caretaker of Hoaiku."

William Brigham explained the secrecy involved with this custom of hiding royal possessions in caves: "More important was the custom of depositing in some cache the especial property of a departed chief. Not by any means with his remains to which they might serve for identification, a thing to be most carefully avoided, ... but in some cave [puoa], possibly on another island from that which concealed his bones, such deposits being left in the care of a **kahu** *who would generally appoint his successors." This tall, ancient container encased in Victorian accoutrements remains today one of the most impressive relics of Kalakaua's reign. It measures 32 3/4" high and 10" across the rim. Together with base and cover, it stands 42" high. The two works are the most successful nineteenth-century attempts to integrate Western and Hawaiian design.*

CHINESE CRAFTSMEN

There is evidence that Chinese craftsmen living in Hawaii in the nineteenth century turned and carved Hawaiian wooden bowl forms. However, very little is known of the craftsmen or their work.

Chinese were living in Hawaii at a relatively early date. In 1794, Capt. George Vancouver wrote of a Chinese man living on the island of Hawaii. In 1819, visitor Adelbert von Chamisso wrote from Honolulu: "Here for the first time I saw the Chinese."

Records of some of the earliest Chinese craftsmen in the kingdom appear in Honolulu merchant William French's first business ledger, in 1826. Listed were locks and hinges purchased by a man named Atai, and another purchase by a "China carpenter."

In 1837, Sir Edward Belcher described how Honolulu had changed since his visit ten years earlier, and noted that Chinese now owned businesses in the town: "The houses of the foreign residents are considerably improved; shops are more numerous and well supplied, and several of them are kept by Chinese."

The following year, a census estimated between thirty and forty Chinese lived in Honolulu, comprising ten percent of the foreign population of the town. While many were merchants and storekeepers, a number were skilled craftsmen. Some were both. Chester Lyman described a Chinese craftsman store owner working in Hilo in 1846: "We called also on another Chinaman who has his shop on the beach. He is a Jack-of-all-trades, carpenter, watchmaker, silversmith, tinker store keeper &c &c., talks English, is ingenious."

The great majority of all craftsmen and merchants in Hawaii, however, were concentrated in

LEFT: *These covered, lathe-turned kou bowls were probably turned by a Chinese craftsman. They may have been part of a larger set intended for poi suppers or luaus. The covers of these bowls, like many traditional Hawaiian and Oriental covers, were intended to be used also as plates.*

Poi supper bowls of Chinese design recall a luau for Kalakaua on the occasion of Chinese new year in 1876 where similar containers were used. The ***Hawaiian Gazette*** *reported: "CHINESE NEW YEAR — This annual festival, which this year commenced on the 25th of the month, passed with the usual exhibition of kindly feeling, and cordial hospitality by the Chinese population. At the residences and stores of all of that nationality, rich and poor, callers were received with manifest pleasure, and invited to partake of the refreshments with which the tables were loaded.*

"At Buffum's Hall, on Wednesday, a dinner was given in Hawaiian style to His Majesty the King, in which a number of other invited guests participated. The hall was hung with festoons of evergreens and flags, and the table, which extended the whole length of the room, was crowded with all the delicacies of sea and land, and flanked on either side with a resplendent array of highly polished bowls of ***kou,*** *filled with the national 'staff of life'. In spite of the almost incessant detonation of firecrackers, and other more noisy explosives, there were but few accidents."*

Although there were several sizes of these bowls made, the two seen here are both 3" high and 7" wide. The covers are 1 5/8" high and 7 3/8" wide. Complete with covers, the bowls stand 4 3/8" high overall.

the kingdom's only large town, Honolulu, on Oahu. Visitor Constance Gordon-Cumming commented on the diversity of Chinese-owned businesses in the town: "The Chinese turn their hand to everything. A considerable proportion of the small wooden stores of the 'business' town are theirs."

By 1852, thirty-seven businesses in Honolulu were Chinese owned. That year, Swedish visitor Nils Andersson wrote: "There is no lack of all kinds of stores; those of the Chinese are generally the neatest ones. Most of the merchandise for sale there, comes from China."

In 1869, the first *Honolulu Almanac and Directory* listed five Chinese as "Carpenters," a generalization that applied to all Chinese who worked with wood, whether carpenters or craftsmen.

The Chinese and their businesses were located together in a particular section of Honolulu. In 1871, visitor Samuel Smiles discovered the Chinese population crowded into tenements behind the storefronts: "Indeed, some of the finest stores in Honolulu are kept by Chinamen. I did not at first observe many of these people about; but afterwards, when exploring, I found whole back-streets full of Chinamen's huts and houses."

In 1873, visitor Isabella Bird wrote of the large Chinese population in Honolulu: "The . . . storekeepers, with a few exceptions, are Americans, but one street is nearly given up to Chinamen's stores. . . . The Chinese, who came here originally as plantation coolies, outnumber all the other nationalities, including the Americans."

In 1876, large numbers of Chinese immigrants began arriving in Hawaii both as contract sugar plantation laborers and independent immigrants. Among them were probably numbers of trained woodworkers, for by 1880, three of the five furniture manufacturers listed in the directory were Chinese.

The *Pacific Commercial Advertiser* took notice of these new craftsmen in 1878: "John Chinaman, as a maker of new furniture, is fast catching up with the American man, and very naturally beats him in cheapness. We recently saw a very handsome koa wood secretary made to order by a Chinese cabinetmaker, the cost of which was over 25 per cent cheaper than would be charged by any other workman."

In 1884, there were just over 5,000 Chinese in Honolulu. The 1884 census noted that six of the town's sixteen wood turners were Chinese. Some of these men would certainly have turned wooden bowls, but little record of these craftsmen or their work has been found.

Only one Chinese craftsman from this period has been identified, and he was not a turner but a carver. One of his masterpieces, however, involved the crafting of a set of food containers for the king. He was first mentioned in the *Hawaiian Gazette* in 1881: "Strolling along Nuuanu Street, we glanced into one of the Chinese carpenter's shops and saw a very fair piece of wood carving." The paper identified the craftsman, Chen Mu, by his Hawaiianized name, Chun Moke. Only one signed work of his, a large ornately carved cabinet that belonged to King Kalakaua, is known to exist. On one drawer pull, he carved his Hawaiianized name in English and his given name, Chen Mu, in Chinese.

In 1885, the *Daily Bulletin* reported on the Chinese section of Honolulu and particularly praised several woodcarvers, again perhaps Chen Mu: "All along the streets in the Chinese quarters are little stores containing tradesmen of every imaginable kind. Each store as a rule consists of but one room in which two, three and sometimes more men are working. Their wood carving is particularly well worth seeing it being all done by hand and with great precision and neatness; one man was working at a large sign-board in Chinese characters, another was working at the finest ornamental carving with ease and rapidity, and a third was making business stamps, that are so generally used, both in Chinese and English letterings.

"The men work on quietly and busily seldom looking up at any chance passer by or allowing themselves to be disturbed by outside occurrences."

It was probably the following year, 1886, that Chen Mu may have been commissioned by Queen Kapiolani to carve a small poi supper table as a gift to her husband, King Kalakaua, for the occasion of his fiftieth birthday. The table top was made from a single piece of kamani wood, and incorporated twelve Hawaiian food containers that were carved as part of the top. This Western-style table with Chinese details and Hawaiian food containers was a unique and highly original work. The table was very probably carved by Chen Mu, for the table legs were carved with flowers of Chinese motif, and the applied plant carvings on the centerpost are of the same style as those found on woodwork in Iolani Palace, for which Chen Mu did carving.

Nothing further is known of him. He became as anonymous as the rest of his countrymen in Honolulu, at least in part because of two devastating fires that destroyed the Chinese section of the town. The first fire was in 1886. The *Daily Bulletin* reported the destruction: "What has long been feared by some, and considered a certain event by others, has happened. The Chinese quarter of Honolulu has been devastated by a fire, that, gaining headway in the dense aggregation of wooden buildings, was quickly beyond control and sweeping in all directions. Practically all of Chinatown proper has been involved in a sudden and vast conflagration. With its narrow alleys, and dark unwholesome courts and hovels; its picturesque ugliness and interesting Oriental features; its immense traffic, on large and small scales, legitimate and otherwise; its social institutions, of good and bad repute, it has been wiped almost completely off the city plot."

The second fire was in 1900; thirty-five acres of Honolulu, the whole of the rebuilt Chinese section, was again razed.

Only one Chinese bowl maker's name has survived. The 1896 business directory listed him as the town's only professional bowl maker in business that year: "Ah Ku, calabash maker, King bet[ween] Achi and Asylum Rd. Palama." Nothing else is known of him.

ABOVE AND RIGHT: *This unique supper table from Iolani Palace was given to King Kalakaua by his wife, Queen Kapiolani, on his jubilee birthday, November 16, 1886. The carving was very probably done by Chinese craftsman Chen Mu, whose work adorns Kalakaua's Iolani Palace, finished in 1883. The table top stands 28 3/4" high and is 22" in diameter. A dozen containers were carved into the thick piece of kamani which also forms the table top itself. The turned bottle and a now missing cup were the only free-standing pieces. The wooden bottle is carved on two sides. One carving depicts the king's private, latticed residence next to Iolani Palace, and includes a portrait of the king looking out from the garden. The carving on the opposite side depicts two royal standards and bases against a patterned background.*

The twelve containers are arranged symmetrically around the table. One of the four large circular bowls has a projection extending from the rim into the bowl cavity. This traditional Hawaiian form clearly identifies the container as meant for the washing of hands, similar to Western "finger bowls." Because of the Hawaiian custom of eating traditional foods with the fingers, etiquette required the presence of these containers at all meals. A small drawer without a pull to identify it, is concealed in the table skirt. The applied plant carvings around the base represent ti, taro, and a flower lei. At least six of the containers and the bottle originally had covers. The top of the table rotates, allowing easy access to all the dishes. At least five different Hawaiian woods were used in constructing the table.

JAPANESE CRAFTSMEN

Japanese first came to Hawaii in large numbers as contract laborers to work the kingdom's sugar plantations. Populous Japan had long seemed to the Hawaiian government a good source of cheap, reliable labor, but attempts to acquire such labor were consistently rebuffed by the Japanese government. A series of severe crop failures in Japan in the 1880s finally paved the way for successful negotiations, and in 1886 Japanese laborers began arriving in the islands. Of the almost 200,000 who eventually came to Hawaii to work, many remained to settle.

In 1924, Albert Palmer wrote about the size of the Japanese population in Hawaii: "By the census of 1920 we had approximately 110,000 of the Japanese race out of our total population of 250,000. There are four Japanese daily papers in Honolulu and upwards of eighty Buddhist temples or Shinto shrines in the territory. The dominant labor group on our plantations until recently and nearly half of our 48,700 school children are of the Japanese race."

Charlotte Cameron, visiting in the early 1920s, made a point of commenting on the large number of Japanese school children living in Honolulu: "As I pass through the streets *en route* I am astounded at the number of Japanese I see. In some districts one might well imagine oneself to be actually in Japan, so many are the Japanese. In passing a street where a school had just liberated the scholars, the entire thoroughfare was blocked by Japanese children. They appeared like so many bunches of flowers in their gay-coloured cotton dresses."

By this time, tourists in large numbers were visiting Honolulu from the United States. As a result, the making of curios had become a small industry in the town. A few individual craftsmen contributed to this industry, but the work tended to be on an assembly-line basis, and run by retail stores. The Japanese made up the majority of the labor force, as they did with most of the skilled and semi-skilled jobs throughout the territory at this time. Visitor Joseph McSpadden wrote humorously of his discovering this fact: "My wife had an amusing encounter with the keeper of a smart shop near the Moana Hotel. In the windows were displayed bowls, cups, platters, and other utensils carved from the koa wood — the native mahogany of light grain and susceptible of high finish. In answer to a query, the shop-keeper said with polite insistence, 'Why yes, these are native. They are made by workmen right here in our shop.' And to prove it she ushered her visitor into a back room where sat several employees — all Japanese!"

One of the finest of the independent craftsmen in Honolulu in this period was a Japan-trained craftsman, Hikohachi Hikokawa. He had emigrated to the Territory of Hawaii in 1913

LEFT: *Turned and covered koa containers like these originated at the Hilo Boarding School on Hawaii in the early twentieth century. The small, delicate bowl in the foreground was made by crafts shop teacher Tadaichi Shintaku, and given as a Christmas gift to the family of his assistant, Takeo Doi. Although Shintaku is credited with their design, they may have originated with his teacher, Masaichi Yamamoto, who retired from the crafts shop in 1920. The design of many of these bowls is similar to traditional Japanese containers used to hold playing pieces for the game of go. The tall bowl is 7" high. The bowl in front of it and the foreground bowl are each 1 7/8" high.*

ABOVE: *Turned koa goblet forms like those seen here were popular curios in the early twentieth century. The design of the base and the combination of turning and carving indicate the bowl in the foreground may have been made by Honolulu craftsman Hikohachi Hikokawa. The body of this bowl was first turned, leaving a thick rim which was then carefully carved in a series of nine undulating waves which emulate organic plant leaf or flower forms. The carving seems deceptively simple, with the bottom of each curve appearing to peel out and away from the bowl in a very natural manner. This bowl is 5 3/8" high and 10" wide. The koa display bowl in the background is 6 1/2" high and 9 3/4" wide.*

ABOVE: *Hikokawa's small Honolulu showroom is seen here with shelves lining the walls, filled with turned koa bowls of various sizes, coconut poi supper sets, koa and coconut curios, and koa plates. A large koa bowl sits on a koa cabinet in the center of the picture and in the foreground is a turned koa goblet placed on the smallest of a nest of koa tables. Hikokawa's workshop was directly in back of the store.*

at age sixteen in order to better support his widowed mother. He married in 1923 and in 1924 opened his own business in Honolulu, The Hawaiian Koa Shop. In the 1925 directory, he ran a large ad listing himself as a general contractor and furniture maker. Like many small, independent craftsmen in Honolulu, Hikokawa and his family lived and worked in the same structure. The showroom was at the front of the shop with the workshop in back; the family lived in small quarters in the rear of the property.

Hikokawa and two employees not only made furniture, but also a large selection of curios that were displayed in the showroom, including polished coconut cups and turned koa bowls in both traditional and pedestal forms. His wife remembered that Prince Jonah Kalanianaole, nephew of King Kalakaua, occasionally purchased turned Hawaiian koa bowls from the showroom. The making of wooden bowls and other curios eventually became the shop's primary business, and in 1929 The Hawaiian Koa Shop was listed under "Curios" in the *Honolulu Business Directory.*

In 1932, at age thirty-four, Hikokawa was forced to close his shop due to a respiratory problem that was related to his long hours of working in an environment of fine wood dust. He died seven years later. None of Hikokawa's traditional Hawaiian wooden bowl forms have been identified, but his pedestal bowls were distinctive for their proportion and shape, and several of these have been tentatively identified.

Perhaps the most successful Japanese craftsman living outside of Honolulu was Tadaichi Shintaku. This locally born cabinetmaker and turner spent the whole of his professional career working at The Hilo Boarding School on Hawaii. He worked there for over fifty years, first as a student, then as an instructor, and finally as proprietor. During this time, he produced a series of distinctive and unique small, covered wooden bowls that integrated Japanese aesthetics with Hawaiian forms.

The Hilo Boarding School was started by Protestant missionaries in 1839. Around the turn of the century, a vocational training program was established to help support the school. One of the most successful departments was the woodcraft shop, which grew to dominate school revenues.

The school itself was small, with just under one hundred pupils. The crafts shop accommodated twenty students. A large part of the shop's revenue was derived from curios made by student apprentices. The boarding school's first advertisement in the 1916 *Hawaiian Directory* stated: "This is certainly the best place in the Islands to procure calabashes, ukuleles, trays and other novelties made of Hawaiian woods." A small undated catalogue was eventually published which listed over one hundred different articles in several sizes made at the crafts shop. Under the heading "Calabashes (Bowls)" the catalogue stated: "All shapes, sizes, and woods made to order. Prices vary as to diameter, depth and beauty of wood." The catalogue then listed twelve different bowl sizes and their prices. The first bowl size listed was five inches in diameter and one-and-three-fourths inches deep for $2.50. For each inch increase in diameter up to twelve inches, the price rose by one dollar. The largest bowl listed in the catalogue was sixteen inches in diameter and five inches high, with a price of $16.

Shintaku had been head instructor at the school for five years when, in 1925, the school closed. The development of the public school system made the school unnecessary. However, it continued to offer boarding facilities in order that students from country areas might attend Hilo schools. To pay for upkeep and maintenance of grounds and buildings, the crafts shop was kept open and Shintaku continued the business with several hired employees. In 1933, the trustees sold the shop to Shintaku, who continued the business until retirement in 1968, when he closed the shop. Tadaichi Shintaku died in 1977.

Takeo Doi, who attended the boarding school after arriving from Japan in 1922, was later hired by Shintaku and worked in the shop until 1940. He remembered Shintaku as a meticulous craftsman and a gifted turner: "He could always turn bowls with very thin even sides. I never learned to turn with his skill. During boarding school days the students also turned some bowls, but the best thin, covered ones were always made by Shintaku. I still have a small covered one he gave to my family as a Christmas present once. Most of them were bought by tourists."

Shintaku turned bowls of varying sizes and shapes and also repaired ancient Hawaiian bowls. His small covered containers, incorporating his most original and distinctive designs, are seldom found in Hawaii today, for they were primarily purchased by tourists visiting from the United States. However, similar containers of Shintaku's design are still made in Hilo.

There were very few independent woodworkers outside of Honolulu in the early 1900s. This was due in part to the economic dominance and the self-sufficient nature of the many sugar plantations throughout the territory. Furniture and furnishings needed by workers and managers were primarily made in mill carpenter shops. The work from these shops tended to be utilitarian and practical. The only twentieth-century plantation craftsman known to have designed and made wooden bowls at his manager's request was Yoichi Watada. Watada was trained as a carpenter in Japan and emigrated to the island of Kauai in 1918, at age sixteen. When a new manager, Caleb Burns, arrived in 1932 to merge Lihue and Kealia plantations, Watada was the building superintendent at Kealia. Burns had Honolulu architect Charles Dickey design a new home for his family, and then interested Watada in designing and making furniture for the house. As part of the furnishings, Watada also designed two massive wooden bowls to sit on either side of the living room fireplace. Watada remembered that Burns was so impressed that he subsequently had him make other bowls as gifts to important plantation visitors: "I made about fifteen or twenty calabashes from 12 inches to 24 inches in diameter, and from 12 inches to 16 inches high. I made them all for Mr. Burns, who used to give them as gifts. I made the bigger bowls of monkey pod because I couldn't get koa trees on Kauai any bigger than about 16 inches in diameter."

Watada explained the effort involved in getting the wood for the large bowls: "I searched all over plantation lands for big monkeypod trees. We found big trees only at remote distances from Lihue. About four trees came from Anahola and Hanalei and two trees came from across the island at Kekaha. The trees were cut by hand sawing and it would take two or three days to cut down a six foot diameter tree and then cut it into six foot lengths. Then a crane was brought from the mill to lift the huge logs onto plantation trucks to take back to the shop.

"Although wood sawn into planks and boards was set aside to dry for two years, I had lathe operators begin turning the big logs for bowls after about three weeks. I drew the bowl shape I wanted on paper and gave the workmen measurements for sizes."

The Burns family still has their large monkeypod bowls designed by Watada and regards them as family treasures.

ABOVE AND RIGHT: *When American Factors Limited, one of the five dominant companies in the Hawaiian sugar industry, asked manager Caleb Burns to relocate from the Pioneer Mill on Maui to the Lihue Plantation on Kauai, they promised as an inducement to pay for the cost of building a new home on the island wherever he and his wife wished.*

In 1933 one of Honolulu's most prominent architects, Charles W. Dickey, was commissioned to design the Burns's home in an isolated spot outside the town of Lihue.

The large monkeypod bowl on the opposite page was one of two identical bowls specially made for the living room of the new house. They were designed by building superintendent Yoichi Watada and were meant to sit on either side of the Burns's living room fireplace. Many bowls in varying sizes of this design were made as gifts by Watada for visiting dignitaries and officials. The making of these bowls was a typical extravagance. The trees, found far from the plantation, required many men, several days of labor, a large crane, and several trucks to retrieve them. Plantation managers were able to allow themselves such occasional indulgences as they were not only in jobs of great responsibilities, they were also expected to be socially prominent in the rural communities in which they lived. As there were few hotels outside the towns, plantation managers were expected to host all visiting plantation representatives and even prominent tourists.

At the turn of the century, visitor Mabel Craft described the typical manager's home: "Plantation life in Hawaii, once the real heart of it is reached, is like life in the South before 1861.... It is patriarchal in a way. There is a big house, where the high-salaried manager lives, with wide verandas and a delightful hospitality, and a little army of soft-footed attendants."

The bowl is 12" high and measures 17 3/8" across the rim.

LEAF-SHAPED BOWLS

In the 1930s, a new form of wooden bowl was developed that quickly became popular with visitors and residents alike. These containers were not patterned after the gourd as traditional Hawaiian bowls had been, but instead took their shapes from broad, tropical 'ape and taro leaves. Although these leaf-shaped bowls were very different in appearance from gourd-shaped bowls, they may be considered a continuation and extension of the Hawaiian bowl-making tradition, for this new shape was clearly an interpretation of the same aesthetics that had resulted in the gourd shape. Both designs were based on Hawaiian plant forms, and leaf-shaped containers, like gourd-shaped bowls, used the dramatic grain of wood to best advantage. Furthermore, like the bowls of old, these new forms were made by hand, for their irregular shapes could not be turned on lathes. Finally, like most old Hawaiian food bowls, the majority of leaf-shaped containers were made in medium and large sizes to hold food for a number of people. However, while the ancient wooden food bowls had been made to hold poi, leaf-shaped ones held salads and condiments.

The immediate popularity of these bowls was due in part to the recognition by residents and visitors that these leaf-shaped containers invigorated and extended an ancient craft tradition. The new bowl form originated in the workshops of S. & G. Gump & Company in Honolulu. Gump, a San Francisco firm offering a very high grade of designer furniture and furnishings, opened a branch in Waikiki in 1929. This store was the first of its kind in the territory, offering designed interiors for island homes and original furniture and accessories created in Hawaii.

Under manager Alice Bowen, the store began designing a range of furnishings based on Hawaiian motifs. This created a sensation. The *Paradise of The Pacific* magazine reported the development enthusiastically: "New and stimulating things in the realm of home decorating have been happening in Hawaii in recent years. . . . Island motifs on textiles, carving, pottery and other mediums give evidence of a sudden, distinctly island, development in those arts and crafts which contribute to the amenities of life. They indicate a renaissance of craftsmanship and design such as the islands have not seen since the days of the tapa and feather cloak makers.

"The new art crafts have taken the form of Hawaii-inspired designs. These are based mostly on the splendid leaf and flower forms of the tropics, such as 'ape, banana, bamboo and fern leaves . . . the three-cornered leaf of an 'ape serving as a platter carved in wood, the exquisite

LEFT: *Leaf-shaped bowls and platters made from koa and monkeypod were very popular in the 1930s. The two bowls in the middle and front are of koa and copy the shape of a taro or 'ape leaf. The light-colored bowl in the background, with several compartments, is of monkeypod. It was one of two matched bowls carved from the same log. The bowls were designed and carved by Honolulu craftsman Carroll Corbaley in 1943, the same year he opened a cabinet shop in the city. He remained in business for thirty years in Honolulu. Corbaley's large condiment platter measures 2 1/4" high, 17 3/4" wide, and 21 3/8" long. The koa leaf-shaped bowl in front of it is 2" high, 8" wide and 12 1/2" long. The small koa piece in the foreground is 1" high, 5 1/4" wide and 7 3/4" long.*

lines of a white ginger flower frosted into a crystal goblet, or the giant buds of the cup-of-gold line serving as a fragile porcelain bowl."

Of all these new products, leaf-shaped bowls were among the most popular and enduring. This new design may have been a collaboration between two employees of Gump, a Swiss carver and a designer from Texas.

George Moody, born in San Antonio, Texas, arrived in Honolulu from New York in 1927 and was eventually hired as head designer at Gump. He may have designed the first prototypes of leaf-shaped bowls, for the *Advertiser* in 1933 reported: "Wooden plates have been quite the rage in the East during the last year. The plates and bowls have Hawaiian motifs."

In 1965, four years before Moody had retired, the *Beacon* magazine credited him with designing the leaf-shaped bowls: "When prohibition was repealed and cocktail parties were born, with them came pupus [appetizers]. To contain these new gourmet tidbits, George designed Kamani food bowls and trays in Hawaiian leaf shapes."

Although Moody may have first designed leaf-shaped bowls, it was probably Swiss carver Fritz Abplanalp who developed the design. In 1935, Bowen hired Abplanalp to oversee the carving of a series of wooden flower-patterned perfume containers for Gump.

Abplanalp had learned carving through traditional apprenticeship in his hometown of Brienz, Switzerland, and at nineteen won a competition for carving the enrichments of the interior for the Convent of the Transfiguration Cathedral in Glendale, Ohio. The carvings took six years to complete. He was then offered a position at Gump in Waikiki carving floral perfume containers. In 1956, the *Star-Bulletin* recalled how Abplanalp came to carve leaf bowls: "He carved hundreds of the lovely wooden flowers, then began looking around for something else that would be practical as well as artistic.

"Studying Hawaii's history, he found the ancient Polynesians developed wood carving as a means of expressing their creative ability, and had also used it for much more utilitarian purposes. Using primitive stone tools, they carved a variety of lovely calabashes or bowls of various sizes and shapes. Some of the old ones may be seen in private collections today. Along these same practical lines, but with a modern artistic touch, the malahini artist began turning out salad bowls; hors d'oeuvre plates, nut dishes in the shape of leaves, 'curled' calabashes, and flowers. The work was successful commercially and a new industry was born."

The woodcraft industry, which Abplanalp helped to start, continued to grow. In 1956, the *Star-Bulletin* reported: "There are more than 20 woodworking firms in the islands today, employing more than 200 people."

Gump closed its doors in 1951; George Moody retired in 1969 and died in Honolulu in 1973. Fritz Abplanalp died in California in 1982. The leaf-patterned bowls that these two artists created at Gump have become accepted as a traditional Hawaiian design and continue to be made in Hawaii.

RIGHT: *In the 1930s Hawaiian design was reinvigorated by artisans working for Gump and Company, who adapted tropical plant forms and Pacific marine life to decorate classical forms. Carver Fritz Abplanalp designed the large 22" platter with flowering 'ape. This became the signature flower for the decade. He also carved the handles of the bleached monkeypod platter. Artist Dorothy Thorpe decorated silver plated bowls and plates with a wide range of exotic flowers in raised relief. She also etched flower patterns on a wide range of glassware like the small 1 3/8" high, 3" wide glass bowl in the foreground.*

FROM ARTIFACT TO ART

It was during the reign of King Kalakaua, between 1874 and 1891, that the Hawaiian wooden bowl evolved from utilitarian object to art object. During this period, bowls began to be displayed prominently in homes as treasured possessions, and large collections became fashionable among both Hawaiian and foreign residents. Even before Kalakaua ascended the throne, there was a growing awareness of the passing of Hawaiian culture and of the rarity of its treasures and artifacts. This rarity had been noted in 1850 by Hawaiian Supreme Court Chief Justice William Lee while he was gathering "a few curiosities" to send to Miss Caroline Scott of Buffalo, New York. He apologized for including no Hawaiian artifacts among his gifts: "I regret that I could not collect you a greater number, and more valuable curios, but they are difficult to procure as the islands have been ransacked for them during the last twenty years."

By 1874, there was a sense that not merely the artifacts of the Hawaiians were disappearing. In fact, the Hawaiian race itself seemed on the verge of extinction. In that year, the population had declined to less than 48,000 throughout the whole kingdom.

Several other important developments contributed to the increased popular interest at this time in collecting Hawaiian artifacts. Among them was the opening of a national museum. In 1872, two years before Kalakaua was elected to the throne, the Hawaiian legislature passed an act establishing the museum. Awareness of the rarity and value of Hawaiian artifacts must have been heightened by the wording in the act: "Every succeeding year is rendering it more difficult to gather from the archives of the past the mementos and relics of our early existence as a nation, as well as of the pre-historic age of these islands. . . ."

The Hawaiian National Museum opened three years later. It consisted of one room on the second floor of the new government building that stood across the street from the king's palace. The *Advertiser* wrote enthusiastically of the small museum: "A number of years ago the subject was agitated here of establishing a national depository of objects of interest in the natural history of the islands, as also mementoes of the past of the native race. These last, however, are now scarce, having been carried away to foreign countries, where they figure largely as curiosities in public and private collections.

LEFT: *This collection of traditional Hawaiian bowls and artifacts, displayed in a cabinet of koa wood, contains an unusual number of ancient gourds. Residents proudly displayed these collections, which were often commented on by visitors. Almira Pitman, visiting in 1917, was impressed with the bowls displayed at the Honolulu home of Miss Lucy Peabody and wrote: "Her home...proved to contain a wonderful collection of Hawaiian things — all kinds of calabashes and* ***poi****-bowls." Later, at Mary Beckley's home in Waikiki, Pitman was again impressed by the display of wooden bowls, noting: "Our hostess has cabinets filled with antique calabashes."*

In 1902, the ***Hawaiian Annual*** *also commented on collections held by well-to-do Hawaiians: "The alii's and many of the better class of natives and part-Hawaiians have large collections, all highly polished, and among them are many cherished heirlooms of ancestry that are held in great veneration."*

"A spacious room in the west corner of the Government House, adjoining the Library, has been set apart for the museum, and there a pleasant hour may be spent by the lover of the curious and the student of geology. Connected with the past history of the Hawaiians may be seen beautiful mats and tapas, the fabrication of which is now a lost art; domestic utensils; ancient war drums; stone hatchets and adzes; and helmets worn by chiefs."

Another factor that contributed to the increased interest in collecting Hawaiian artifacts was the Victorian custom of possessing a "curio cabinet," which became popular in Hawaii at this time. Visitor Isabella Bird traveled among the islands in 1873 and wrote that: "Many of the residents possess . . . cabinets of minerals, volcanic specimens, shells, and coral, with weapons, calabashes, ornaments, and cloth of native manufacture."

By the 1880s, serious collections began to be formed and prominently displayed in homes. In 1883, Minnie Grant visited the Charles Reed Bishop home: "Their home in Honolulu was a very beautiful one, with lovely gardens, and the house itself a perfect museum of Hawaiian curiosities."

Private collections were not limited to homes in Honolulu. That same year, Grant visited Alexander McBryde's ranch at Eleele on Kauai and saw another early collection: "There was a collection of native curiosities in the room of the young master of the house, calabashes, mats, spears, stone poi pounders, etc."

One of the earliest private collectors of Hawaiian artifacts was Joseph Emerson, whose father had first arrived in the islands in 1835 as a missionary sent by the American Board of Commissioners for Foreign Missions. Emerson was born on Maui in 1843. He attended the Massachusetts Institute of Technology and graduated in 1874 with a degree in civil engineering.

In 1877, Emerson was hired as a government surveyor and worked at that job for twenty-six years. As a surveyor, he traveled to different parts of the kingdom and, in talking with elder Hawaiians in the course of his job, he developed an interest in Hawaiiana. He later recalled: "The gathering of first hand information from the older Hawaiians regarding their folklore and curios has brought me much in contact with a most interesting people now fast passing away."

Emerson began purchasing Hawaiiana from natives in 1882, but it was in 1884 that he began collecting seriously. The following year, he was stationed on Hawaii and purchased a large number of artifacts from Hawaiians: "During the year 1885, I had occasion to spend some little time at Kailua, Hawaii, and with my friend James Alexander camped in the old ruined house at Laniakia, formerly occupied by the Thompson family. Natives came to see me from time to time

RIGHT: *This extensive collection of Hawaiian artifacts, part of which is displayed here in a converted bookcase, was collected by William Deverill on Kauai. A wide range of ancient domestic artifacts make up the collection, including stone implements, musical instruments, ornaments, fishing paraphernalia, tobacco pipes, tapa sheets, and a large number of tapa beaters and bamboo stamps. Also displayed in the case is a shelf of Hawaiian seashells.*

A long, thick, wooden tapa anvil leans against the display case on the left. On the right is a long board used in the making of cordage. The few Hawaiian containers included in the photograph are rare and choice. On the floor to the left of the cabinet is a lidded storage container covered with ieie. On the other side of the case sits an unusually large patterned water gourd. Among the wooden containers on the bottom shelf is a fragment of an ancient refuse bowl inlaid with teeth. In 1908, Deverill's Hawaiian collection, composed of 321 items, was purchased by the Bernice Pauahi Bishop Museum.

about land matters." Emerson recorded every purchase, writing down the amount paid, where and from whom he bought each artifact, and its history. In 1886 and again in 1889, he sold collections of artifacts to Charles Bishop for the future Bernice Pauahi Bishop Museum totaling 1,161 pieces.

The growing popularity of Hawaiian artifacts was also due in part to the influence of the king, who became an avid collector. When King Lunalilo died in 1874, he had not designated a successor. In a subsequent election, the Hawaiian legislature voted High Chief David Kalakaua king. Kalakaua was the first chief to assume the throne who was not a member of the Kamehameha dynasty. Although his ancestors had been prominent chiefs on the island of Hawaii, the new king was able to bring to his office few ancient patrician possessions to corroborate his noble ancestry. However, Kalakaua soon began collecting rare Hawaiian objects of every description. He may have acquired many of these by direct appeal to his Hawaiian subjects. Records show several gifts of ancient artifacts which he received from Hawaiians who had removed them from caves where they had been stored. His growing collection was displayed in the two-story, lattice-work wooden building that was his residence next to Iolani Palace. By 1883, he had acquired an extensive collection that very much impressed visitor Minnie Grant: "On taking our leave, the King said he was then going into the town to shew Mr. and Mrs. Lambert some ancient Hawaiian curiosities which were at the palace, and most kindly invited us to accompany them. We considered ourselves most fortunate, as now-a-days, unless in the houses of the high chiefs, one cannot see any good native work.

"Accordingly we drove back to the town behind His Majesty's carriage, and in a short time drew up in front of the lattice-worked veranda which we had seen on the day of the procession. The door, as usual, opened at once into the drawing-room and here were the cabinets containing the interesting relics of ancient Hawaii, and there was a good show indeed. Rolls of the finest tapa cloth, of which the dresses of both men and women used to be made, were unfolded for inspection. . . . We saw beautiful calabashes; bowls of elaborately carved cocoa-nut, shining like ebony, quantities of fragrant sandlewood. A perfect model of a native grass hut quite small, but most exact in each detail, was much admired, as were also the immense strings of tiny white shells, only found on Niihau, and which formed a lei to be worn by royalty.

"The great feather robe was also produced; and it was indeed a wonder.

"The tall Kahilis, or rods of white feathers with long handles of tortoise shell, to be borne before the monarch on occasions of state, also were shown to us — and after conveying our warmest thanks to Their Majesties for the kindness extended to us, we left the Palace with a bright remembrance of one of the happiest days in Honolulu."

In 1886, the king celebrated his fiftieth birthday with a week-long series of special events. Hundreds of wooden bowls of contemporary design, made in cabinet shops throughout the city, were received by him as presents from citizens, officials, and Hawaiian organizations, and were displayed throughout the palace. Photographs of the king's collection of birthday gifts were sold commercially in Honolulu for years after, along with photographs of the ancient Hawaiian artifacts he had collected. In both royal collections, the wooden bowls were displayed most prominently, which inspired others to value and collect these wooden artifacts.

Hawaiian handmade bowls and ancient artifacts had never been easy to obtain. However, between 1873 and 1885, an unprecedented series of auctions brought on the market hundreds of bowls that had belonged to Hawaii's highest chiefs. The first large auction of Hawaiian artifacts in the kingdom was that of Mercy P. Whitney. Held in 1873, it included a number of old wooden bowls. The auction house was clearly unfamiliar with the nature of these artifacts and advertised them inaccurately as "Koa bowls." At the end of the advertisement for the auction, placed in the *Pacific Commercial Advertiser,* the auctioneers added this unusual commentary: "This sale affords the best opportunity that will ever be furnished for obtaining Hawaiian Curiosities, which have become very scarce."

The *Advertiser* staff also found the sale unique and in a separate article wrote: "An opportunity is afforded today at Adam's Auction Room, to purchase curios of the Islands which will probably never occur again." This, however, was only the beginning. Four years later, in 1877, High Chief Charles Kanaina died. His son, King Lunalilo, had reigned for only one year before dying in 1874. Having no direct heirs, Kanaina's property was put to auction. This was the first time that the personal furniture and furnishings of a high chief had been available at auction in Honolulu. Among the furnishings for sale were "SEVERAL HUNDRED CALABASHES!"

For the first time, the general public was able to purchase finely made wooden bowls that had been crafted for Hawaiian nobility. The *Advertiser* reported the enthusiastic response of Honolulu residents: "Mr. Bartow had large audiences at his sale of household effects of the late High Chief Kanaina. Pretty steep prices were realized for some articles, owing to the competition, though a number of excellent bargains were obtained."

Three more auctions of royal property followed between 1883 and 1885, and many collections were probably formed from them.

In 1883, High Chiefess Ruth Keelikolani, a great-granddaughter of Kamehameha, died. Ruth was perhaps the wealthiest of the Hawaiian royalty. She perpetuated many of the ancient Hawaiian customs and possessed a large collection of Hawaiian artifacts. A collection of her wooden bowls was put up for auction after her death. The auctioneer, E. P. Adams, advertised them prominently: "A large collection of Kou and Koa Calabashes. Many of them of the Old Ancient style, and valuable as Momentoes of the Chiefs." The *Pacific Commercial Advertiser* later reported: "The auction at the late residence of Her Highness Ruth Keelikolani was largely attended yesterday. High prices were obtained for calabashes, etc."

The following year, 1884, the last direct descendant of the Kamehameha line, Princess Bernice Pauahi Bishop, died. She had inherited Princess Ruth's estate and reserved many of her inherited royal artifacts for display in a proposed museum. As with Princess Ruth's estate, however, a large collection of bowls was auctioned off. The *Advertiser* described the bowls to be sold: "There are a great many calabashes in the collection, from a massive one made of hard dark wood down to tiny ones fashioned from thin coconut shells." The auction was reported under the title, "High Priced Curios." The article went on: "The auction sale by Lyons and Levy yesterday, of articles of Hawaiian manufacture and use belonging to the Estate of the late Mrs. C. R. Bishop was attended by a large number of people, many of whom were Hawaiians, and the articles offered for sale brought high prices. . . . calabashes that can be purchased new for $1.50 brought $5 to $7 each. . . . Everything Hawaiian was energetically bid for."

In 1885, the death of Dowager Queen Emma, widow of Kamehameha IV, brought the Kamehameha dynasty to an end. Queen Emma, like Bernice Pauahi before her, set aside "all my native curiosities, such as Kahilis, Calabashes, Feather Capes, and Leis, and all and sundry the various articles belonging to me coming under the head of Hawaiian curiosities." These were to be placed in a future museum. Nonetheless, a large auction was held and the *Evening Bulletin*

ABOVE AND RIGHT: *In these two pictures are displayed King Kalakaua's collection of traditional Hawaiian objects. The photographs were probably taken shortly after the king's birthday in November 1886, for several birthday gifts may be seen in the pictures. Prints of these pictures were sold commercially in Honolulu and may have contributed to the growing fad of collecting Hawaiiana which became fashionable about this time among residents.*

At least fifty wooden bowls and twenty gourds are displayed with capes, kapa, Niihau mats, and other ancient articles on the second floor hall of Iolani Palace. Mixed in with ancient objects were some relatively new ones. Near the center of the picture on the right is the poi supper table given to Kalakaua on his birthday. Three contemporary lathe-turned covered bowls of Kalakaua's Hale Naua Society are also displayed.

reported: "SALE OF QUEEN EMMA'S RELICS. The sale yesterday by E. P. Adams & Co. of shawls, kahilis, native mats and calabashes at Queen Emma's late residence was a very successful one. The house was crowded all day and the prices realized were such as to show not only the skill of the auctioneer, Mr. Morgan, but plainly demonstrate that in spite of hard times there is plenty of money in town. . . . About two hundred calabashes were sold, realizing from $5 to $27.50."

The high prices paid for bowls at Queen Emma's auction reflected a growing public awareness and appreciation of these traditional Hawaiian heirlooms. In comparison, the government had purchased several fine bowls at High Chief Kanaina's auction nine years earlier, in 1877, paying only one dollar for a kou bowl and $1.50 for a kou spittoon. Several other spittoons had also been purchased for only one dollar each. But fine bowls would, from now on, be hard to find, for Dowager Queen Emma's auction was the last of the great royal auctions to be held in the nineteenth century.

In 1889, the Bernice Pauahi Bishop Museum was founded. Opened in 1891, it housed the Hawaiian collections of the Kamehameha dynasty, which included an unrivaled collection of ancient wooden bowls. Displayed in an institution and preserved as important and rare objects of the past, these bowls gave even more lustre to those in private collections. Hawaiian "calabashes" were quickly becoming icons, symbols of "old Hawaii," conferring on their owners the status of having connection with Hawaii's history.

In 1893, the Hawaiian monarchy was overthrown, and the following year Hawaii was declared a republic. The last vestiges of the Hawaii of old were about to vanish and every object of the past was eagerly collected.

At the same time these royal auctions were taking place in the 1880s, the first curio shops were opening in Honolulu, selling both old and new bowls. These stores further popularized Hawaiian bowls by making it easier for residents and visitors to purchase them. Prior to this time, souvenir hunters sought out bowls and curios wherever they could find them.

A typical experience of souvenir hunting was recorded in 1876 by visitor Anne Brassey, who had stopped at a residence to rest on the way to view Kilauea volcano on Hawaii: "The woman of the house, which contained some finely worked mats and clean-looking beds, showed us some *tappa* cloth, together with mallets and other instruments used in its manufacture, and a beautiful orange-coloured *lei,* or feather necklace, which she had made herself. The cloth and mallets were for sale, but no inducement would persuade her to part with the necklace." Brassey was not able to strike a bargain until returning from the volcano two days later, when she once again stopped at the house: "I made an unsuccessful attempt to induce the woman of the house to part with her orange-coloured *lei.* I bought some *tappa* and mallets, however, with some of the markers used in colouring the cloth, and a few gourds and calabashes, forming part of the household furniture."

Honolulu photographers James Williams and Menzies Dickson were among the earliest in Honolulu to regularly stock curios. Dickson's successor, Williams, offered them for sale along with the souvenir photographs that made up a large part of his business. The *Daily Bulletin,* in 1887, reported a number of turned wooden bowls for sale at his store: "Mr. R. Rycroft, of Puna, Hawaii, has on view and for sale at Williams photographic parlors, about 30 calabashes made of milo wood. Mr. Rycroft, who has been handling native wood for the past several years at Puna, Hawaii, has collected during that time a fine assortment of milo wood which he has converted into the calabashes referred to. These calabashes are splendidly proportioned and are of remarkable size, considering the scarcity of the wood, from which they were made." The following year, Williams was one of the first two businessmen to be listed in the kingdom's *Directory* as a seller of curios.

In the 1890s, curio stores began opening at a steady rate; by the turn of the century, the *Directory* listed eight stores in Honolulu, one on Maui, and two on Kauai.

When bowls of particular interest were displayed for sale in these shops, the newspapers reported it. The *Daily Bulletin*, in 1892, was particularly impressed with a large bowl being offered for sale: "A CALABASH made of kou wood is on exhibition in a window of the Golden Rule Bazaar. It is six feet two inches in circumference and seventeen inches in depth. The size of this receptacle indicates the enormous size of the trunk of the tree, seeing that it is all one piece."

The purchasing of bowls by collectors was also considered of interest. The *Advertiser*, in 1895, treated one such event as news: "Christian Conradt made a purchase of seventeen calabashes yesterday, some of which are over eighty years old and the ownership of some of them may be traced back to several very high chiefs."

Even the provenance of bowls was published. In 1898, the *Advertiser* reported: "Historic Calabash. W. F. Love displays in the window of the Pacific Hardware Co. one of the largest and oldest calabashes in the country. It has a written history as far back as Kamehameha II, and probably antedates that time by fifty years. The calabash is of the finest koa. It is considerably worn inside. There is a legend that it was used many years in feeding the shark god, the meat being thrown out from it. The calabash is held at $200."

By 1899, Hawaiian wooden bowls were becoming very difficult to find. The *Advertiser* that year interviewed Evelyn Oliver, manager of Woman's Exchange, a store offering "fancy goods and curios." In an article titled "Rare Calabashes," Oliver predicted there would soon be no bowls left in Hawaii to sell: "Miss Oliver, of the Woman's Exchange, says that she is of the opinion that in two years more there will not be for sale in these Islands a single handmade calabash. The demand for calabashes of this character has been steady and people of Honolulu have travelled all over the group buying them. Every tourist of means takes a handmade calabash away and no new ones are appearing. The few stocks on the market are quite small at this time. Island people and natives in good circumstances prize the handmade calabashes highly, and of the many private collections here very few indeed can be broken under any circumstances."

A newspaper article published in the United States in 1900 warned tourists what to expect if trying to purchase an old bowl as a souvenir: "Calabashes are placed before anything else in the eyes of the people of Hawaii, not only by the natives, but more particularly by the Kamaainas, the old timers in the islands. Visitors who come to the island do not appreciate the value of the calabash, nor can they fathom the cause of the high prices. The tourist who comes and tries to buy at a curio store a wooden bowl, highly polished, it is true, and finds that the prices range from $5 to $200, is a trifle surprised, and complains to his nearest friend that the people here have been trying to rob the unsuspecting visitor. And when he goes to a second store, with his heart set on one of the wooden bowls, and picks out a calabash that looks worn and patched, in the hope that it will come within the limits of his pocketbook, he is amazed and angry when an even higher price is placed upon it. For the people here much prefer a calabash with patches as proof of its antiquity."

The article went on to state that the demand for old bowls was so great in Hawaii that ancient burial caves throughout the islands were being ransacked: "The old calabashes are greatly prized, particularly since Hawaii became the home of so many white persons, who prize the beautifully carved and polished pieces of wood more than the natives. The demand for the wooden utensils has increased so rapidly that there are now natives who spend their entire time in searching for old caves in which calabashes might be hidden. It was formerly the custom to bury Hawaiians in caves, generally inaccessible and guarded over either by warriors or spirits, and the personal property of the chief was buried with him. There are many of these caves in the islands, all of volcanic origin and many still undiscovered, so well did the old natives conceal the entrances to the caves.

"At Napoopoo, where Captain Cook landed upon discovering the islands, is a series of caves the entrance to which is below the sea level and along the side of an abrupt cliff. Recently adventurous white men gained entrance to the old burial caves here by means of a rope, and found many calabashes of great rarity within."

By 1902, the popularity of Hawaiian bowls had reached such proportions that the *Hawaiian Annual* published an article on the phenomenon: "There has been considerable interest manifest the past few years by residents and visitors alike in making collections of the wooden calabashes of Hawaiian manufacture. The subject has developed to such a degree as to be quite the 'fad' to be the possessor of an array of from a dozen to fifty or more of these specimens of ancient handiwork of various sizes and shape, and, incidentally, of different varieties of wood. Among our foreign residents in this city there are several large collections, and we learn of one in San Francisco that is the admiration of all beholders.

"As these former household utensils are rapidly disappearing their prices naturally are steadily advancing, and many kamaainas are bemoaning their neglect to improve opportunities that have slipped by them when they might have selected many at a comparative small expense.

"There are several places in this city, and in Hilo, where a variety of polished Hawaiian calabashes are kept in stock for sale.

"In these days nothing is done, of course, among the Hawaiians in the way of reviving their ancient handiwork in this line. The supply therefore of the 'legitimate' handmade article is limited, and this fact adds zest to the collector and assurance of value to his gatherings that is not likely to be diminished by an overstock of the market."

By 1908, Hawaiian wooden bowls seldom came on the market. Bishop Museum Director William Brigham wrote in a publication in that year: "The ancient hand-made bowls are very uncommon now, although the turner makes tolerable imitations and applies French polish in a way unknown to the old natives, but which suits the taste of modern customers."

In 1913, William Castle commented on the now costly rare old bowls: "There are, of course, shops which sell Hawaiian curiosities, most of them things which few people except 'curio' hunters would care to own. Old calabashes, which are often wonderful in colour and texture, are becoming hard to find, and are, therefore, very expensive."

In 1930, Margaret Cullen, writing in *Paradise of the Pacific*, commented on the proud display of these bowls in island homes: "If you are fortunate enough to be a guest in some old-time Hawaiian home, you undoubtedly will see in a place of honor a collection of polished wooden calabashes of various sizes and shapes."

ABOVE: *This group of wooden containers and other artifacts was collected by James McGuire. The photograph, displaying seventy bowls, may have been taken before the turn of the century. When McGuire died in 1941, his probate listed well over one hundred bowls, appraised at that time to be worth $7,532.80. This collection was very impressive, and the* **Star-Bulletin** *reported: "The appraisement, one of the most unique in recent years, was three pages long and included such articles as papa kahi olona or boards for kneading mulberry bark into fishing lines, ie oopu or fish baskets, weapons, gourds, drums, leis, fish nets, kahilis and ipu kuhas or cuspidors.*

"The most valuable single item was a rare feather lei, which was appraised at $800.

"A fine meshed fish net was valued at $120.

"The two cuspidors were valued at $45."

McGuire was custodian of Iolani Palace under King Kalakaua, and served in that position until the king's death in 1891. An article in the **Advertiser** *in 1937 stated that "then he went into business, and is known to most of Honolulu's kamaainas as the proprietor of downtown curio stores."*

In 1900, another newspaper article wrote of similar collections: "One of the finest collections of calabashes in the city is owned by Prince Cupid and Prince David, having formerly been the property of King Kalakaua. This is valued at $20,000. The Queen has a fine collection, as have also some of the wealthier and older residents of the city and territory."

These collections became, and have remained, a source of family pride. Minnie Crawford, visiting a prominent home in Honolulu, commented on the large wooden bowls displayed: "The old Damon house is open to visitors and is filled with antiquities of many kinds; beautiful *kou-wood* bowls, the largest I have seen."

Almira Pitman visited Honolulu in 1917 and wrote, "it was Miss Peabody who sat beside me the day of our first big reception. Her home is up in [Nuuanu] Valley, above Mrs. Holloway's home, and proved to contain a wonderful collection of Hawaiian things - all kinds of calabashes and *poi* bowls, war implements, drums, and musical instruments, and a wonderful cedar chest full of feather *leis* - no doubt of untold value."

Visitor Isabel Anderson also described bowls being displayed in Honolulu residences: "There were knickknacks everywhere, and teakwood tables and chairs, *poi* bowls made by hand, and primitive stone tools." At another home she observed: "Here were also royal feather plumes in vases and more polished poi bowls."

Albert Taylor, writing of social life in Honolulu for *Western Tours* magazine, best described the place the Hawaiian wooden bowl continues to hold in the imagination of residents in twentieth-century Hawaii: "The calabash, too, is ours. It is a great wooden bowl round or oval, all the more valuable when old and freely patched. It was formerly used for poi, but now its jeweled brilliancy of polish is its own excuse for being."

The handmade Hawaiian wooden bowl, in the twentieth century, had become art.

ABOVE: *This array of over seventy wooden bowls was part of a large Hawaiiana collection assembled on Kauai by Walter McBryde. Visitor Minnie Grant viewed this collection while visiting the McBryde home in 1883, and wrote of seeing "calabashes, mats, spears, stone poi pounders, etc., and the most perfect specimens of tapa cloth I saw while in the Islands." Part of this collection of bowls is now in the Kauai Museum. As wealthy residents began purchasing bowls and putting together collections, ancient wooden bowls became harder to find and prices rose accordingly. In 1899, visitor Mabel Craft wrote: "The* ***kapa*** *and the* ***poi*** *calabashes are becoming rare. Good prices are obtainable for both articles, and the natives are learning that porcelain is cheaper than* ***poi****-bowls and coverlids than* ***kapa****. And so, as with the peasantry of other countries, the choice old things are disappearing from the cottages." In 1912, visitor May Lawrence commented on the rising prices: "People to-day appreciate the beautiful handwork on these old calabashes and pay much more for them than for the modern machine-turned ones. Some of them are worth a great deal of money."*

Visitor Grace Harlow also could not help commenting on the value of wooden bowls even while viewing the Bishop Museum collection in 1925: "We take a trip to the other side of the city, to Kamehameha School and Bishop Museum....There are calabashes of all sizes, some of which if handmade sell in the stores for $15.00 when only about a pint size."

ABOVE: *Mrs. Charles Cooke founded the Honolulu Academy of Arts in 1927. Among the treasures she gathered from around the world was this collection of Hawaiian wooden bowls. No other Hawaiian artifacts were assembled by Mrs. Cooke for the academy. In selecting only this collection of wooden bowls as representing the finest of the arts of Hawaii, she influenced people to change their perception of calabashes as artifacts and to consider them also as art.*

*The **Hawaiian Annual** of 1927 listed the different collections assembled for the academy: "Mrs. Charles M. Cooke's gift includes examples of old and modern painting; early American china; English furniture; Philippine embroideries; Hawaiian calabashes; Chinese ceramics, textiles, paintings, carving, crystal, glass; Japanese lacquers, wooden figures, screens; Korean ceramics."*

FAKES AND DECEPTION

Around the turn of the century, when antique wooden bowls were in great demand, tourists and residents seeking them out became vulnerable to fakes and deception. Newly turned bowls were sometimes altered and sold to gullible customers as "antique." A newspaper article published in the United States at this time warned visitors, stating that residents "much prefer a calabash with patches as proof of its antiquity to the new ones the whites are turning out in large numbers and foisting upon the public as the genuine article."

In a 1908 publication, the director of the Bishop Museum, William Brigham, stated that some turners tried to give the appearance of age to bowls by intentionally damaging and then repairing them. According to him, however, these attempts were usually not very successful: "It is seldom that one sees the fine curves of the old bowls in these modern mechanical imitations, and the makers seem to recognize their shortcomings when they put in patches and make cracks only to fill them again and thus impart a flavor of antique art where the age and art are both wanting."

There was less commercial profit in fabricating antique Hawaiian wooden bowls in the nineteenth century, however, than in fake artifacts of other kinds. One of the first recorded instances of selling fake artifacts in Hawaii was in 1825. The English ship *Blonde* had returned to the islands the bodies of King Kamehameha II and his wife, who had died in England while visiting.

The crew and officers avidly searched out relics and antiquities to take back to England. Capt. Lord George Byron, the cousin of the English poet, wrote: "We remained with them until

LEFT: *The four wooden bowls displayed on the counters of this Honolulu curio shop may or may not have been handmade. The responsibility of authenticity lay solely with the buyer.*

Although authenticity was seldom an issue when purchasing curios from Hawaiians themselves, the purchase itself could be an ordeal. Visitor Clarence Webster recorded his experience in 1892: "In financial matters the Kanaka is peculiar. If they are conducted on a basis of friendship one is loaded with an excess of good measure if not a gift outright, but if it is straight business your friend becomes as keen as an oriental and as cold as a chattel mortgage shark.

"One day when we were ashore at a little landing on Hawaii, I picked up a primitive lamp cut out of lava in the refuse of a door-yard.

"I asked the gentleman with me to buy it, as he spoke the native language.

"He took me up to the hut and introduced me to the old lady who lived there....

"She very gladly gave it and was sorry she hadn't another one to present me.

"I caught sight of a gourd calabash with a nice color, which would make a good wall decoration. It was cracked and useless.

"I proposed to buy it of her and started to negotiate for it, using an interpreter. This was business, and she modestly demanded $4 for it. The price of a good one in Honolulu is about 50 cents. Yet the lamp, which is one of the kind which is now only found in old graves, had a value of something between $15 and $25."

the 12th, during which time a most friendly intercourse was kept up between us, and many exchanges, purchases, and gifts, were made; we being anxious to possess curious things from the Islands, and the natives no less desirous of having whatever we could furnish them with from our country."

Among the items most sought after by the visitors were carved religious images. The abolition of the native religion in 1819 had caused most of them to be destroyed. As a result, Hawaiian craftsmen in Honolulu apparently set to work immediately carving and antiquing images to sell to the crew.

The ship's artist, Robert Dampier, wrote that although the native craftsmen attempted to fool the visitors, the deception was discovered: "Observing that several of us were eager to possess some of these ancient Idols they diligently set to work, and soon fabricated a great number of grim looking deities. To these they endeavoured to give as ancient a look as possible hoping thus cunningly to impose upon our credulity."

American surgeon William Ruschenberger, visiting Hawaii in 1836, was apparently given to understand that the ruse had worked: "The officers of H.B.M. ship Blond, when here, were anxious to procure some of the ancient idols, to carry home as curiosities. The demand soon exhausted the stock on hand: to supply the deficiency, the Hawaiians made idols, and smoked them, to impart to them an appearance of antiquity, and actually succeeded in the deception."

Another instance of the making and selling of fake idols was uncovered by the *Pacific Commercial Advertiser* in 1872: "A Manufacturer of Images . . . In Hawaii Nei, there has long been a brisk demand for ancient stone and wood idols, and the supply of the veritable gods having given out, native ingenuity manufactures *facsimiles*. The man who may be seen every other day, trundling about a wheel barrow load of plants in pots for sale, is also a dealer in first class heathen deities. He will on short notice accommodate you with a wooden or stone god with a long name and a longer pedigree, bearing all the apparent marks of a venerable age. If closely questioned, however, he will acknowledge with a quiet smile that he made the *Akua* [deity] himself, and that the time-worn appearance was produced by dragging the image vigorously through the mud a few times."

In the 1860s, regular transportation between the kingdom of Hawaii and the United States was begun. Laura Judd remembered: "In 1865 a line of steamers was established between San Francisco and Honolulu, which has developed into a continuous monthly service."

As tourists from the United States began arriving on these steamers in the 1870s, there was an increased demand for curios and artifacts. Although tourist traffic was not yet able to support specialized curio businesses, these items were sold in stores as a sideline, along with merchandise meant primarily for residents.

Visitor Constance Gordon-Cumming, shopping in Honolulu in 1879, found that the Chinese merchants were among the first to take advantage of this new trade: "The Chinese turn their hand to everything. A considerable proportion of the small wooden stores of the 'business' town are theirs; and there are shops for the sale of Japanese and Chinese *curios*, and everything else that any one can reasonably be expected to want, including old Hawaiian stone gods, necklaces, and various implements (none of which can possibly be really obtained). These are sold for a ransom to the innocent steamboat passengers, who are told how they were dug up in trenching the fields, but are not informed of their recent burial in those places by their astute Chinese and other manufacturers."

The manufacturing of fake antiquities was carried on not only in Honolulu, but on other islands also. Christopher Hofgaard remembered a Hawaiian man who manufactured artifacts on Kauai: "When I came to Waimea to live in 1885 I shortly afterwards made the acquaintance of Kanakahelela. . . . He was a very steady attendant to the Hawaiian Church. . . . He lived about half a mile up the valley in a little house between the Peekauai Ditch and the road. His son W. S. Oka . . . was a prominent businessman in Waimea, when I got there. He was a very old man and had been a carpenter, as was his son W. B. Aka. Kanakahelela was a manufacturer of antiquities. He had a lot of hardwood and with a good American Rip Saw and a good American jack-plane and with sandpaper and glass he made ancient spears and when he had them finished he put a lot of dust and cobwebs on them and put them away under his house waiting for curio-hunters. With the assistance of good hammers and cold chisels he was also making antique stone lamps, poi-pounders and probably other utensils, all of which was duly deposited under his house and covered with dust and cobwebs.

"He also bought and otherwise acquired some real antiques from the Hawaiians, so he really had some genuine articles, and consequently the people in the valley steered curio-hunters to his place.

"He was a nice and guileless looking old man and I saw him polishing spears many times. He seemed to enjoy the joke (as he called it) on the curio-hunters."

In 1890, visitor John LaFarge even accused King Kalakaua of having altered ancient idols in his collection to make them more important: "He collects, or has collected; but is little addicted to the civilized habits of curators of museums, and is fond of arranging his remains and fragments . . . and remaking old idols which are fragmentary, not without surmises of his taking more than an outside scientific or artistic interest in them."

In 1886, King Kalakaua celebrated his fiftieth birthday. On this occasion he received over 200 turned wooden bowls of various designs made by Honolulu cabinetmakers. Each container was later branded with the king's monogram to identify it. The reason for this form of identification is not clear. These bowls may have been branded to identify them as jubilee presents or to distinguish the king's personal property from that of the Hawaiian government. Whatever the reason, this brand now makes the bowls valuable as royal curios.

Sometime in the twentieth century, unscrupulous dealers or collectors began branding similar bowls in order to affect their market value. These copied brands make it difficult now to determine whether certain branded bowls are authentic or not. It is not known how many counterfeit bowls exist, or even if the brands are still being used.

Another deception having to do with Kalakaua's jubilee gifts was the creation of two royal pieces from one. Almost all of the containers given to Kalakaua were made with covers, and both base and cover were branded to identify them. By simply switching covers with an unmarked lidded goblet, a stamped, but counterfeit, royal piece could easily be created. The unsuspecting buyer would assume that only one stamping was used to identify each covered bowl.

Many old lathe-turned bowls were probably sold as ancient and handmade near the turn of the century. This deception may not have always been intentional. Lathe-turned bowls were made in Hawaii probably since the introduction of commercial lathes in the 1840s. Many of these early bowls were made to be sold as practical utensils. Their owners would have used, cherished, and repaired these bowls equally with those that were handmade, for their machined perfection would have made them expensive and unique. When wooden bowls became popular to collect in the late 1800s, many of these early lathe-turned bowls would have been fifty or more years old. Such bowls remain difficult to distinguish from handmade bowls.

RIGHT: *This brand was burned into each turned wooden bowl and cover given to Kalakaua on his fiftieth birthday in 1886. On all pieces, both the underside of the lid and the bottom of the bowl carried the brand.*

In 1896, visitor Mabel Craft noticed these brands while visiting the king's former residence, Hulihee Palace at Kailua, on Hawaii: "Kailua was the old capitol of the islands and the health resort of later kings. There is a fine royal residence there, now the property of dowager Queen Kapiolani. It is a big house with a wide hall and immense rooms.

"The big dining-hall across the vestibule has a fine carved sideboard, and on it are a number of **koa** *calabashes, polished, and marked inside with the crown and royal coat-of-arms, etched with a poker. These calabashes all have covers, and were designed for pink* **poi**. *It requires all of one's moral nerve to refrain from becoming a kleptomaniac." In the twentieth century, ordinary kou goblets were sometimes stamped with an almost identical brand to counterfeit a royal provenance. These fakes are very difficult to detect.*

PART II

CALABASHES OF OTHER MATERIALS

LEFT: *Seen here are containers of coconut, gourd, and basketry. Fine Hawaiian storage baskets were probably always rare and coconuts were used primarily as drinking cups. It was the gourd that was the most common and versatile container used by all levels of Hawaiian society. Gourds remained in general use from ancient times well into the middle of the nineteenth century. Visiting in 1840, Lt. Charles Wilkes wrote of their continued use by Hawaiians in Honolulu: "Instead of baskets, they use a kind of gourd, which grows to a large size, and seems peculiar to these islands; these are thin and brittle, but with the care the natives take of them, are extremely serviceable: they are used for almost everything, as dishes, for carrying water, &c."*

The gourd is 10 1/4" high and 8 3/4" wide across the rim, the basket 17 1/2" high, and the coconut 4 1/2" high and 5 1/2" wide.

GOURDS

Wooden calabashes have become highly prized symbols of traditional Hawaiian culture and art, but the most common calabashes of the ancient Hawaiians were made of the Hawaiian gourd *Lagenaria siceraria.* The Hawaiians made more use of this hard-shelled fruit than did any other Pacific culture. On Kauai, in 1778, Capt. James Cook observed "great numbers of gourds. These . . . grow to a very large size, and are of a vast variety of shapes."

The expedition surgeon, David Samwell, also noted the many specialized uses to which gourds were put by Hawaiians: "Gourd shells they have of various Shapes, some like bottles in which they fetch & keep Water with a stopper of Cloth or green leaves, they have others with large Covers fitted to them in which they keep their thin puddings, others are long & just wide enough at the Mouth to admit a man's hand — in these they keep fish hooks & lines and various other things. . . . they find these shells very convenient for many purposes and they apply them to various Uses according to their different shapes & sizes."

Ernest Dodge, author of *Hawaiian And Other Polynesian Gourds,* wrote of their importance in Hawaiian life: "The conditioning of a Hawaiian was particularly influenced by the presence of gourds, and countless were the manifestations of this plant upon his life. He was brought up on the myth that the heavens were the top of an enormous gourd, that the earth was its lower half, and the celestial bodies were the seeds and the pulp thereof. Throughout life he drank his water from gourd bottles, ate his food from gourd bowls, danced to the rhythm of gourd drums, called his lover with the low notes of a gourd whistle, and at last, after death, his bones were perhaps cleaned and kept in an ossuary urn made of a gourd."

Gourds were cultivated on the hot lowlands of the southern and western coasts of all the islands. They were planted at the beginning of the winter rainy season and matured in about

LEFT: *Gourds were the common containers in Hawaii. Historian Samuel Kamakau wrote: "Gourds were highly valued for their usefulness....From [the gourd] came everything needed by man for the inside of the house."*

Displayed are both decorated and undecorated gourd containers. The bottle-shaped gourd in the foreground, with a Terebra shell stopper, was the traditional form of water container. Unusually short-necked gourds like this were said to be carried by travelers.

Decorated gourds were the reserve of nobility, and the decorating technique, which still remains a secret, was known only on the island of Niihau and perhaps parts of Kauai.

As late as 1846, gourds were still in common use on the island of Hawaii. In that year, visitor Frederich Walpole wrote: "All their cooking is done in the ground, and their only articles of use are calabashes: they have them of every size, and excellent they are, adapted to every species of work. They serve for tubs, clothes-boxes, tureens, but are hardly strong enough for seats, as I learned by frequent practical experience."

The covered storage gourd stands 17 1/4" high. The decorated gourd on the left is 7 7/8" high and 7" across the rim. The one on the right is 9" high with a 6" opening. The gourd bottle, with its netting of coconut, is 7 1/4" high.

six months, during the hot, dry summer. Edward Handy, in his 1940 publication, *The Hawaiian Planter,* wrote: "Gourds grew best on the hot shores and lowlands of leeward and southerly coasts where there was moderate rain fall and plenty of sun. Niihau was famous for its gourds. On Kauai the section from Waimea to Mana was the gourd country. Keahi Luahine remembered that relatives exchanged fish from Wahiawa for gourds from Mana. It is said that gourds once grew abundantly in Kekaha district.

"On Oahu, the southwestern section, especially coastal Waianae and presumably Ewa, was the best gourd country. Gourds are said still to grow wild and cultivated at Ewa. A few gourds have recently been grown at Waimanalo, Hauula, and Laie.

"The southern coast of eastern Maui was formerly the best gourd country, although some were grown on the windward side in sheltered lowlands.

"Kau, Kona, Kawaihae, and Kohala were the gourd raising areas on Hawaii. In Kau some varieties still grow wild, and at Keauhou and Honaunau in Kona they are still planted by Hawaiians."

Young gourds were carefully tended by farmers to insure they grew full and rounded, without deformities or blemishes. The Hawaiian newspaper *Kuokoa* described the care taken by gourd growers: "Among the plants grown by the Hawaiians, there was no other plant that was cared for like a baby like the bitter gourd during the growing period, the blossoming and the fruiting.

"When the fruit grew larger, the farmer watched carefully by spreading grass and setting the fruit upright. The idea back of this was to make the fruit round out well and stand by itself so that it could be used for a poi container, a hula drum, a container for his fishing paraphernalia, a place to keep his kapa garments or anything he wished to use it for. There were many uses."

Handy described another method of preventing defects: "As the gourd grew big, a little prop or frame (*koo laau* or *haka*) was made with three sticks, set so that the gourd hung suspended between them: this made the fruit symmetrical. Stones and pebbles were removed from beneath the gourd, and a 'platform' (*paepae*) of grass or leaves (in later times, a board) was laid out under the gourd."

Once the fruit ripened, it was picked and cleaned. Cleaning simply meant the removal of the soft, pulpy interior. Once this was done, the gourd was ready for use. The *Kuokoa* described the process: "The fruit was watched untill it was ripe enough to pluck from the vine, then it was put in a good place for a few days, after which the top was cut and the contents removed. It was done with patience and care. All the pulp clinging to the shell was removed, then it was filled with water. Care was taken not to let the water remain in it too long lest it rot. At this time, when the water was poured out, scrapers were put in to clean it. The purpose of the water was to soften the remaining pulp.

"When all the pulp had been removed, then the cleaners were put to work, and then we could see, O reader, the way that cleaning was done. Stones from the beach were the sandpaper of that time. The cleaning was done in the evening, after eating, when one sat down to talk. As the mouth talked, the hands rubbed. That was how it was done untill it was very clean. Then it was rinsed with water."

The long-necked water gourds were difficult to clean because of the restricted size of the opening. Ernest Dodge explained the process: "Extracting the pulp from any gourd to be used as a water bottle was more difficult because of the small opening. Water was poured in to hasten the decaying process. When the pulp was well rotted it was shaken out and stones and sand shaken around inside until all the soft parts were eliminated and the hard shell was clean. After cleaning, water was left standing in it untill it became sweet."

A "sweetening" process was especially important for the variety of gourd called the "bitter gourd." This container was favored throughout Hawaii for its hard shell, but required a neutralizing process before it could be used to hold food. Edward Handy was familiar with the traditional method of doing this: "The cleaning process for the 'bitter gourd' consisted in cutting off the top, and filling the gourd with sea water. The water was changed each day for ten days. This eliminated the acidity and softened the tough flesh. The flesh was scraped out slowly with pumice. . . . The flesh of the 'sweet gourd' could be cleaned right out, the calabash washed and used immediately."

Historian Mary Pukui recorded how some Hawaiians bartered for gourds: "This is what Keahi Luahine told me when we were on Kauai. The place where gourds were much cultivated was on Mana where the sun was very warm. She was a native of Pa'-a but reared at Wahiawa where no gourds grew because it was a little too damp for it. Her people used to fish and dry more fish than their family could possibly use. The surplus they saved to take to Mana in the late summer or fall after the gourds had been picked. They took fish and turtle meat to relatives in Mana and remained there a few days. The gourds were lined up on the stone walls to dry, some cut open and some whole. It was fun to join in the rubbing and washing of gourds with the people of Mana. Then when it was time to go home, they took gourds back to Wahiawa."

Gourds used by the chiefly class were often decorated with designs by a process now lost. Capt. Cook was impressed with the decorated gourds he saw in 1778: "They stain their gourd-shells prettily with undulated lines, triangles, and other figures of a black colour." Cook's second lieutenant, James King, was also impressed and wrote: "They have likewise a method of scoring them . . . so as to give them the appearance of being painted, in a variety of neat and elegant designs." The process of decoration left areas of dark brown against the natural light orange tan of the gourd itself. The surfaces of these gourds were smooth and sometimes shiny, leaving no trace of the method by which they were decorated. Patterned gourds were noticed and commented on by many early visitors. In 1786, Capt. George Dixon wrote of them: "Many of these are very prettily stained in undulated lines, which at a distance appear like paint."

In 1819, French voyager Louis de Freycinet noted: "The calabashes used for holding water or liquor are ornamented with elegant designs." In 1823, Rev. William Ellis commented on decorated gourds he saw while visiting a chief on Hawaii: "Arapai is evidently a chief of some importance . . . his house was large, well built, and stocked with a number of useful articles, among which we noticed some large and handsomely stained calabashes, marked with a variety of devices." Ellis was quite impressed with these gourds and went on to remark: "The calabash . . . is used to contain water and other fluids, by the natives of all the islands in the South Sea; but the art of staining it is peculiar to the Sandwich Islanders, and is another proof of their superior powers of invention and ingenuity."

Traditionally decorated gourds were said to come from the island of Niihau, although some may have been made on neighboring Kauai. Throughout the islands in the nineteenth century, decorated gourds were called Niihau gourds.

In 1931, the Hawaiian newspaper *Hoku o Hawaii* stated: "The best gourds are found in Ni'ihau and also patterned water bottles. That is the land where the natives do not weary in making designs. There are good gourds elsewhere but not many."

ABOVE AND RIGHT: *Here are two undecorated gourds typical of those used by commoners. The larger gourd held food or dry goods, the tall-necked vessel was a water bottle. The* ***1892 Preliminary Catalogue of the Bernice Pauahi Bishop Museum*** *noted of these: "Na Hue wai or gourd water bottles were formerly in universal use. Those with a long thin neck, or of unusual size were for home use, while the short-necked, globular ones were for the use of travellers. There were still other forms used by fishermen. For stoppers, a Terebra shell or a neatly folded palm or hala leaf served well."*

The bottle gourd with Cerithium shell stopper is 13" high. The large gourd is 8 3/4" high with an opening that measures 7 3/4" across.

These patterned gourds do not reveal the secret of the technique used to decorate them. The surface is as smooth and perfect as undecorated ones. Patterned gourds were said to have been traditionally made on the small island of Niihau at the northern end of the eight major Hawaiian islands. An unidentified correspondent wrote: "The canoes gathered from Niihau with the men and women of that Island with their patterned mats, 'ihiloa water-bottles and calabashes nicely made by skilled artisans. For these things the men and women were noted and it was said that the very best mats and calabashes came from Niihau."

The large storage gourd was collected during the visit of the HMS **Blonde** *in 1825. It stands 13 3/4" high.*

The patterned bottle is 12 1/2" high and was collected by Rev. Elias Bond who arrived in Kohala, Hawaii, in 1840, where he remained for his lifetime. He sent this gourd, along with other Hawaiian articles, to Bangor Theological Seminary in Maine, from which he graduated shortly before sailing for Hawaii.

Freycinet indicated that the most decorated kind of gourd was that used for holding water. This gourd was in common use on all islands, and probably represented a large portion of Niihau's gourd trade. Decoration was lavished on such gourds perhaps because water bottles were the Hawaiians' most essential containers. Dodge stressed this: "These various types of gourd water bottles . . . were among the native Hawaiians' most important vessels. The entire water supply of a household was kept in them, they were used for carrying water from streams and springs, for transporting salt water, and they also contained the water supply of fishermen and voyagers."

Water gourds remained in general use in the nineteenth century even by foreign residents, for there was no container available that was more efficient for transporting and storing water. Rev. Sereno Bishop, who grew up in Kona on Hawaii in the 1830s, recalled their usefulness: "Twice a week one of our ohuas or native dependents went up the mountain with two huewai, or calabash bottles, suspended by nets from the ends of his mamaki or yoke, similar to those used by Chinese vegetable vendors.

"These he filled with sweet water and brought home, having first covered the bottles with fresh ferns, to attest his having been well inland. The contents of the two bottles filled a five gallon demijohn twice a week."

The bearing poles that Bishop wrote of, which were used to transport gourds and their contents, were generally between four and six feet long; they were round, and thickest in the middle, tapering to notched ends. They allowed one man to carry two large gourds, each suspended in a net hung at each end of the pole.

Journals written on the Cook expedition do not mention burden poles. These poles may have been introduced in the eighteenth century through contact with Chinese. Hawaiians travelled to China as sailors during the latter part of the century and would have seen them in use. Also, Chinese were in Hawaii very early, at least as early as 1792, according to Capt. George Vancouver, who visited the islands then.

ABOVE RIGHT: *The gourd in the background is from the Kauai Museum. It measures 8 1/2" high and 8 1/2" across the rim. It is decorated with a series of nested "X's" drawn with thin, serrated lines that form diamond shapes at the edges.*

The bowl in the foreground is 8 1/4" high with a 6" opening. As these gourds illustrate, traditional designs relied heavily on combinations of dots of various shapes and straight lines that were thick, thin, serrated, and undulating.

BELOW RIGHT: *These two small gourds from the Honolulu Academy of Arts may have been spittoons. The larger gourd, decorated with a series of stylized spiny shellfish designs, is 5 1/8" high with a 2 3/4" opening. The bowl in the foreground is 4 1/2" high and 3 1/4" across the rim. Incorporated into the design of this bowl is an unusual shield motif.*

Spittoons of gourd may have been more common than those of wood, particularly among chiefesses. In 1819, artist Jacques Arago wrote of a gourd spittoon used by Kaahumanu, a widow of Kamehameha I: "A young woman brought to her at intervals, a small vase made of the calebash, as a spitting-dish; it was half filled with flowers."

In 1836, William Ruschenberger visited the home of Nahienaena, daughter of Kamehameha I, and also noted gourds used as spittoons: "Small gourds, with a few blades of fresh grass in the bottom of each, were on the table, and were used as spittoons."

ABOVE: *These two water gourds were thought to have been collected on Capt. Cook's third voyage.*

The British Museum's accession record for the gourd in the foreground reads: "Small pear-shaped gourd of a light brown color. On it is an old label on which is written, 'calabash in which they carry their water.' Probably brought by Capt. Cook's ships." This gourd stands 8 3/4" high.

The patterned bottle is 12 3/8" high. The basic design is repeated four times around the circumference. The short, stout neck may indicate this gourd was carried by travelers.

ABOVE: *These two gourd containers from the Vienna Museum of Ethnology were collected by members of Capt. James Cook's crew.*

The plain covered gourd in the foreground has a cord which passes through the top of the lid twice, with each end tied on opposing sides of the bowl's rim to secure it. This covered gourd stands 5" high.

The decorated gourd in the background is 11 1/4" high. The pattern is divided into two parts. One side is decorated with continuous vertical lines; the other side, seen here, is divided into two sections, one with vertical lines and the other with horizontal patterning. The short neck on this gourd identifies it as a traveler's water container.

To carry calabashes, Hawaiians attached open-mesh net bags to these poles. This development may have also been the result of foreign influence.

John Stokes, in "Hawaiian Nets and Netting," speculated that open-mesh net bags of advanced design may very well have been introduced: "Foreign sailors have closely associated with the natives since 1778, and the sailor with his knowledge of knots on the one hand and the native on the other eager to learn the foreigner's way would make it a simple matter to introduce a new method into their work." Visitor Gabriel Franchère, in 1811, noticed such a craftsman working in Hawaii: "Near the palace I found an Indian from Bombay, occupied in making a twelve-inch cable, for use of [a] ship."

Stokes also noted that there was no mention of these koko, or carrying nets, in Hawaiian oral or craft traditions: "It might be here mentioned that enquiry among the older generation of living natives elicited almost no information concerning the manufacture and use of koko. . . . One old man explained that he had seen his grandfather make them, but that he himself had had no use for them so did not take the trouble to learn. . . . There are a few natives in Honolulu who make koko for sale to tourists, but they unfortunately did not acquire the art by inheritance, merely having picked it up by unravelling some old specimen. . . . Only two works mention the existence of the koko."

Stokes was also suspicious of the origins of these bags, for they are not mentioned by eighteenth-century explorers. He noted that they "were surely too remarkable to have escaped observation."

Open-mesh bags and carrying poles were most often used to support very large gourds capable of holding up to ten gallons. This variety of great gourd was found nowhere else in the Pacific. It was in use extensively into the nineteenth century but is now thought to be extinct. Lt. James King described the great gourds seen during Cook's visits in 1778 and 1779: "The gourds, which grow to so enormous a size, that some of them are capable of containing from five to ten gallons, are applied to all manner of domestic purposes." In 1786, Capt. Nathaniel Portlock had Hawaiians on Oahu bring water out to his ships in gourds, among which were some great gourds: "The natives now began to bring us water pretty briskly, and some of their calabashes contained near ten gallons; for one of these we gave a ten penny nail."

Great gourds were still very much in use in 1850 when Frederich Gerstaecker visited Honolulu: "There is a great quantity of produce carried about through the town by single men, who commonly bear two very large calabashes attached to the extremities of an elastic pole, about five or six feet long, which they balance on one of their shoulders, having one calabash hanging before and the other behind. These calabashes, sometimes twenty inches in diameter, and fitted with a cover of the same material, are enclosed in net-work, and frequently contain their favourite poe for the use and benefit of the natives only, also eggs, vegetables, &c., taking back from town, in the same way, merchandise which they want or do not want at home."

This was one of the few ways to transport goods overland. Henry Lyman, growing up in Waimea on Hawaii in the 1830s and 1840s, remembered: "Since there was neither cart nor wheelbarrow, nor any beast of burden, in the place, everything had to be carried by hand or on the backs of men."

Elizabeth Kinau Wilder, born in 1831, remembered a childhood excursion from Honolulu to Waialua on Oahu using great gourds: "Two natives with long poles on their shoulders and large calabashes tied to each end of the poles carried the food and clothing for the family, as they

ABOVE: *Niihau was a small, semi-arid island which supported a small population. Besides decorated gourds, the island was renowned for very finely plaited decorated mats. How the people of this island originated the technique of staining gourds, and why these techniques were not disseminated to other islands, is simply not known.*

This uniquely shaped patterned gourd container from the Bishop Museum is an example of the many forms into which gourds were shaped, both naturally and artificially. It stands 8 1/4" high, is 6 1/8" across the rim, and was part of Queen Emma's collection.

ABOVE: *This carved burden pole is supporting two large covered storage gourds suspended in net bags. These net bags are of a highly developed style reserved for nobility and are termed koko puu puu. Ethnologist John Stokes wrote of them: "The koko puupuu was reserved for the sole use or service of the alii, who were exceedingly jealous of their dignity, promptly punishing by death any presumption on the part of a plebeian in making personal use of such a koko....This koko took its name from...the steward of a person of high rank, deputed to carry and care for the alii's food."*

Both this style of weaving and the double-loaded suspension poles may have been introduced after Western

contact. They remained the common form of transporting goods in Honolulu into the 1850s. Lt. Charles Wilkes, visiting in 1840, commented on their use in Honolulu: "Some of these gourds will contain upwards of two bushels. For travelling on these islands, they are almost indispensable.

"The gait of the Kanaka moving with his load is a quick trot, and he takes very short steps. The loaded calabashes, when suspended from the sticks, have a see-saw creaking sound that is heard from an easy old-fashioned chaise."

Both covered gourds stand approximately 13" high. The burden pole is 49" long.

(the calabashes) were light and completely water-proof and almost indispensable to island travel in those days."

Furthermore, there were no true roads on any of the islands other than Oahu, and on that island the only roads were in the small town of Honolulu. Sereno Bishop remembered visiting Honolulu from the Ewa district in the 1830s: "The road was only the native trail, winding up the various palis on the way. There were no bridges in these islands until after 1840."

Even in Honolulu, transportation was limited, and most of the water and produce for the city was carried to town on the shoulders of Hawaiians bearing great gourds suspended from carrying poles. Bishop recalled: "At that time there was scarcely a wheeled vehicle in the city. . . . Saddle horses were here in very small numbers.

"The native population formed the great body of the population then seen upon the streets. They were always moving about and at work. They bore burdens upon the Hawaiian yoke, or mamake, which with its load at both ends, very much resembled the method of carrying which is followed by the Chinese at the present time."

In 1840, visitor Francis Olmstead described a unique method employed to balance loads: "All articles of merchandise of this kind [food] are transported in calabashes, large flat gourds, eighteen or twenty inches in diameter, fitted with a cover of the same material, and suspended in net work, attached to the extremity of a pole, which the native balances across his shoulder, preserving the equilibrium by a corresponding calabash containing merchandise, or with admirable sagacity, substituting a large stone in preference to dividing his load."

In 1850, Gerstaecker found this unusual method of balancing a load still practiced, though the sagacity that Olmstead perceived eluded him: "The awkwardness with which they very frequently divide their load is peculiar. After selling one part, they never think of dividing the left into two equal parts to preserve a balance, but leave the one half in its own calabash and put an adequate stone in the other scale, even taking such a weight home with them for miles over the mountain."

In 1842, visitor George Simpson was particularly appreciative of the cool water brought in calabashes from the streams above Honolulu, for the town had no water system and relied on brackish wells: "Early in the morning, a crowd of natives may be seen flocking into Honolulu, all carrying something to sell. Most of them have large calabashes, suspended in a netting, at each end of a pole, which they carry across one shoulder, the contents being all sorts of small

RIGHT: *Pictured here are the ends of several burden poles. The carving on each end would be of identical design. The notches secured the open-mesh net bag which hung from it. The most notable of these poles has two carved heads facing each other between which was hung the net bag. It is 72 3/4" in length and was collected by Joseph Emerson, who recorded its history: "Auamo or Mamaka Kii, the latter is the common name in Kona, Hawaii, kauila wood. Bought of Kaili of Laaloa, Dec. 7, 1885 for $10.00, this elegant piece of carving was made by Kipola, the father of Kapolena....It was made in the reign of Kamehameha III....The widow of Kipola is still living in Pahoehoe, near Laaloa, Kona, Hawaii, an aged woman named Polohe from whom my agent, Kaili, bought it. Her father Koehe was a pili alii, or aipuupuu [personal steward] of Kamehameha I."*

The longest of the poles pictured is 92" and the shortest 41" in length.

The burden pole shown here on top of the one with carved heads was made for Emerson in January 1887. Mahiai of Pahoehoe, South Kona on Hawaii, charged Emerson $1.00.

articles, *kalo* and *poi,* and fruits and vegetables, and milk and eggs, and, what is the safest speculation of all, water fresh from the cold atmosphere of the mountains."

Water was carried to Honolulu in this way until 1850, when a system of pipes and a reservoir were constructed in the back of the town. That year, Robert Evans wrote: "There are some wells in the City for drinking water but the larger part of that is brought from the valley in Calabashes or large gourds on the heads and backs of natives. The citizens are building a large pool or reservoir, which will be filled by pipes from the springs above, and thus supply the town with plenty of pure sweet water." Perhaps because of this project, the town declared itself a city that same year.

As a result of the water project, and with the introduction of more horses to carry burdens, the need for great gourds decreased and they began disappearing from Honolulu streets altogether. By 1865, gourds were rarely found in the city. In that year, a Catholic nun, Sister Catherine, returning to Europe, had to write to Judge Azaria Kahalewai on Maui to try to procure great gourds as curios: "I find difficulty here in getting a *very large* calabash, and *also* a *small* bottle calabash, both of which I am anxious to take with me to show in England, and I have been told, that they grow on your land. If you would kindly give me one of each I should be greatly indebted to you." Gradually, great gourds disappeared entirely from Honolulu.

Outside of Honolulu, great gourds were most in use on the island of Hawaii, for transporting the provisions and luggage of tourists viewing the Kilauea volcano. Visitors were transported from Honolulu on the monthly steamer, landed at the small port town of Hilo, and lodged with residents before starting on the thirty-five-mile trip to the top of the 4,000-foot-high volcano. All baggage and provisions for the overland trip were carried in great gourds by Hawaiians.

This transportation and guide service for tourists eventually became very organized. Small caravans of Hawaiians, all carrying identical great calabashes on burden poles, formed picturesque trains wending along the ascending trail to the volcano. Although Lord Byron, captain of the *Blonde,* and a large party visited the volcano in 1825, the earliest of these organized tours

RIGHT: *This rack for storage of gourd containers, seen here in front of a thatched house in Bishop Museum's Hawaiian Hall, may have been developed after contact with the West, for no such device was described by early voyagers. In 1779, surgeon David Samwell described the storage of utensils on a shelf within the house: "In one Corner of the House are two long pieces of wood stuck in the ground with a board between them forming a kind of shelf; on this they put their Bowls & other household furniture & hang their Calibashes of water &c. to the Poles."*

In 1809, visitor Archibald Campbell described containers hung on the interior walls of houses: "Their household utensils, consisting of wooden dishes and calabashes, are hung, neatly arranged, upon the walls."

William Ellis, in 1823, was the first to write of the specialized hanger shown here: "When the house was finished, it was soon furnished....a few calabashes for water and poë, and some wooden dishes, of various size and shape, together with a haka, were all they required. This latter article was sometimes like a stand used by us for hanging hats and coats on. It was often made with care, and carved, but more frequently it was a small arm of a tree, with a number of branches attached to it. These were cut off within a foot of the main stem, which was planted in some convenient part of the house, and upon these natural pegs they used to hang their calabashes, and other vessels containing food."

The simply knotted woven bags holding the covered storage gourds were the kind used by commoners. They were called koko pualu. John Stokes wrote of these: "The koko pualu was a plain netted bag....and a coir koko of the class pualu would be referred to merely as **koko***....The mesh was always large and plain."*

came about when a large party of naval officers with the United States Exploring Expedition wanted to visit the volcano in 1841; it was less than well organized.

At that time, there were no facilities for such a trip so gourds were sent from Honolulu for the purpose. The American mission station in Honolulu arranged for the gourds to be transported to Hilo for the overland trip to the volcano. Lt. Charles Wilkes was impressed with the practicality of these unique trunks: "[The Honolulu mission] kindly offered to take all the preliminary steps in reference to the arrangements with the natives, and to procure suitable travelling equipments, in the shape of large calabashes, &c. These last are deemed on these islands a most necessary appendage for travelling, and are admirably adapted for the purpose, being exceedingly light and having great capacity. When in the care of a native, although extremely fragile, they are quite secure; they are surrounded by a net made of fine twine or sennit of the cocoa-nut."

This first large tour to the volcano, as Wilkes described it, was no doubt comic in its disorganization, "more allied to a May-day morning in New York, or a vast caravan. It consisted, as my friend Dr. Judd informed me, of two hundred bearers of burdens, forty hogs, a bullock and bullock-hunter, fifty bearers of poe (native food), twenty-five with calabashes, of different sizes and shapes, from two feet to six inches in diameter. Some of the bearers had large and small panels of the portable house on their backs; others, frying-pans or kettles; and others, tents or knapsacks. Then there were lame horses, which instead of carrying their riders, were led by them; besides a large number of hangers-on, in the shape of mothers, wives, and children, equaling in number the bearers, all grumbling and complaining of their loads; so that whenever

RIGHT: *Displayed here are the kinds of containers used by fishermen. Fish was a staple of both commoners and chiefs, and fishing was an important occupation of all classes. The narrow container lying on its side is 18" long and held a fisherman's supply of water. Of these containers William Brigham wrote: "The fisherman's huewai were long and almost without necks, that they might be laid on the bottom of the canoes out of the way."*

The tall, covered gourd is 18 1/2" high and held fish lines. The smaller covered container next to it held hooks and snood lines, as seen in the foreground. Unlike the gourd in the foreground, however, the body of the smaller standing container is of wood, which may identify it as belonging to a chief. This container stands 7" high and was the property of Kamehameha IV.

*About this class of utensil, Brigham wrote: "While a fisherman would doubtless have many of the implements of his calling in and about his house, such as fishing sticks, traps, nets, hooks, etc., many of the Alii were also fishermen (**e.g.**, the Kamehameha family) and kept their choicer implements in their dwellings, especially **ipu le'i**, a container of fish hooks or hooks and line also; the smaller part was an umeke of wood and the cover, much larger, of gourd: some choice ones were all of gourd and of small size. The common fishing line container was a bottle gourd with a large neck capped with a small coconut shell. In these the fine oloná lines were so carefully kept that it is no wonder that one would last several generations of fishermen."*

The fish hooks are of bone and tortoiseshell. In 1822, Gilbert Mathison visited Hawaiian Prime Minister Kalanimoku and observed him inspecting similar hooks and lines: "He was sitting in his hut, surrounded by a large family of women, children and attendants, and occupied in the examination of his fishing apparatus, lines, hooks, &c.

"He had a great number of these hooks in his possession, putting a high fancy price upon them, and refusing to part with any for less than a dollar each."

and wherever we stopped, confusion and noise ensued."

Despite the disorganization of that first tour, Hilo chiefs realized that tours were profitable. Great gourds and carrying poles were procured and hikes to the volcano became very organized as more visitors arrived on the monthly steamer.

In 1842, Sarah Lyman wrote to her sister about the phenomenon of tourists: "It has become quite fashionable for individuals in civilized lands to make a trip to these fair Ocean isles in search of health, and then the Volcanoe attracts them to this island."

By 1844, volcano tours were commonplace. A visitor recalled the novelty then of traveling with a caravan of gourd carriers: "Some on horseback, and some on foot, we got away from the village about eight o'clock, attended by thirteen natives, to whose calabashes our prog and clothing had been transferred; these calabashes answer this purpose admirably; they are gourds of enormous size, cut through rather above their largest diameter, which is from eighteen inches to two feet; the half of another gourd forms the lid, and keeps all clean and dry within; when filled they are hung by network to each end of a pole thrown across the shoulders of a native, who will thus travel with a load of fifty or sixty pounds about three miles an hour."

That same year, William Wood hired bearers and described the amount of luggage great gourds would hold: "It was surprising to see what a number of articles could be stowed in one of these vessels. Mine were not filled (the two) by three shirts, two pairs of stockings, two blankets, one great coat, one pair of cloth pantaloons, two pair of shoes, toilet articles, towels, patent liquor flasks, several books, &c. These gourd trunks are exceedingly light, and of course completely impervious to water. During our halts, the tops served very well for dish-tubs and wash basins."

In 1846, Danish Capt. Steen Bille visited the volcano and was impressed with the endurance and the honesty of Hawaiian bearers: "He, with a load of fifty or sixty pounds marching over rocks and stones, generally at the rate of one mile an hour, [is] indifferent to even the heaviest shower, sure that his things keep dry if only the cover is tight and without any cracks. There is not even a question about locking anything up; it is quite unheard of that something thus confided to a Kanaka should be missing."

In 1848, Lt. Henry Wise toured the volcano and found that tours had become even more sophisticated. Calabash bearers now started out ahead of tourists to set up camp and to allow tourists, who now often rode horses, to travel at their own pace: "Each was provided with a

RIGHT: *These long gourds with covers may have been general storage trunks holding the personal treasures of their owners. Surgeon David Samwell described their uses in 1779: "Gourd shells they have of various Shapes, some... are long & just wide enough at the Mouth to admit a man's hand — in these they keep fish hooks & lines and various other things."*

William Brigham described them as also used to store the most valuable articles of the nobility, the feathers and featherwork which symbolized their rank: "Long thin varieties of this Curcubita were also used for storage of the feather capes and leis, and were sometimes so curved that they could be hung over a beam or rafter."

*Ernest Dodge, writing in **Hawaiian and Other Polynesian Gourds**, also stated these gourds were for storing featherwork: "Gourds used only for storing feathers and featherwork in the Hawaiian Islands were long and curved." The largest of the covered storage containers pictured here is 40 1/2" long, the shortest is 12 1/2" in length.*

kanaka as a sort of body-servant to take charge of extra luggage and wardrobe, stowed in two huge calabashes, with the half of other shells laid over the round orifices on top, which effectually shielded their contents from the weather: they were then slung by a net work of bark braid to each end of a short pole, like a pair of scales, over the swarthy shoulders of our valets.

"There were a full half-a-dozen more fitted with the like contrivances filled with edibles. All were sent off at daylight, while we remained to a delightful breakfast of fresh water fatted mullets, new eggs, and butter."

Most of the tours involved small parties of visitors, but occasionally a large contingent would arrive and disrupt the economy of the village. In 1849, Sarah Lyman wrote to Lucy Wilcox to complain of the effects of the USS *Ohio,* which remained in port four weeks: "The Ohio left nearly $20,000 here, and the natives are so rich, they are entirely above work. No body can be obtained for love or money to mahiai [farm] or thatch a house. Food is very scarce and fetches a high price. Fish is exorbitant. This getting money so easy as they do of Men of War is a serious evil."

As late as 1876, though tours were conducted regularly, the actual number of visitors remained small. Anne Brassey, visiting the volcano that year, wrote: "Visitors to the island are not numerous and can only arrive by the monthly steamer from Honolulu."

In 1866, a small hotel was erected at the volcano. Visitors now did not need to carry provisions; only their personal luggage needed to be packed on horses. Visitors like Hezekiah Geiger, who visited the volcano in 1874, never mentioned gourds: "To carry all this luggage we had three pack mules." The great gourds had disappeared from Hilo.

In contrast to the great gourds, household gourds generally ranged from a pint to five gallons in size. They were the universal container in Hawaiian households and continued in common use into the third quarter of the nineteenth century.

In 1825, Andrew Bloxam described the interior of a typical commoner's grass house: "The furniture of it was simple — a dozen or two calabashes of different sizes and forms to contain poe, water, and other little things."

The following year, another visitor, Lt. Hiram Paulding, found that High Chief Boki possessed more furniture than did commoners, but used the same simple gourds: "Two or three old

RIGHT: *The hourglass-shaped gourd bottle resting on its side is of a form popular in the nineteenth century. It is 9 1/4" high. The standing water bottle is 10 1/2" high.*

The standing water bottle incorporates the words "KA MAI" into the design. One translation of ka mai means "the sickness" and this nineteenth-century gourd container may possibly commemorate a series of epidemics that swept through Hawaii in 1848. It was estimated that 10,000 Hawaiians, one-tenth of their number, died throughout the islands.

Rev. George Rowell wrote in January of 1849 from Kauai: "Death still rages among us. Some 200 or more I think have died in this field including Niihau....A terrible influenza setting in with the rains and the cold, has followed hard on the heels of the measles and whooping cough."

This may have been the worst of a series of epidemics that had been introduced to the islands as a result of Western contact. Little was recorded of these devastating diseases or their consequences. A previous epidemic on Oahu in 1804 thwarted Kamehameha's eminent attack on Kauai in an attempt to bring that final major Hawaiian island and its satellite Niihau under his rule. This delayed the unification of the Hawaiian Kingdom until 1810, when the king of Kauai peaceably ceded his island to Kamehameha.

MAI

chairs; a plain table of small dimensions, and a dressing-case with a mirror in it, was all of Boque's furniture, either useful or ornamental. Besides these may be mentioned a few hollow gourds for poye, (a favourite food of the Sandwich Islanders, made from the tarrow,) hanging at the side of the hut."

It wasn't until Kamehameha III moved from the island of Maui into his new, Western-style palace in Honolulu that he began to forgo private family meals served in traditional containers of wood and gourd. In the 1840s, Laura Judd and her husband were instrumental in influencing King Kamehameha III and his family in the daily use of Western crockery: "It is the custom of the chiefs to keep crockery, table-linen, silver, etc., packed away in bundles and distributed among their attendants, to be forthcoming when called for, which is only on great occasions, as they usually eat fish and poi served in a very simple manner, requiring little else than a calabash, fish dishes, and finger bowls. The king now has a table spread regularly for breakfast and dinner, under the supervision of a well-trained English steward and purveyor."

In 1846, Capt. Steen Bille commented on the numerous functions for which household gourds were still commonly used: "These calabashes serve the inhabitants as chests of drawers, as dishes or pots, as buckets, as water jugs, in short they serve all possible purposes."

Although by 1852 Western utensils were generally available in Honolulu, apparently gourds continued in common use elsewhere on the island. In that year, Swedish traveler Nils Andersson visited a family on Oahu and found gourds in daily use: "Around the walls stood calabashes which are used as spittoons and water containers. . . . In the second hut they kept, as I said before, eatables and kitchen utensils, the latter consisting merely in a cooking pot, a frying pan, and a few calabashes, as more are hardly useful in a country where fish and poi are the common diet." Andersson described the gourd as a common household container even in wealthy Hawaiian homes: "The houses of the well-to-do are covered with mats, and full of domestic utensils, such as calabashes, which are used as dishes, and plates, as cooking utensils, boxes and trunks."

On the other islands, gourds also remained the only utensils for most rural Hawaiians. In the 1860s, Henry Baxley visited a Hawaiian family living outside of Hilo on Hawaii: "Around the room hung a score of calabashes of all sizes, from half a foot to two feet in diameter, serving as cupboards, closets, pots, trunks, and general table ware."

In 1870, Frank Vincent visited a family along the remote Hamakua Coast of Hawaii which was still using gourds: "The family took their supper, simply a calabash of poi and a saucer of kukui-nuts and salt."

Even well-to-do Hawaiians in country districts in the 1870s continued to span two cultures. In 1873 on Hawaii, Isabella Bird visited "Halemanu, a great man in the district, for, besides being a member of the legislature, he is a deputy sheriff." She later wrote of his ease with both Western and Hawaiian utensils and manners: "I was surprised to find everything in foreign style — chairs, a table with a snow white cover, and table napkins, knives, forks, and even saltcellars. I asked him to eat with us, and he used a knife and fork quite correctly, never, for instance, putting the knife into his mouth. I was amused to see him afterwards, sitting on a mat among his family and dependents, helping himself to *poi* from a calabash with his fingers."

In 1884, the *Hawaiian Directory* listed only one calabash grower in the kingdom: "Pihi, Banana and calabash planter, res Nuuanu Valley." However, Hawaiians living in remote areas continued to use gourd poi calabashes well into the twentieth century. Handy recorded that:

"At Hamoa, in Hana [Maui], one family was cultivating *ipu awaawa* [bitter gourds] in 1933."

Old Hawaiian gourds, once the most common and plentiful of containers for all classes of society, are now extremely rare, and seldom found even in private collections. Their thin shells were easily broken, and unlike bowls of wood, they disintegrated rapidly once discarded. Even when cared for, gourds were at risk from rodents which were ever present on all islands. Author Ethel Damon recounted the loss of a famous Kauai gourd owned by Paul Kanoa, governor of the island from 1847 to 1877: "The governor owned a famous calabash which was thought to be the largest gourd calabash on the island. To keep it well, it was always hung up inside the house in a koko, or net. When the governor called for it one day and found that it had a large hole eaten in it by the mice, he scolded his retainers roundly, using the proverb: Aole malama i pau i ka iole, A thing taken care of the mice will not get at."

The gourd plant grew throughout the isolated Hawaiian Islands for centuries, but had little resistance to imported diseases and insects. Gradually, as farmers ceased to cultivate and protect it, it died out.

REPAIRING GOURDS

Like wooden calabashes, gourd containers were repaired when they were broken or cracked. They were most commonly repaired by sewing. Holes were drilled through the gourd on alternating sides of the crack line the length of the break. A cord of native fiber was then sewn through the holes, from one side of the break across to the other and back again. The crack was sewn the length in one direction and then back in the opposite direction.

The cord was then tied off and the repair was complete. The finished repair would appear to zigzag back and forth along the length of the crack. If a particularly strong repair was desired, the steps of sewing the length of the crack and back again would be repeated two or more times. The repair would then look like a connected series of "X's."

Broken gourds may also at one time have been repaired with the aid of glue. Capt. James Cook, in describing gourds he saw on Kauai in 1778, mentioned that "on other occasions, they use a strong size, or gluey substance, to fasten their things together."

Kekahuna, however, described a method of filling the drilled holes in gourds with a putty-like substance after repairing: "It would perhaps be well for the writer to explain a most important phase of this work. If the gourd to be mended with cord were a water-gourd the ancestors would get the gum of the breadfruit ('ulu), papala (tree of the genus Pisonia), or that of other gum-producing trees (laau hu). When the gum was prepared pumice-stone from the seashore was first secured, or perhaps red-ochre or clayey soil were pulverized. . . . If olona were the cord, coral-pumice would be used, and if sennit were used, red-ochre would be used, or perhaps dark clayey soil.

"When the gum was obtained it was heated in large opihi-shells until of the proper constituency, when it was mixed with the pumice, red-ochre, or clayey soil until thick like the putty of this new period. It was then stuffed into the little openings or cracks and left a few days to harden, when the process was repeated if the first gum put in had shrunk, and again repeated if necessary till shrinking had ceased, when the pumice was used till the article was smooth, and the trouble was ended. That is the way all injured articles of this class, both wooden and gourd calabashes, were treated."

LEFT: *Pictured are typical gourd repairs. Damaged areas were literally sewn together through holes drilled along either side of the break. The finished repair created a zigzag pattern running the length of the crack, as seen here on the lighter gourd. The darker decorated bowl has a repair that creates a series of "X's" the length of the break. Written just under the rim are the words KUIHELANI M LA MAKA. Both the letters and words are written backwards. Joseph Emerson purchased this gourd and another similar one on February 3, 1888. Both bowls had this inscription encircling the rim. They belonged to Mary Kapola of Niihau who was given them when a little girl.*

Kuihelani is a Hawaiian name. The rest of the inscription may be interpreted several ways. This bowl and its twin may have been heirloom decorated gourds, made for Kapola or a member of her family as their first personal poi containers. The darker bowl is 5 1/2" high and 4 5/8" across the rim. The plain covered gourd is also 5 1/8" high overall.

COCONUTS

In addition to making calabashes of wood and gourd, Hawaiians also fashioned containers from coconuts. The coconut palm, *Cocos nucifera*, grows on sandy shores throughout the tropics, and this graceful tree may reach a height of one hundred feet. Coconut trees may live for more than a hundred years, each bearing up to fifty coconuts annually. The nut, which ripens in about ten months, is enclosed by a smooth, thick husk. The nut itself has a hard, thin shell, which is used by all races and cultures living within range of the tree. William Brigham wrote: "The coconut is so widely spread through the tropics that many other races have exhausted their ingenuity in devising implements from the hard, durable shell of the coconut."

In Hawaii, which is near the northern limit of the tree, the coconut is not abundant and the fruit is small, lending itself to only a few uses. In 1779, surgeon David Samwell observed: "The Cocoa nut shells they use as Cups for drinking, others are made with a lid to them in which they carefully keep their red & yellow feathers." Samwell also noticed a coconut cup used to hold religious offerings: "They brought us out a small rude image. . . . He was tyed to a small round Cup made of the Cocoa nut tree with a Cover to it, in which they kept some provisions for him."

Robert Dampier, visiting in 1825, noted yet another use for the nut: "Its fruit presents to them drinking cups, & musical instruments." Although the nuts were indeed used occasionally as musical rattles, drums, and small storage containers, they were used throughout the islands primarily as drinking cups. Hawaiian nobility in particular used coconut shells as the preferred vessels from which to drink the mildly soporific awa. These shells were formalized to the extent

LEFT: *In the background is an unhusked coconut and in front of it a hard shelled nut after husking. The once highly polished coconut container on the right is an awa drinking cup of the priestly class. The awa cups used by the priest of the ancient Hawaiian religion were cut lengthwise from the nut, and at an angle, eliminating the three pores at one end. The cup pictured is 5 3/4" long and bears a label reading: "drinking cup from the Sandwich Islands." It was collected by Reverend Elias Bond in the 1840s and sent back to Bangor Seminary in Maine. A residue of awa coats the interior of the cup. These cups were no longer made after the abolition of the Hawaiian religion in 1819.*

The small 4 7/8" long coconut container in the foreground with a carved wooden stopper was used to hold tobacco. It was found together with a wood pipe near Kiholo on Hawaii. This was the site of a very large fishpond built by Kamehameha in 1801.

Early western voyagers introduced tobacco to Hawaii and by 1807 Isaac Iselin noted the Hawaiians' affinity for smoking: "The men seemed fond of smoking, several of them have pipes and green tobacco." Smoking had quickly become an integral part of Hawaiian culture, with distinctive brass-lined wood pipes and coconut tobacco holders developed by island craftsmen. In 1817 visitor Peter Corney described these pipes and paraphernalia as part of a Hawaiian woman's everyday dress: "A tobacco pipe is hung ... round their necks, and they do not consider themselves dressed without them." Corney went on to comment: "Both young and old are very fond of smoking tobacco. They also cultivate the tobacco plant, of which the natives use in immense quantity, as men, women and children smoke a great deal." After 1820 smoking was vigorously suppressed by American missionaries.

that coconut awa cups reserved for priests had a distinctive shape, which Brigham described: "The Hawaiians made a distinction between ordinary cups (*apu niu*) and those exclusively for the use of the priests to which the name *olo* was given. The former were cut at right angles to the vertical axis while the latter were cut parallel to this determinant. . . . A coconut cup was the orthodox form for awa drinking, and such cups by long use gather a fine *patina* which is as much valued by awa experts as the rich color of a meerschaum pipe by its smoker."

Coconut cups were also traditionally given by chiefs as commemorative gifts. Brigham had personally observed this custom: "Here we may mention a pleasing custom of the Hawaiians which has survived within my own observation, for a chief to bend down a young coconut tree in token of taking possession, and ever afterwards the tree was known by the name of that chief, and on gathering the first nuts, the chief had them made into cups for presents to friends. Several such cups are in this Museum, as the cup of Pauahi, the mother of Keelikolani, that of Queen Kamamalu, and that of Liliha, Madame Boki and daughter of Hoapili; the last two cups were from the famous grove of palms at Kalapana on Hawaii."

When the ancient Hawaiian religion came to an end in 1819, so did the priestly class and their distinctive coconut cups. Coconut bowls continued to be used in Christian services well into the 1800s, however, particularly in remote areas, where there was very little access to Western goods. In 1850, Rev. Lorenzo Lyons, stationed in the district of Waimea on the island of Hawaii, was still using them in the churches of his district: "Natives in remote districts know nothing of flour. Some manufacture sacramental bread from kalo and pia (arrowroot). Molasses diluted with water is pretty generally substituted for wine. Neat cups are made of coconut shells."

Sometime in the middle of the century, craftsmen began fastening polished coconut-shell cups to turned wooden bases to form goblets. These often had turned, knobbed covers of the same wood as the base. The base and cover would be a Hawaiian wood, often koa, kou, or milo. The nuts themselves were often large, imported coconuts from the southern tropics. These may have been popularized by Queen Pomare IV of Tahiti, who sent coconuts to Queen Emma in the 1870s. Queen Emma wrote to her mother about Tahitian coconuts in February 1871: "This is the news I have to tell you, Pomare has written me a letter. It says in the letter that all the coconut shell containers ordered by Hakaleleponi are for me, but there is no ship to ship them on. It is unusual to have the Queen of Tahiti write to me." The Bishop Museum has in its collections a coconut cup on a silver stand with the engraving: "H. M. Queen Emma from H. M. Queen Pomare of Tahiti. . . ." Ethnologist Roger Rose wrote of this commemorative cup: "A touch of Polynesian sentiment is apparent in this royal token, believed to have been sent from Queen Pomare IV to Dowager Queen Emma. Ambitious and proud, both women faced political intrigues in their own countries, so the humble coconut perhaps helped reaffirm their kindred Polynesian ancestry."

RIGHT: *The coconut and kou goblets seen here were typical of the elegant form developed in Hawaii. The light colored coconut in the foreground belonged to Princess Kaiulani, niece of King Kalakaua and Queen Liliuokalani and heir apparent to the Hawaiian throne. The dark goblet, 11 1/8" high, is made of a Samoan coconut, typically much larger than the Hawaiian shells. Often, these goblet forms were commemorative pieces, like the goblet in the background which was made from a "calabash tree,"* ***Crescentia cujete****, grown on Samuel Damon's Moanalua estate on Oahu. This goblet is 11 7/8" high.*

As it became fashionable to have parties in the form of luaus, which were traditional Hawaiian feasts, coconut goblets were used to hold individual servings of poi, replacing the wooden bowls that were disappearing into collectors' cabinets. Along with turned, small wooden bowls for condiments, coconut-shell goblets became standard tableware for Hawaiian-style parties, and remained in common use into the twentieth century. In 1908, Brigham wrote of their popularity: "As the coconut shell takes a beautiful polish the manufacture of cups, bowls and small dishes has been much modified under foreign influence. Among Hawaiians these polished nut cups, foreign even to the glue that unites cup and base, the latter the work of the turner, are still popular for individual poi bowls at feasts."

Almira Pitman, visiting Hawaii in 1917, was particularly enchanted with them: "One thing that made the table unusually attractive was the *poi*-bowls. Beside each plate, with the glasses and finger bowls, stood an individual *poi*-bowl containing a portion of *poi* without which no feast is complete to the Hawaiian. These individual *poi*-bowls are made from cocoanut shells, polished so highly that they have the appearance of mahogany. Thus the table, instead of being bright with much silver, as in own our homes, with these two rows of rich brown bowls — each standing upon a base of the same color . . . is rich in warm coloring."

Coconut and wooden goblets were not only used as food containers but also became popular as souvenir items. Henry Howell and his wife, visiting near the turn of the century, fondly remembered being given such a gift by their hosts: "When the time came to say good-night we found that the carved cocoa-nut bowls, which we had admired so much at the *luau,* were placed in our carriage — a gift from these kindhearted people; they saw that we were pleased with them, that they were a novelty to us, and so, they reasoned, we ought to have them."

In the 1880s, a few craftsmen began carving designs into the shells intended for purchase by the tourist trade. The first notable craftsman to carve such scenes on coconut shells, mounted on turned stands, may have been Frederick Otremba. Originally from Germany, he trained as a carver in Italy before emigrating to Hawaii in 1882 at age thirty-one. In 1883, a year after his arrival, he displayed a carved coconut at a Honolulu coffeehouse. Two Honolulu newspapers reported it as newsworthy, indicating that nothing like it had been seen in town before.

The *Saturday Press* wrote: "At Mr. Nolte's deservedly popular Beaver Coffee Saloon may be seen a polished coconut shell, curiously carved by Mr. Frederick Otremba, a German wood carver, now employed in Mr. Miller's upholstery shop on Hotel Street. On one portion of the shell is carved a section of palm grove, with the sea in the foreground and mountains in the background; in another portion is the Royal Coat-of-Arms; and in still another place, an inscription."

The *Pacific Commercial Advertiser* also reported the display in an article titled "A Souvenir." Since the scenes described on this shell seem to be different, Otremba may have carved several coconuts: "A German recently arrived in Honolulu, who has some talent in wood carving, is exhibiting a specimen of his work at Mr. Nolte's. It is a coconut shell highly polished and carved with figures representing Captain Cook's Monument, native huts, etc. The work is well done and the ornament would make a pleasing souvenir of the Hawaiian Islands."

Two years after Otremba first exhibited his carved cups, the Kaumakapili Church Hawaiian crafts fair of 1885 included a display of carved coconut tableware. The *Advertiser* noted: "There are also a large number of dishes, cups, plates and other containers made of coconuts, and beautifully polished. The carving on some of them is very pretty and original." These may have been done by Otremba, for a month before the fair, in April, he was reported in the *Bulletin* as having opened a curio shop. Besides "statues, calabashes, canes, plaster ornaments, etc.," the paper noticed "a number of articles made out of cocoanuts" and also "some beautiful carving on cocoanut."

The shop probably did not stay open for more than a year, for the kingdom's directory for 1888 did not list it.

Otremba worked in Honolulu for twenty-eight years, until his death in 1910. Much of his wood carving has survived but the early carved coconut goblets remain largely unidentified. He probably carved relatively few and stopped entirely after his store closed.

Only one other notable craftsman in Honolulu, August, or Aukukuokalani, Herring, is known to have carved scenes on coconuts. He may have been inspired by Otremba's work, but unlike Otremba, Herring's potential as an artist was never fully realized.

In July of 1886, J. M. Oat, Jr., & Co., sailmakers in Honolulu, displayed in the shop window two paintings and a carved coconut cup. They were the work of the sixteen-year-old German-Hawaiian. The works attracted much attention around town, for Herring's father was a laborer and Herring had no training as an artist or carver. King Kalakaua was so impressed he purchased the carved coconut calabash and conferred upon Herring the Medal of the Royal Order of Kapiolani. The *Pacific Commercial Advertiser* published a lengthy article describing Herring as "an adept at carving. He has taken a cocoanut shell and turned it into a most beautiful ornamented cup, which is now in the possession of His Majesty the King. It rests on a stand made of kou, with four claws, on which are carved fern leaves. On the bottom of the nut is engraved the invased Order of Kamehameha, also of Kou. The lid, which is of the same wood, has the Order of Kamehameha carved on it, also fern leaves, and is surmounted by a crown. On the nut itself four medallions are carved — one of His Majesty the King in uniform, and on the opposite side Her Majesty the Queen. These are good likenesses. The other medallions represent the old grass house, Kailua, Hawaii, now used as a residence by His Majesty, with the stone church steeple in view, and Diamond Head with a fringe of coconut trees in front. There is a highly artistic finish to the entire work which will bear the closest inspection, and would do credit to an experienced artist."

Two months later, the young artist opened his own "Engraving Establishment" in a little shop on Fort Street. He was now called by his Western name, August. He specialized in coconut carvings, which were fully described in an article titled "NATIVE GENIUS" published by the *Daily Bulletin:* "He has in various stages of embellishment many cocoanut ornaments engraved in rare artistic style. One cup bears a very presentable likeness of the American Minister, Mr. Merrill, also representations of the United States arms and of the King's house at Kona, besides a cocoanut grove. Another not so far advanced under the graver has a portrait of Mrs. Merrill, recognizable at first sight, very finely engraved. A third shows pictures of Emperor William of Germany, King Kalakaua, Cook's monument, and a sea view at Kona. An egg shaped nut-shell has His Majesty and Cook's monument. A large round shell has engravings of Kamehameha, from the statue; Kamehameha in a spear-catching bout; Waiakea Bay, Hawaii; and the hula dance. The artist has made some elegant vases for Queen Kapiolani, also cocoanut wine cups chased with grape vines and clusters."

The paper went on to say how remarkable it was that Herring had acquired his skill without a teacher and suggested that the government educate him, stating: "He certainly has claims to share in the appropriation for educating Hawaiian youths abroad." The government took up the suggestion and the following year sent Herring to Italy.

In September of 1887, Samuel Nowlein chaperoned Herring and another scholar to Europe. He wrote back to the minister of foreign affairs: "I have now placed Mr. August Herring with professor Tabacchi at Turin. This gentleman has the repute of being a very successful instructor in the art of sculpture. Mr. Herring will receive at his studio instruction in drawing as well as in sculpture, and from what I have seen of the young man I feel no doubt that he will do justice to his instructor and to the Hawaiian government which has so handsomely provided for his future career."

This was the high point of Herring's life. From this time, things began to go wrong.

In 1888, Herring and several other students were recalled as the result of political turmoil in the islands. A Hawaiian government order was issued to "notify those in Italy . . . that if they wish to remain any longer there it must be at their own expense."

Herring must have been extremely disappointed. He had been in Italy barely six months and he was dependent on government support. Having studied Italian for only a few months, he probably would not have known the language well enough to find employment to support himself. Thus, he returned to San Francisco. When it came time to board the ship back to Honolulu, he was found in bed in his hotel, claiming to be sick and unable to sail. Sixteen days later, when the consul-general, David A. McKinley, returned to Herring's hotel to accompany him to another ship, Herring ran away. The consul-general was incensed and perplexed: "The boy reached here in rather straightened circumstances, or at least so he claimed, and his appearances tended to bear out his claims and I therefore gave him some few clothes and several dollars for pocket money, besides paying his hotel and doctors bill never once suspecting his dishonesty.

"In all my intercourse with the wards of the government, this is the first instance of any deception being practiced upon me, and I cannot account for the young man's reason or purpose for acting as he has, for I cannot see what he expects to gain."

Herring sought out his foster father in California and apparently stayed with him. His father later complained: "I had to pay debts for August in San Francisco, Sacramento and Suter City for one pair of boots $6.00 while I was sick and poor besides $400 while he was coming from Itale." According to the *Advertiser*, Herring remained in San Francisco with his father for two years.

Sometime after he returned to Honolulu, about 1890, Herring apparently opened another curio shop. The *Daily Bulletin* later recorded: "After his return he kept a turning shop on Fort Street, where he made a specialty of Hawaiian curios in the shape of cocoanut dishes and calabashes, engraving Hawaiian scenery on them, and so forth."

It does not seem that his shop was very successful, for in 1893 he was employed at painting a private home on the slopes of Punchbowl in back of Honolulu. He had earlier been arrested for eloping with a Hawaiian girl and was fined for carrying a gun. He was also described as being "in with the radical element of politics for some time." In May of 1893, he shot and killed a close friend whom he suspected of being involved with his wife. Herring was convicted of manslaughter and sentenced to ten years in prison. In 1899, after serving almost six years, he was pardoned. The Council of State, in reconsidering his sentence, stated: "The deed of shooting and killing Huntsman was done under circumstances which would leave room for a

ABOVE: *This coconut goblet depicting Diamond Head was carved by craftsman Frederick Otremba and is still owned by the family. It may have been carved shortly after he arrived in the islands in 1882, for newspaper articles in 1883 described in great detail similar carved coconut curios by Otremba. It stands 10" high.*

great deal of excuse for Mr. Herring."

Herring was twenty-nine years old when he was released from prison. During the following years, the *Hawaiian Directory* listed him under several occupations, none of them apparently successful. In 1903, he was a partner in a sign painting business. In 1905, he was a "Fresco Artist." In 1907, he was listed as "sculptor." The following year, his occupation was listed simply as "painter." For each year he had a different address. He did not appear in the *Directory* again until 1911. Living in the small sugar town of Waipahu, outside of Honolulu, he seemed to make one more attempt to succeed, listing his occupation as, "House, sign and general painting, scenic painting a specialty." In 1912 and 1913, he was listed simply as "sign painter," before disappearing from the directories.

Herring's works are rare and his body of work was probably relatively small. Sadly, in only one year, twenty years after sailing for Italy to study sculpture, did Herring list himself in the *Hawaiian Directory* as a sculptor.

Although few other craftsmen in Honolulu carved coconut goblets, fine plain ones were made in large numbers and were popular with tourists and residents, as well as with royalty.

Helen Mather, visiting Iolani Palace in 1890, wrote of seeing "glossy bowls, made from the cocoa-nut" displayed there.

Cabinetmaker John Daniel Wicke may have produced a large number of these undecorated coconut cups and goblets around the turn of the century. Wicke took over his father's cabinet shop in 1886. His father had been one of the better craftsmen in the town and had been regularly favored with royal commissions. However, part of his father's business had apparently come from making polished coconut cups in the shop for tourists and residents. Visiting Hawaii in 1882, Mrs. Joseph Brewer recorded in her diary bringing coconuts to "Mr. Wiki" for finishing: "Call at Mrs. Allen's and she gives me three rough cocoa-nuts and 1 mounted. Take them to Mr. Wiki to be polished."

In the 1890s, as tourism increased and the collecting of Hawaiian wooden bowls became fashionable, John Daniel Wicke began turning out numerous bowls and curios. He first ran a modest advertisement in the 1894 *Directory* only mentioning curios: "J. D. Wicke Cabinetmaker. Furniture made to order, repaired and upholstered. Curios of natural wood for sale or made to order." However, two years later, in the *Directory* of 1896, he barely mentioned the making of furniture. The majority of his business now came from the making of curios. His advertisement in the *Directory* that year read: "J. D. Wicke — Cabinetmaker. Curios of Hawaiian wood for sale or made to order. Cocoanut shells carved and polished. Calabashes a specialty." He listed himself in the *Classified Business Directory* under the heading "Curios" from 1898 until his death in 1904 at age thirty-eight. In those years no other cabinetmaker advertised as a manufacturer of curios.

In the twentieth century, the popularity of the coconut pedestal bowl as a souvenir faded, but

RIGHT: *This coconut curio may have been carved by August Herring between 1886 and 1893. It stands 10" tall with cover and is composed of several pieces of coconut and a stem of turned kou. Four circular carvings around the body of the piece depict scenic Diamond Head, portraits of Queen Kapiolani and King Kalakaua, and a view of the king's residence, Hulihee Palace, at Kailua, Hawaii. The turned kou stem is attached to a coconut shell carved in the outline of a Hawaiian royal order. The fern leaves twining around the four legs and circling the cover are separate pieces fastened with small metal brads.*

its use at Hawaiian luaus remained an essential part of that traditional event. Almira Pitman, visiting in 1917, remembered admiringly: "*Poi*-bowls, which are made of cocoanut shells and polished until they shine like glass, were placed at every plate."

In 1930, the governor of Hawaii, Lawrence Judd, declared the coconut tree the "Territorial Tree." The proclamation was an eloquent tribute to the coconut, reading in part: "Its commanding presence is recognized in romance; it is stately; it is ornamental, and in addition has a very definite economic value. Breathing the spirit of the tropics, it is recognised as a symbol of hospitality, and stands as a sentinel casting a magic spell that no one has been able to resist."

The coconut remained the territorial tree until Hawaii became a state in 1959. In that year, the kukui was declared the state tree.

RIGHT: *The curio in the foreground has a cover and base of turned kou and stands 8 7/8" high. On one side of the coconut body is carved a scene of Waikiki and Diamond Head. On the opposite side is carved "ALOHA NEI HAWAII" in high relief against a modified heart-shaped background. This gift to the Bishop Museum was from Rear Admiral Armin Farenholt. According to Farenholt, this piece may have been given to his wife's (Henrietta Afong Whiting) first husband, Rear Admiral William Whiting, and could possibly have come from King Kalakaua, as they were friends. Farenholt stated the goblet was at least fifty years old when he gave it to the museum in 1940.*

Polished coconut containers were often given as gifts to visitors. Ida von Holt wrote of one such gift given by Queen Emma: "Another gratious act of hers was to invite the sister of the Bishop of Oregon (who was paying us a visit) to have tea with her at Waikiki. During the afternoon the Queen asked Miss Morris if she had ever tasted a fresh coconut. Miss Morris replied that she had never before even seen a coconut tree. Whereupon Queen Emma told one of her attendants to fetch down a good nut. The boy tied his feet together about a foot apart, to aid in climbing, climbed the tree, screwed off a nut and brought it to Miss Morris. She drank the milk and ate the meat, enjoying both very much. When she was returning to San Francisco, Queen Emma sent a parcel on board for her, and there was the very coconut she had seen picked, beautifully polished and made into a bowl."

The coconut curio in the background depicts an unidentified building, coconut trees, and the word "Honolulu" carved near the rim. The carving does not appear to be the work of a trained craftsman. The serrated rim and base give this piece particular charm.

FIBER

Hawaiian craftsmen used a particular mountain vine, the ieie, to twine tight-fitting coverings that completely encased very special gourds and wooden containers. These are now very rare. Little is known now about the craftsmen who made them or the craft itself.

William Brigham wrote that these containers were "for solidity and durability of workmanship, I believe to be unsurpassed in this Pacific region, nor do my limited studies in the field of basketry embrace any baskets of any region which may justly be accorded a higher rank than pertains to the baskets made from ieie by the Hawaiians."

The ieie, *Freycinetia arborea,* is a native Hawaiian plant growing in high forests both as ground cover and in trees. Brigham commented on the Hawaiians' familiarity with the vine: " 'Born is the tangled ieie in the forest' is a common saying of the old Hawaiians, for the plant is found in abundance in the forests, especially the more elevated ones, all over the group."

The aerial roots of the climbing vine were the parts of the plant that were used in weaving. Marie Neal described how these roots were used: "The many long, narrow, aerial roots emitted from the stems formerly furnished material for baskets of Hawaiian workmanship, excelled nowhere in the Pacific. These roots are uniform in size, strong and pliable, and can be used whole or split in half and combined with other materials. They were made into close-fitting coverings around wooden or gourd calabashes and bottles, into baskets for household goods, fish baskets, fish and shrimp traps, idols, and helmets.

"The 'ie'ie was formerly considered sacred and was dedicated to ceremonial purposes."

Of these baskets woven over wooden or gourd bowls, Brigham could gather little information: "Exactly how these were made I cannot say, and the technic must be gathered from the specimens, for in the early days of my explorations on this group I never saw any such baskets, and have not been able to learn much about them from the present generation of natives."

Although these containers were seldom mentioned by early visitors, they are apparently an ancient art form. No journal from the Cook expedition mentions them, yet there is a covered basket of ieie in the British Museum that is listed as "Cook Collection."

Capt. George Dixon's published account of his voyage in the Pacific between 1785 and 1788 included an engraving of a covered ieie container. Unfortunately, no mention was made of it in

LEFT: *The ieie container in the foreground was collected during Capt. James Cook's visits to Hawaii in 1778 and 1779. It stands 21 1/2" high. The British Museum accession record reads: "Large basketwork cover for a big gourd, with semi-spherical detachable lid of the same material. It is oviform and has remains of a network of sennit-cord round the neck. The gourd which was once contained in the basketwork has disappeared."*

The wickered covered gourd in the background has faded red-and-black designs woven in. These colors, which originally were bright, were achieved by dyeing the ieie vines before plaiting. The accession card at the British Museum states that this type of container was "for carrying a chief's clothing."

In the extreme foreground is another example of Hawaiian weaving, a finely crafted fan.

the text.

French Capt. Louis de Freycinet visited Hawaii in 1819 and also included an illustration of a covered ieie container in the publication about his voyage. The ieie's scientific designation, *Freycinetia,* was in honor of this explorer. Of these containers, Freycinet wrote: "One works in the [ieie], some patterns in the taste of those of our basket-work, but perhaps better finished; there are ones of solid shade; others (of which are helmets, fans, baskets, wickering of the calabashes where one stores valuable items, etc.,) are of hues of various colors. These patterns bespeak the delicate hand of a woman and offer forms and dimensions which are quite diverse."

One of the few references to baskets of any type in the nineteenth century was made by Rev. William Ellis in 1823. Touring the southern side of the island of Hawaii that year, Ellis purchased two ieie baskets at the village of Kaau, near Hilo: "Before we left the place, the people offered for sale some curious deep oval baskets, with covers, made of the fibrous roots of ie. We purchased two, intending to preserve them as specimens of native ingenuity."

Only a few surviving specimens of this basketry, preserved primarily in museums, give evidence to the high quality of this extinct Hawaiian craft.

RIGHT: *The storage containers seen here, one wood and one gourd, are both encased in twined ieie coverings. French Captain Louis de Freycinet wrote in 1819 that these containers were for storing articles of great worth.*

The descriptive catalogue of the Hawaiian National Museum collection described similar containers as "used for containing clothes, featherwork, hairwork, ivory and other valuable property of the natives of olden times. A netting was generally woven into them so that by pulling draw strings, the top was securely fastened on by the netting."

In 1920, the Peabody Museum of Salem, Massachusetts, published a catalogue of their Hawaiian collection, among which were containers similar to these. The catalogue stated: "The hinai poepoe, or globular baskets, were tightly woven over bowls of wood or gourd and supplied with a cover of the same which was tied on. These were used as receptacles for their most valued possessions."

The wooden covered container is 21 1/4" tall, and the gourd container in back is 16" high.

Both the feather cape and banded lei are made from the feathers of two Hawaiian birds. The black and yellow feathers are from the o'o, the red from the i'iwi.

A bracelet, kupee, and neck ornament, lei niho palaoa, both of whale ivory, are also pictured.

The 1895 **Hawaiian Annual** *explained the value of these royal raiments in ancient Hawaii: "In the economic system of ancient Hawaii a higher valuation was set upon bird feathers than upon any other species of property, the next rank being occupied by the whale tooth, a jetsam-ivory called palaoa pae, monopolized as a perquisite of the king."*

RIGHT: *Assessing the quality of Hawaiian basketry, Dale Kronkright, senior objects conservator at the Pacific Regional Conservation Center, had this to say: "The examples of Hawaiian basketry that I have examined at the Bishop Museum are of very high quality. They are also interesting in that, unlike the weavers in most basketmaking cultures in the world, Hawaiian weavers apparently varied their weaving technique for both functional and creative reasons. In most cultures, weavers work in a single direction. For instance, if the weaver begins twining in a clockwise direction, that direction is usually maintained throughout the work.*

"In addition, the direction in which weavers work is usually fixed and distinct to a culture and there is little variation. Hawaiians, however, seemed perfectly comfortable changing directions two or three times or more in a single work. If the weaver came to a curve where it was more practical to change direction, they did so. At other times, they appear to change direction for no apparent reason. In such instances, the stitches will not appear to have changed. This is very difficult to do.

"Not only does the weaving direction change back and forth freely and flawlessly, the weaving is technically quite sophisticated. Almost all basketmaking cultures use a plain twining technique with two wefts over every warp. A more difficult and demanding technique is to use three or four wefts in twining; that is, three strands or even four woven over each upright fiber. This makes the work stronger and in other cultures is used primarily only in areas of stress and wear, like the bottoms and rims of baskets. Hawaiian craftsmen, however, frequently used three- or four-strand twining throughout their work, for both strength and decorative effect.

"Among world cultures, then, the basketry of ancient Hawaii may be considered a highly developed artistic tradition."

Ethnologist Roger Rose wrote of this craft: "Some of the finest and most delicate twining was applied directly to the outer surfaces of wooden and gourd vessels, in a manner perfected by Hawaiian artisans. The twining is so expertly executed on some examples that even natural imperfections in the underlying gourds are perfectly reproduced. The finest examples were presumably reserved for use by the chiefly classes for protecting valuable personal ornaments and clothing, such as their costly feather capes and cloaks, or perhaps for their carved wooden images of the gods. Unfortunately, the need for these fancy containers rapidly declined after imported European and Chinese chests became generally available, and all knowledge of the more elaborate, specialized twining techniques disappeared by the mid-nineteenth century. Were it not for the relatively few examples surviving in such places as the Bishop Museum in Honolulu, one of the Pacific's most distinctive basketry traditions might have vanished almost without a trace."

PART III

CALABASHES, FOODS, AND FEASTING

LEFT: *This humorous carte de visite of Alan Wilkes Judd identifies him on the back using the Hawaiian form of his name, Alani. Judd was the fourth son of Dr. Gerrit Judd, who arrived with the third company of American missionaries in 1827 and later served the Hawaiian government as secretary of state for foreign affairs, minister of the interior, and commissioner to France, Great Britain, and the United States.*

Judd has seated himself on the floor, a fish in one hand, the other dipping into an uncovered poi gourd, perfectly imitating John Townsend's 1835 description of a Hawaiian at table: "He seats himself cross-legged upon the ground with his calabash before him, and a fish and a little pile of salt on a wooden dish by his side. His two first fingers are immersed in the paste."

Joseph Ingram wrote of Hawaiians insistence on dining in this traditional manner: "The natives take their meals sitting on the floor. They will adopt every other innovation of civilization but to surrender their primitive mode of eating. This custom of their ancestors is held as a sacred legacy and around it cluster so many memories that they cling to its form with tenacious loyalty. The king himself never looks so happy as when seated on the floor with his people, eating out of the calabashes."

POI, THE STAFF OF LIFE

Wooden and gourd containers in Hawaii in the late nineteenth century were commonly called "poi bowls," reflecting the importance of taro, *Colocasia esculenta,* to the Hawaiians. In 1837, visitor William Ruschenberger found this vegetable not only a major food source, but often the only one available: "The food of these natives consists almost exclusively of taro, and when they occasionally get a little meat or fish, they esteem themselves fortunate." The tuber is an excellent carbohydrate, and both the tuber and leaf are high in minerals and vitamins.

Although taro was a food source for all Polynesian cultures, it was most highly developed in Hawaii, where over 50 varieties and 300 different Hawaiian names have been recorded. Some varieties were cultivated for their leaves, stalks, or sprouts, all of which were edible. The great majority of taro, however, was cultivated for the tuber, which was baked, kneaded into a paste with the addition of water, and set aside to sour slightly. In this form, it was called poi and was traditionally eaten at all meals.

The use of taro in this soft, semi-liquid form was unique to Hawaii and was very likely the major reason for the high degree of sophistication in the development of wooden bowls and the cultivation of gourds. Dr. James Beaglehole, in *The Journals of Captain James Cook,* commented that "the Hawaiian poi, a standard food of mashed taro diluted with water, was a liquid, unlike the other Polynesian foods; and so gourds, and gourd-shaped bowls, were a distinctive Hawaiian utensil."

Visitors were fascinated by Hawaiians' predeliction for this staple food. In 1841, Sir George Simpson wrote: "To see the natives eat it, or to hear them speak of it, one cannot but conclude that, in their estimation, it is the greatest luxury in the world. The passion for poi pervades all classes, from the king downwards; and the chiefs make no secret of the fact, that, after dining with foreigners on the collected dainties of both hemispheres, they take a little poi at home, by way, as they express it, of filling up the corners."

Capt. Nathaniel Portlock, in 1787, commented on Hawaiians' strong reaction when poi was not available: "They frequently make a pudding of it, which they keep till it becomes a little sour, and then they are very fond of it, preferring it to every thing else. The Indians that were a little while at sea with me almost fretted themselves to death when their stock of po-e was exhausted." Capt. Frederick Beechey also discovered, during his visit in 1826, just how important taro was to Hawaiians. None of the Hawaiian chiefs and chiefesses who had accompanied King Kamehameha II and his wife to England in 1824 wanted to return to that country in large part because of their having to do without poi: "The want of their favourite dish Poe was, besides, so serious an inconvenience, that when allusion was made to England, this privation was

LEFT: *On a small lauhala placemat sits a kou calabash filled with poi and beside it a banana leaf plate with red Hawaiian salt as a condiment. The Hawaiian term for a bowl of poi is umekepoi. When American missionary Lorrin Andrews produced the first Hawaiian dictionary in 1865, he defined: "**Umekepoi** A poi calabash full of food, much valued by Hawaiians."*

ABOVE: *In this photograph the pail of water beside the seated worker indicates that taro corms were in the final stages of conversion to poi; after a thorough first pounding, usually immediately after cooking, taro corms were reduced to a thick paste called paiai. In this state it could be stored for long periods of time. In preparing poi from paiai, pounding was resumed, with small amounts of water added until a creamy consistency was achieved. It was then put into a calabash where more water was gradually added and carefully stirred by hand until the desired consistency was reached.*

Mabel Craft, describing poi during her visit in the 1890s, wrote: "All ***poi*** *is allowed to ferment slightly before it is eaten, and iconoclasts say that it tastes like sour bill-sticker's paste, which is a libel. It seems to me that* ***poi*** *is almost tasteless, and makes a good background for a meal."*

Clarence Webster, visiting in 1892, wrote of poi: "It looks like sour paste, it smells like sour paste, and it tastes like sour paste. The appetite for it is usually acquired quickly and easily, and when one gets to be confirmed in the habit, there is nothing which will take its place.... I became a shameless poi fiend."

LEFT: *This 1880s photograph shows a Honolulu street vendor posing with his wares in a photographer's studio. On either end of his carrying pole are harvested taro plants, complete from root to leaf. The large bulbous roots have yet to be cooked, peeled, and thoroughly pounded into a thick, creamy liquid to become poi. Researcher Margaret Titcomb recorded the difference between two varieties of plants: "Dry land taro reached six to eight feet in height; lowland taro between three and four."*

In 1841, Sir George Simpson visited Hawaii and, quoting a Honolulu newspaper, wrote: "In regard to cheapness of food for the natives, it is proper to state, that forty feet square of land, planted with ***kalo****, affords subsistence for one person for a year. A tract of land one mile square ... will feed 15,151, and probably not more than one-twenty-fifth of that number would be required in its cultivation."*

Simpson was writing of wetland taro, which was the more common variety in the nineteenth century.

always mentioned."

That same year, visitor Lt. Hiram Paulding was surprised that chiefs invited to a meal onboard ship ignored their hosts' Western-style foods and brought their own poi: "Instead of partaking of what we had provided for our guests, they, with one or two exceptions, unceremoniously uncovered their poye pots, which had been brought with them by an attendant, and ate heartily of their favourite food, using their fingers as is the native custom."

There are two basic varieties of taro, wetland taro and dryland taro. One was planted wherever there was a water source for irrigation, and the other was commonly grown on those parts of the islands without streams.

Peter Corney, who visited the islands several times between 1815 and 1818, described the two varieties: "Tarrow, which is the principal vegetable, grows in abundance; there are two sorts; the first and best is planted in large square patches, banked up about six feet, and beat down very hard at the bottom and sides, so as to hold water; the growers then put a quantity of loose mould, turn some water on, and plant the tarrow in straight lines, or circles; and the water forms a fish pond as well as tarrow patch. This root takes about nine months to come to perfection. They manage it so as to have the patch always full, for as they dig up that which is ripe, they plant the suckers in its room, and by the time they come to the end of a patch, that which was first planted is ripe, and by this means they are never without it. They turn the water from the mountains, bring it down in streams to the tarrow ground, and take it in rotation to turn it on to the different patches. Round the banks of these patches there are beautiful walks, planted with sugar canes and plantain trees.

"The other sort of a tarrow is planted in dry ground, and takes a year to come to perfection."

When ripe, the tubers were harvested and baked. Taro is inedible in raw form due to a high concentration of oxalic acid crystals that are a severe irritant when swallowed. Once baked, the tubers would keep for a long period of time, although commonly the taro went through the first stages of mashing before being stored. This partially prepared poi was termed paiai.

The Rev. Ellis explained the baking process, which was the most common cooking process employed by Hawaiians for all their foods: "The oven was a hole in the earth, three or four feet in diameter, and nearly a foot deep. A number of small stones were spread over the bottom, a few dried leaves laid on them, and the necessary quantity of sticks and firewood piled up, and covered over with small stones. The dry leaves were then kindled, and while the stones were heating, the man scraped off the skin or rind of the taro with a shell, and split the roots into two or three pieces. When the stones were red-hot, they were spread out with a stick, the remaining fire-brands taken away; and when the dust and ashes, on the stones at the bottom, had been brushed off with a green bough, the taro, wrapped in leaves, was laid on them till the oven was full."

Mary Pukui described the sealing of the oven: "Several thicknesses of [ti leaves] were used, the leaves spread out, fanwise, and over them more banana leaves, so placed as to keep the next covering — three to four inches of soil — from trickling through to the food, enough also to keep the steam within. By the time sufficient soil had been piled on top of the imu it looked like nothing more than an earth mound. An imu of this size required two or three hours to cook its contents; large imu took longer. Sometimes an imu was left all night, especially those for taro."

Once cooked the taro was ready to be beaten into paiai or poi. The process of pounding the tubers to a thick, smooth consistency was long and hard. It was done seated on the ground straddling a thick plank of hardwood that had been carved into the shape of a platter. Typically, these planks were from three to five inches thick, three to five feet long and about fifteen to twenty-four inches wide.

When large amounts of poi were to be readied, two men sat at either end of the longer poi boards, each working independently. The pounders themselves were of shaped stone, the most common formed like an exaggerated pestle. In ancient times this work was done exclusively by men because of the strenuous labor involved.

Lt. Frederich Walpole described the pounding process: "The quantity required, generally about enough for a week's consumption, is placed on a large flat surface . . . and a man with a stone mallet, which he uses with both hands, beats it, and kneads it about, mixing water with it every now and then, till every lump is pounded, and the whole is of the consistency of paste. This requires much labour, and it is several hours' hard work to make a calabash of poe. When made, it is put into one of the large calabashes of the country, and allowed to stand two or three days, till it has a slight acid taste, and it is then fit to eat. . . . The quantity they eat is wonderful."

The making of poi required the addition of water during mashing to produce a creamy thickness. It was then put into a gourd or wood calabash where more water was stirred in by hand until the desired consistency was reached.

Different varieties of taro caused poi to be different colors. Rev. John Sheepshanks noticed this in 1866, when he observed that poi had "the consistency and somewhat of the appearance of paste. The colour, however, varies somewhat, being sometimes white, sometimes with a blue, sometimes of a reddish tint, according to the species of the kalo."

Poi was always eaten with the fingers, from a gourd or wooden calabash, even after utensils came into general use. In 1849, Robert Elwes wrote of the accepted etiquette when eating poi: "Taro . . . is always eaten from a calabash with the fore-finger — the natives, from long practice, being able to take up a good mouthful with that alone. . . . A spoon seems never to be used with poe; and even when it is ladled from one vessel to another, they resort to the hand."

Hawaiian society affected a manner of eating poi according to its consistency, with one, two, or three fingers. Writing in 1820, pioneer missionary Lucia Ruggles Holman was among the first to note this practice: "They have a kind of pudding which they call poa, made of Tarrow, and which answers the purpose of bread for them. They have one kind which they eat with one finger, which is about as thick as hasty pudding; another, which is made thinner, and requires 2 fingers, and a third, 3."

George Cannon, writing of Hawaiian manners in 1882, stated: "Usually they are particular about having their hands clean, and eating with due respect to each other's rights. One waits for the other to put his finger in the *poi* and their ideas of decorum and manners, such as they are, are as strict as ours."

Not only manners, but a proper attitude was demanded as part of Hawaiian dining etiquette. Mary Pukui remembered: "All unpleasant topics were avoided during eating. No business was discussed. Talk was often in funny tales and humorous banter." Visitor Joseph Ingram noted: "Their happiest hours seemed to be at their meals. There they abandoned themselves to jollity of manner, and are never so merry as when gathered around their banquet gourds."

All visitors tried poi, and reactions varied widely. Andrew Bloxam tried poi in 1825 and wrote: "I tasted some of the *poe* brought off yesterday in the canoe. It resembled in external appearance a thick, creamy custard and to my taste somewhat similar to a very rich gooseberry fool turned rather sour." In 1896 Adelbert Cronice tried to describe poi: "The taste is hard to

ABOVE AND RIGHT: *A favorite subject for professional artists and photographers was Hawaiians eating poi in the traditional manner. Seen above is an oil painting by San Francisco artist Theodore Wores who in 1901 painted this young Hawaiian girl in a white muumuu sitting on a lauhala mat before a beautifully polished kou bowl filled with poi. On the right are commercial photographic prints taken by Joaquin Gonsalves between 1900 and 1910. Hawaiian women sit in front of painted backdrops with wooden poi bowls prominently displayed.*

dispute
However I
I am always glad
to hear from you
I did hope to see

define, but there are sensations of something soft, slippery and slightly sour. Although it is not half bad, a longing for it has to be acquired." Tourists were still describing their reaction to poi in the twentieth century. In 1917, Almira Pitman rendered her judgment: "The *poi* is made from the taro root, and when cooked looks like strained oatmeal porridge. I cannot say that I liked it, but the Americans say it is an acquired taste, like olives."

The commercial price of poi varied widely during the nineteenth and twentieth centuries. In 1930, the *Paradise of the Pacific* reported that: "Poi can be purchased in almost any Honolulu market and sells for between five and seven cents a pound. It is enjoyed by many *haoles* (white persons) and is served at least two or three times a week in *kamaaina* homes." In the early nineteenth century, however, the poi sold in Honolulu was primarily eaten by Hawaiians who formed the majority of the labor force in the town. To feed this urban population, enterprising Hawaiians transported poi to town in large calabashes to sell at the markets. Prices rose and fell according to availability.

The *Pacific Commercial Advertiser*, in 1863, recalled an early attempt by the merchants to form a cartel to sustain exorbitant prices for the product: "Our friend 'Kentuck' recalls to our memory an incident which many may remember as having occurred in the good old days of '48 or 49, when the governor's word was law and gospel. There was a famine in those days, or rather high prices prevailed, and a calabash of poi, which formerly commanded 25 cts sold for 75 cts. The rise in the price of poi, and the complaints of the people soon reached the ears of Governor Kekuanaoa, who said it was purely speculation and must be stopped. So the next day, taking his cane, he walked out to the poi market, where the calabashes were all ranged in a row, and the speculators in the 'staff of life' were assembled and hawking their wares as eagerly and noisily as brokers in a modern stock exchange. His Excellency watched them a little while, when, walking up to the first calabash, he asked the price. 'Ekolu hapahs' (75 cts) said the owner, and the Governor drew up his cane and smashed the container, scattering its contents, here and there. Passing on to the second calabash, he made the same inquiry and received the same answer, when it and its contents were scattered in the same manner. The next seller wisely dropped his price to 50 cts, and the governor spared his lot, and found no one above that figure. The price of poi suddenly collapsed, and no further complaints were heard of the combination of poi dealers."

In the 1880s, Chinese began to monopolize the manufacture of poi. This shift was first noticed by the *Hawaiian Gazette* in 1881: "Poi making is largely going into the hands of the Celestials." Visitor Minnie Grant, in 1882, found that the street vendors were no longer Hawaiians with burden poles carrying large calabashes of poi. They were now Chinese carrying metal cans: "Poi is made by the Chinese, and sold in all stages by them, a common sight in the streets of Honolulu being a Chinaman . . . bearing on his shoulders a pole at either end of which, is suspended a five gallon kerosene tin can, filled with pai-ai or poi."

In 1891, visitor Ash Silvers wrote humorously of poi but included a veiled caution about poi made by Chinese: "The adhesive quality of poi is remarkable. It makes an excellent paste for putting on wall-paper, and is warranted to stick to the appetite, like bad luck to an indolent man. It is not, however, generally relished by foreigners, on first acquaintance, it is so cold and unsocial; but one quickly acquires a taste for it, and if he can only avoid going where it is manufactured by the Chinese, will soon learn to enjoy it."

The 1888 report of the Board of Health to the legislature noted the dominance of Chinese poi factories in Honolulu: "There are within the limits . . . 47 establishments where poi is made and sold, and with one exception they are all carried on by Chinese." The Chinese section of Honolulu was cramped and crowded. Food preparation under such conditions was difficult. Awareness of these conditions by some residents led them to choose their poi manufacturers carefully. That same year the government passed a law regulating poi making through the Board of Health. Thus, in the twentieth century, poi factories were so sanitary that visiting them became a standard part of a visitor's tour. A typical visitor, Minnie Crawford, wrote in 1920: "I have been having an interesting time this week, all my days being full. I have visited a *poi* factory."

To appease the tourists' curiosity and make it more palatable, hotels served fresh poi that had not soured, and even added sugar to insure a positive response. Visitor Mary Wetmore stayed at the Hawaiian Hotel in 1888 and wrote of poi: "It is served generally in sauce plates with sugar sprinkled over it, and eaten with spoons." This was so successful that not only sugar but cream was added. In 1920, Crawford reported: "Nearly everyone visiting the Islands eats *poi*, but *not* in *kanaka* style. At the hotels it is served like mush and eaten with sugar and cream, or made into a cocktail and served as an appetizer."

Residents derived much enjoyment from visitors' frequent awkwardness at first eating poi at a luau, and in 1884 the *Chicago News* published a tourist's typical experience: "I don't know whether you have ever seen poi or not, but it is as like melted lard in appearance as possible, and contains the element of food and drink. . . . The natives eat it with their fingers, fetching it to their mouths by a graceful gesture which the whites in vain attempt to follow. I remember the first time I saw poi eaten was at a native feast. . . . After the roast pig and cocoa-nut milk came poi. . . . I glanced around; the foreigners were watching me. I made a resolve; down went my fist, up came about a teaspoonful, dripping everywhere, and flying off the tangent of my hand, it reached — No, I beg your pardon, not my mouth, but, in equal quantities, my shirt front and the lady's cheek. The people yelled with delight, and I made shift to clean myself from the plight I was in."

Although poi was still considered a novelty to visiting tourists into the early twentieth century, it remained a staple food item for residents, and was found in most food stores and markets.

In 1932, Charles Liu, poi inspector for the City and County of Honolulu, reported to the *Star-Bulletin*: "Nine poi factories are in operation in Honolulu, six by Chinese, one by a Korean, one by a Japanese and one by a Chinese Hawaiian. The country districts have four poi factories, two at Laie operated by Hawaiians, one at Kailua operated by a Chinese, and one at Waialua operated by a Japanese.

". . . In the city there are 127 places where you may buy poi to take home and 77 cafes and restaurants where you may order it served. In addition, two Honolulu hotels serve poi each day. The rural districts report 16 dealers, one cafe and one restaurant. The largest of the factories is the Oahu poi factory, which during August turned out 231,000 pounds of poi, or nearly 3,000 pounds each working day." For many island residents, poi continued to be "The Staff of Life."

However, as the traditional containers of wood and gourd were recognized as art objects and withdrawn from use, no new form of specialized vessel was developed to celebrate this unique Hawaiian food.

LUAU AND PAINA

Ancient Hawaiian religious practices kept men and women apart during meals. Men and women ate in separate, extended family groups with their own utensils in their own areas. Commoners and women of all ranks were forbidden to eat certain foods; only men of rank had the possibility of unrestricted diets.

In 1819, as a result of growing Western influence, traditional Hawaiian religious practices and observances were ordered abolished by Kamehameha II. The symbolic act which ended the ancient religion was the king eating with women at a feast he hosted. What are now considered traditional Hawaiian feasts, luaus, began after that date.

Luaus were simply large feasts where men and women ate traditional Hawaiian foods together in the traditional manner, with the fingers, usually seated on mats on the ground.

Pioneer missionary Reverend Hiram Bingham described what had become a traditional luau laid out for Hawaiian royalty in 1823, only four years after the abolition of the eating kapu: "Their supper scene along the beach exhibited a good specimen of the customs of the nobility, to which the mild atmosphere and clear sky of their evenings, on the leeward of their islands, were favorable.

"Animals, larger and smaller, baked whole, are set forth, in full size on heavy wooden platters, placed on the ground or on mats. At intervals are set calabashes of *poi*, potatoes, cresses, sea moss, and fruit. [They] drank cold water from gourd-shell bottles."

The *Pacific Commercial Advertiser* explained the term luau in 1875: "The principal dish at these parties affords the name. The young and tender leaves of the taro plant, when boiled or baked with meats in native style is called *luau*."

Author Margaret Titcomb, in her notes on Hawaiian feasts, stated of these leaves: "It is so important a food at feasts that the term luau has replaced the old term for feast, *'aha 'aina*."

Resident Mary Pukui explained the table setting at a traditional luau: "Before serving . . . a mat was spread on the floor, then another about three feet wide, was laid upon it and covered with green ti leaves, perhaps some ferns added for ornamentation.

"Down the center of this went the rows of poi-filled calabashes. On either side of this row went the platters of meat. The two who sat side by side generally ate from the same platter. Dry foods like sweet potatoes, salt, dried fish or meat covered in ti leaves, were laid right on the clean ti leaves."

LEFT: *Seen here are place settings for a paina, a small intimate version of a Hawaiian luau or feast. The setting was part of a 1989 exhibition at the Honolulu Academy of Arts titled* ***The Hawaiian Poi Supper****. In this setting the meal is served in traditional Hawaiian style, on the ground. Ti leaves serve as a tablecloth and are laid over a large lauhala mat, with ferns running as decoration down the center. Place settings are made up of a mixture of wood and coconut containers, each to hold a particular food that is to be eaten with the fingers. Place names are indicated at each setting, and a traditional laulau, pork and taro leaves cooked in a wrapping of ti leaves, sit at each place as a first course. Vintage Hawaiian soda bottles complete the setting.*

ABOVE: *Alonzo Gartley photographed this small community luau at Honaunau, Hawaii, between 1900 and 1910. Various foods are served on Western dinnerware, but the poi is served in traditional containers of wood and gourd. Ash Silvers, visiting in 1892, noted that poi was the first food served at a luau he attended: "The first course served to us was a calabash of poi, rattling good poi it was, too; and then came raw fish, and roast pig, fresh from the ground-oven in which it had been cooked, sweet and delectable, and half a dozen other dishes, besides, that I knew nothing about, but all clean and palatable. Not wishing to be considered 'tenderfeet', we partook of everything freely and in native fashion, eating poi, pig, and all, with our fingers, as if to the 'manner born.' "*

LEFT: *This 1890s afternoon outdoor luau for Honolulu high society was held at the home of Charles Brown at Waipio, Oahu. Brown is seated in the foreground on the right. Low tables hold the food as guests sit on woven mats on the ground. Covered wooden goblets were used on this occasion as centerpieces.*

Ash Silvers, visiting in 1892, wrote of attending a similar luau: "We took our seats on the ground . . . our feet doubled up Turk-fashion beneath us. The table consisted of rough boards resting on 'horses' of wood about a foot from the floor, and was covered with a thin spread of clean, fresh fern-leaves, which answered admirably the purposes of a table-cloth; and on this the different articles of food were spread in abundance."

At traditional luaus, all the different foods were eaten directly from common bowls and platters or guests placed individual portions on ti or banana leaves. In 1846, Danish Capt. Steen Bille described the practice of using leaves as plates: "A small pig, a turkey, a chicken or even a dog . . . is served on a wooden dish; if things are to be done in great style everybody places a large leaf in front of him as a plate."

Leaves were traditionally used as plates; John Ledyard described them used by Hawaiians hosting Capt. Cook in 1779: "The navigator and his officers were sumptuously feasted on baked hog and potatoes, neatly spread out on green plantain leaves." During the nineteenth century, the tradition of using eating utensils in common slowly gave way to the Western tradition of individual place settings. However, instead of just a single plate, a number of individual dishes, each holding a different Hawaiian food, would accompany a plate to make up an individual place setting. These individual place settings were developed primarily for parties called paina or "poi suppers." A poi supper differed from a luau primarily in the number of participants. Poi suppers included fewer people and would generally be somewhat more elegant and intimate.

Author Maili Yardley described these dinners in the 1930s: "Hostesses of that era favored the poi supper as a charming way of entertaining in the home. Hours of work went into preparing this special occasion to give it the innate Hawaiian atmosphere. Shiny ti leaves were laid closely down the long table as a tablecloth and down the center were delicate ferns, low floral arrangements or leis and cut pineapples and watermelons. The table sparkled with crystal, coconut dishes and calabashes, finger bowls and double damask napkins, but no silverware. Guests prided themselves on the graceful art of eating with their fingers and mastering one or two finger poi.

"These dinner parties were referred to as a *paina* and the menu consisted of succulent laulaus of pork with either salmon or butterfish wrapped in luau and ti leaves, Lawalu pond mullet wrapped in ti leaves, lomi salmon topped with crystals of ice, chicken luau and rich coconut cream, squid luau, soft shell crabs, opihis, baked taro, sweet potato and bananas, haupia, kulolo, poi and condiments of Hawaiian red salt, green onions, kukui nut, limu and dried fish. Dessert was a rich coconut cake with a custard filling topped with seven-minute frosting sprinkled generously with moist grated fresh coconut.

"These were the days of prohibition when a host prided himself on serving the finest *okolehao* his bootlegger could provide. Kegs of this liquor were delivered under cover of night and then left to age to a mellow nectar.

"Coffee was served on the lanai or on the lawn under protective spreading trees - sometimes even with a full moon shimmering on the water. There was a rare relaxed air of aloha at these gatherings. Hawaiian hospitality at its best!"

In 1917, visitor Almira Pitman described a typical place setting at a poi supper: "I never could imagine so sumptuous a table. There must have been at least twenty dishes of as many kinds of food, all so tastefully arranged around each plate that it looked tempting beyond description."

It became fashionable about this time for these settings to be made from island woods. In 1930, visitor Joseph McSpadden recorded what became known as a "Poi Supper Set": "A koa-wood plate for each guest, and around it several smaller dishes. Some sort of drink is ready in a calabash, which is a cocoanut shell with scalloped edges."

Large collections of these poi supper sets were purchased by wealthy residents for private parties. Most of these collections have been scattered, and they are now rare and costly.

Another nineteenth-century use of wooden bowls and gourds was to receive voluntary cash donations at benefit luaus. Residents often held luaus as a means of raising money. Friends and neighbors would be invited and a wooden bowl or gourd would be left in some inconspicuous spot, in which guests would place their donations when they had finished eating. There was no set charge, everyone paid what they wished.

Lorenzo Lyons lived in Waimea on Hawaii and wrote of this practice in 1860: "In America, concerts, sewing parties etc. are got up to raise funds. With Hawaiians, a festival is found to be a successful expedient. Hence a great feast is got up and guests invited from all the surrounding country. They have a pleasant and sociable time, intermingled with singing, speechifying, etc. A collection is taken up to aid in paying off the debt. Sometimes the collection is quite satisfactory — again it is so meager that the makers of the feast feel not only disappointed but indignant. They would have got more if they had sold their pigs, fowls, poi, and cattle. We have had four of these festivals during the year. They were quite pleasant seasons, though I cannot say they were very profitable."

The Hawaiian wooden bowl or gourd was understood by all to act as collection plate at these luaus and was somewhat ignored by the host to avoid any confrontation or embarrassment over the amount any guest might contribute. Visitor Charles Nordhoff wrote a travel book, published in 1874, describing the custom: "If now you look you will see a calabash somewhere in the middle of the floor, into which each, as he completes his meal, puts his quarter or half dollar."

Thomas Knox, visiting in the 1880s, hired a guide who took him to a luau and then explained the custom: "He pointed out a calabash bowl lying on the ground as the receptacle of the money, as it was a matter of etiquette for the master not to receive the cash directly from the hands of his guests."

One of the most pleasant of luau traditions is the lavish use of decorative greenery and flowers. Resident Mary Pukui recalled: "I have never seen a feast (in my childhood nor heard from the old folks of my mother's or grandmother's generation) in which mountain greenery was omitted. Ti leaves and ieie vines were generally the favorite but hapu leaves, whole banana plants (without the fruit) and gingers have been used. The people wore leis of maile mixed with palapala ferns and the fragrance of these plants added much to the joyousness of the occasion."

Minnie Grant was visiting in Honolulu during King Kalakaua's coronation luau in 1883 and wrote of the extravagant floral decorations used to celebrate the event: "Tables were draped with white, but the entire tops were covered with ferns and leaves massed together so as almost to form a tablecloth of themselves; quantities of flowers were placed about mingling with the ferns. . . . The natives had turned out in great numbers, and the scent of their leis of flowers and maille leaves was almost overpowering."

Another tradition of the Hawaiian luau was to eat seated on mats on the ground. Sitting on the floor often came as a surprise to visitors, such as Henry Howell in 1891: "The feast was laid *on the floor!* Down the centre of the room was spread a roll of matting, and on this were great quantities of ferns, vines, leaves large and small, and hundreds of flowers; arranged among these lay the various dishes."

Eventually, low tables were introduced. The *Pacific Commercial Advertiser* reported on a luau attended by Kalakaua, in 1882, and somewhat humorously described the discomfort of luau tables only six inches high: "A long, low platform . . . only raised about six inches from the

ABOVE: *Seen here is a single setting from Queen Liliuokalani's poi supper set displayed at the Honolulu Academy of Arts in 1989. All the containers that make up individual place settings are of coconut. The large oblong serving platter at the top right is of wood, and an ancient wood finger bowl is at the top left, identified by the raised projection in the center. The ti leaves that form a placemat on the koa table are interwoven in the manner favored by the Queen at poi suppers she hosted.*

LEFT: *A typical poi supper setting is made up of coconut and wood containers of various sizes and shapes. Each held a different food, the largest usually reserved for poi, the smallest for condiments such as salt and grated kukui nuts. Plates were rare, but when used were usually of wood, like the 11" monkeypod plate seen here.*

Mabel Craft, visiting in the 1890s, wrote of these feasts: "Invitations to a dinner are always invitations to attend a ***luau,*** *and the modern feast is modeled after the old ones at which the Hawaiians, from king to lowest peasant, made merry.*

"The tables are almost entirely covered with ferns and garlands of ***maile****. Calabashes of polished cocoanut-shells, small gourds, or wooden bowls of the brilliantly polished* ***koa,*** *are at each place, for* ***poi,*** *generally the prized pink* ***poi,*** *is served at all these ceremonious affairs."*

ground and beside which the hundred guests sat on mats in the recumbent or cross-legged fashion. . . . On this occasion some long limbed guests found it difficult to dispose of the superfluous portion of their extremities, some knees being elevated above the platform, and some feet were scattered about in promiscuous directions. However, with abundant courtesy, good humor, and jocularity the guests adjusted themselves and partook heartily of the Hawaiian luau."

An essential part of Hawaiian luaus was the ancient custom of eating with one's fingers. This was considered a traditional form of table etiquette and, even after the introduction of silverware in the nineteenth century, many chiefs continued the custom. In 1816, Russian explorer Otto von Kotzebue was told by King Kamehameha of his firm adherence to the ancient etiquette: "Tamaahmaah, who, during the whole repast, had made use only of his fingers, perceived very well that I attentively observed his motions, and said to me, 'This is the custom in my country, and I will not depart from it!' "

This custom surprised Almira Pitman as she sat down to her first luau in 1917: "Now prepare for a shock. There was no sign of knife, fork or spoon upon the table! One must go back to nature at a *luau* and eat with one's God-given implements! The dainty manner in which these people used their hands, and Hawaiian hands are proverbially beautiful, was a revelation."

Visitor Ash Silvers was also won over after attending a luau in 1892 with Queen Liliuokalani present: "Her majesty proceeded to business at once. Down into the royal calabash went the royal fingers, scooping up poi in wholesome morsels, which forthwith was transferred to the royal lining with many a royal smack. Here a piece of roast pig was sampled, there a strip of raw fish; and crabs, and jellies, and jams, and comfits, and no one knows what else besides, all floated away to the regions of the imperial duodenum in reckless confusion.

"But the meal went on quietly, orderly, and in good form; and so far as I was able to observe, the Queen did nothing, either there or elsewhere during the day, that a cultivated lady might not have done anywhere, except to eat with her fingers."

Residents were greatly amused at the inconvenience of visitors attending their first luau and finding no utensils with which to eat. At Princess Ruth Keelikolani's birthday luau in 1882, the *Advertiser* wrote: "Knives, forks, and spoons were not in the programme and it was amusing to watch the perplexed faces and bungled manoeuvres of some of the guests, who were present at a Hawaiian *luau* for the first time, and seemed to be mentally resolving that it would also be the last."

At Kalakaua's coronation luau, Minnie Grant recorded what would be a typical menu: "At every second or third place was a great calabash of the inevitable poi, without which no Hawaiian meal is complete. At each plate was a small bundle of the ti leaves enclosing various fish which, being cooked in the leaves and also served in them, preserves the delicate flavour immensely. Sweet potatoes of enormous size, boiled and baked taro, sea weeds of different kinds boiled and eaten hot, kukui nuts grated up as a kind of salt relish, native onions, bananas, and native fruits in quantities, — all these go to make up a native Luau; and above all, the noble pig baked in a hole made in the ground for that purpose, which is filled with hot stones and leaves, covered up for a certain length of time, and he finally emerges in a state of perfection. . . . Raw fish plays a conspicuous part at Luaus too. . . . The only liquid served on the day I speak of was soda water, a bottle of which lay at each place."

One of the most notorious foods served to visitors at luaus in the early nineteenth century was dog. Small, short-legged Polynesian dogs were brought by emigrating Hawaiians not as pets, but as a food source. They were fed on vegetables and prepared the same way as pigs. Dogs were a principal part of the diet of nobility, particularly the women, to whom pork was forbidden. In 1792, Thomas Manby, master's mate with Vancouver's expedition, noted the large number of dogs on Niihau: "We saw but few hogs, and no fowls of the domestic kind. Dogs, they had great numbers of. These animals indeed constitute a very considerable part of the food of the inhabitants of all the Sandwich Islands." Lt. James King noted in 1779: "They are, in general, fed, and left to herd, with the hogs; and I did not recollect one instance in which a dog was made a companion in the manner we do in Europe."

Despite Western abhorrence, dogs continued to be a staple food among Hawaiians at feasts through the 1820s. William Ellis wrote of that decade: "In their feasts the flesh of the dog constitutes the principal meat. I have seen nearly two hundred dogs cooked at one time; and during the last visit which Taumuarii, late King of Tauai, and Kaahumanu his queen, paid Kuakini, the governor of this island, a feast was prepared for them by the latter, at which Auna [a Tahitian mission teacher] was present, and counted four hundred baked dogs, with fish and hogs, and vegetables in proportion."

In the 1830s, dogs became somewhat less of a staple and were raised mainly for luaus. In 1832, Francis Bishop commented on their continued popularity at feasts: "The greatest dainty among the Sandwich Islanders is dog flesh. The puppies intended for the oven are carefully fed, fatted on poe and vegetables only, no flesh being allowed them. These curs are served up at the grand entertainments sometimes given by the King and chiefs, and the flavor of baked dog when fed on poe alone resembles that of young pork."

The serving of dog to visitors during luaus became a large source of enjoyment for residents, for Westerners were both horrified and fascinated. Visitor William Ruschenberger, served dog at a luau, had a typical reaction: "Near my place at table was a fine young dog luäued, the flesh of which was declared to be excellent by all who partook of it. To my palate, its taste was what I can imagine would result from mingling the flavour of pig and lamb, and I did not hesitate to make my dinner of it, in spite of some qualms at the first mouthful. I must confess, when I reflected that the puppy now trussed up before us might have been the affectionate, and frolicksome companion of some Hawaiian fair . . . I felt as if dog-eating were only a low grade of cannibalism."

Jeremiah Reynolds, visiting in 1832, recounted a luau he attended where an attempt was made to disguise the dog: "The whole party soon set down to a most abundantly-furnished table, loaded with savoury viands, cooked after the native fashion — or *luaued.* At one end was a *dog;* which, in order to induce us to eat, had the head and feet of a pig sewed on, instead of its own. But without this stratagem, all would have eaten of it, as we had heard so much said about this animal. It was difficult to tell it from pig, so much did the taste resemble the flavour of that animal. These dogs are a peculiar kind, and are fed for the purpose on nothing but vegetables; and though not numerous, are always eaten on great occasions of this kind. The dinner was served up in a very handsome style."

In describing an 1836 luau for the officers of the American naval ships *Peacock* and *Enterprise,* the editor of the *Sandwich Island Gazette* gleefully reported: "Food, in the native style, was abundantly served up, — *baked dog,* (dog! only think of it,) was among the dishes! and, — 'it was not to be sneezed at.' "

The great hilarity occasioned by the attempts of visitors to differentiate between dog and pig caused the dog to be even further disguised, and residents continued to pretend dog was served long after it was discontinued. Fitch Taylor attended a luau in 1839 hosted by Kamehameha III and never did find out if dog had been served: " 'And which is the dog?' was the general murmur of interest. . . . That is the dog, said one; and that is the dog, asserted another; and I will take a piece of the dog, said all in their turns. But are you sure that this is dog? . . .

" 'Let me try a piece, I can tell,' said Mr. S., a gentleman near me — 'Calo, here, will not eat it if it is dog,' added Mr. S., as he pitched a small piece to his favorite pointer. But Calo was a gentleman's dog, and it was not his part to refuse aught that was set before him; and therefore Calo ate it without a murmur.

" 'Dog don't eat dog,' they say, and incredulity, in our neighborhood, seemed rather to prevail.

"The politeness of Calo did not fail him, even the second time; and the conclusion now inevitably was, that either dog will eat dog, or else no dog graced the feast of the Pari. And it is equally true, that if the piece to which I was helped was dog, I did not distinguish it from the choice rib part of a pig, though in the passing amusement of the moment, I confess I did not particularly call into requisition my most particular powers of discrimination."

The town's newspapers could not resist joining the joke. The *Polynesian* of 1840 teased officers of the United States Exploring Expedition after a luau held for them: "Two long tables set out in a manner that might excite envy in Apicus. Profusion of every luxury the Islands afford. Luaued dog included, (numbers by the way, went the whole hog upon this national dish). . . . Baked dog — thought delicious by some — Governor suspicious of its being pig in disguise — no mistake though."

By that year, the aboriginal Hawaiian dog had, for the most part, disappeared through unchecked breeding with dogs imported as pets. Frederick Bennett found them rare in 1835 when he visited: "The aboriginal, or poë dog . . . is now a rare, and will probably be soon an extinct species — lost amidst a mongrel race of dogs partaking of every foreign variety."

Residents could not help continuing to tease even themselves about eating dog. In 1847, a luau sponsored by the king was reported in the *Hawaiian Annual* as containing perhaps a hint of dog: "The dinner — the feeding of the immense crowd of men, women and children — was a sight to be remembered. . . . Beef, pork, fish, and poi, the staples were in profusion (with a suspicion of dog)."

Residents perpetuated among themselves the myth that dogs were being cooked and eaten at luaus as late as 1907. In that year, the *Paradise of the Pacific* printed this tongue-in-cheek news item: "Reports an undated note from the *Sunday Advertiser* to the effect that a citizen complained that her pet dog was taken to the pound by the dog warden and killed before the legal time limit had expired, to furnish food for a luau given by one Supervisor Kealoha and others."

The legend of the Hawaiian luau dog continued to fascinate visitors also. In 1921, visitor John Anderson was able to find a resident who claimed to remember the taste of dog. He was no less than the first director of the Bernice Pauahi Bishop Museum: "I was most fortunate in meeting Dr. William T. Brigham, who was sent by Harvard University in 1864, to Hawaii and was privileged to spend many hours with him, a real, living encyclopedia. . . . I asked which he liked best, roast pig or roast dog, cooked in the same fashion on hot rocks covered over with earth — the original fireless cooker — and with a most delightful smile, he said, 'Roast dog is more delicious.' " The native Hawaiian dog, once a common food source in old Hawaii, had by Anderson's visit in 1921 been extinct for many years.

Luaus tended to be large affairs, often with hundreds of guests. One of the largest ever held was hosted in 1847 by Kamehameha III celebrating the restoration of Hawaiian sovereignty by England in 1843. The *Hawaiian Annual* printed the king's steward's list of foods prepared: "271 hogs, 482 large calabashes of poi, 602 chickens, 3 whole oxen, 2 barrels salt pork, 2 barrels biscuit, 3,125 salt fish, 1,820 fresh fish, 12 barrels luau and cabbages, 4 barrels onions, 80 bunches bananas, 55 pineapples, 10 barrels potatoes, 55 ducks, 82 turkeys, 2,245 coconuts, 4,000 heads of taro, 180 squid, oranges, limes, grapes and various fruits."

Most luaus were smaller than this but still impressive. When Princess Ruth Keelikolani celebrated the completion of her new home in Honolulu in 1882, the *Advertiser* assessed the huge amount of foods served: "For the Luau or Feast, given by Her Royal Highness Ruth Keelikolani on the occasion of the opening of her palatial residence, there were killed and eaten 20 head bullocks, over 200 hogs and pigs, besides numberless chickens, ducks, and turkeys. As for poi, kalo, sweet potatoes, etc., the quantity can only be reckoned by tons."

When King Kalakaua held a large birthday luau in 1886, the *Daily Bulletin* could only report: "Pigs, in almost continual streams, are coming in from the country, for His Majesty's birthday."

Luaus were usually held in the afternoon. When very large numbers of guests were expected, they were fed in relays or several seatings, as at King Kalakaua's fiftieth birthday luau. Fifteen hundred guests were invited and tables set for 500, with the guests eating in turns. The *Daily Bulletin* reported: "The guests began to arrive at the scene of the festivities a little before two o'clock. . . . Probably not less than 15 hundred guests partook of the feast, which lasted from the time of commencement till the shades of night began to gather. As the guests retired from the tables, making room for fresh relays, they wandered around the grounds and through the palace, enjoying themselves."

Few luaus in the twentieth century have been as large as those hosted by Hawaiian royalty in the 1800s. The luau, however, continues to be a popular entertainment throughout Hawaii.

As the traditional wooden and coconut luau containers disappeared into curio cabinets, the luau began to be served on disposable paper plates and in paper bowls. These containers, often decorated with a printed Polynesian design, have come to symbolize the luau in the twentieth century, replacing the fine wooden bowls and the gourds that were once so plentiful.

GLOSSARIES

Presented here are two Hawaiian glossaries relating to Hawaiian containers and their appurtenances. The first was compiled from *A Dictionary of the Hawaiian Language*, published by Lorrin Andrews in 1865 and revised by Henry Parker in 1922. Andrews's 1865 work, the first published Hawaiian dictionary, contained approximately 15,500 Hawaiian words. Parker used contemporary annotations to the original work, with additions and clarifications by various scholars, to republish the dictionary.

The second glossary was compiled from a work by Mary K. Pukui and Samuel H. Elbert entitled *Hawaiian-English Dictionary*, first published in 1957. This glossary makes use of the 1971 edition which was retitled *Hawaiian Dictionary* and which contains approximately 26,000 entries. The glossaries list the words in these dictionaries that define the names of traditional Hawaiian containers, tools used in making them, and appurtenances such as netting and carrying poles.

A Dictionary of the Hawaiian Language
By Lorrin Andrews, revised by Henry Parker
Honolulu, 1922

aa (a'a), n. 7. A pocket; a bag. *Aa moni*, a purse; a scrip; a bag to carry provisions for a journey.

aahoa (ā'ā-hō'-a), n. A food container or wrapper.

aapu (ā-ă'-pu), n. 1. A cup. 2. A concave vessel.

apu (ă'-pŭ), n. A small drinking vessel, usually made of coconut shell; a cup. 2. Any hollow vessel of whatever shape, size, or material, used for serving food at meals; a cup or bowl; a dish.

apuauhuhu (ă'-pŭ-āu'-hŭ'-hŭ), n. [*Apu*, cup, and *auhuhu*, the fish-poison plant (*Tephrosia piscatoris*).] A cup for containing the *auhuhu*; hence, a cup of poison.

apuawa (ă'-pŭ-ă'-wa), n. [*Apu*, cup, and *awa*, a plant (*Piper methysticum*) of the pepper family.] A cup containing beverage prepared from this cup.

apukoheoheo (ă'-pŭ-kō-hĕ'o-hĕ'o), n. [*Apu*, cup, and *koheoheo*, deadly.] A cup containing a mixture of several poisonous ingredients, principally *auhuhu* (*Tephrosia piscatoris*) and *awa* (*Piper methysticum*); a cup of poison prepared for the purpose of suicide or for the execution of criminals.

eo (ĕ'o), n. 2. A calabash or other vessel brimful of food.

hanai (hā'-nai), n. 1. The four strings that hold a hanging calabash.

haona (hā-ō'-na), n. 1. Name of certain calabashes for cooked food. 2. A receptacle, or repository.

hinai (hi-na'i), n. 1. A container made or braided ie [vine] or other materials. 2. A basket.

hinaipoepoe (hi-na'i-pō'-e-pō'-e), n. 1. A round basket. 2. A basket braided around a calabash.

hipuu (hī'-pu'u), n. 3. A bag for carrying small things.

hoaha (ho'-ă'-ha), v. [*Ho* for *hoo* (causative prefix), and *aha*, a cord.] 1. To make or braid together the strings for a calabash with netting. 2. To tie up a calabash.

hokeo (ho'-ke'-o), n. 2. A long calabash used as a receptacle for clothing or for a fisherman's outfit. It was made of the gourd of the vine *Lagenaria vulgaris*, also called *hulilau*.

holeie (hō'-lē-ī'-e), v. [*Hole*, to peel, and *ie*, a vine.] 1. To peel the bark from the *ie* used in basketmaking.

hue (hū'-e), n. 1. A gourd; a water calabash.

huewai (hū'-ĕ-wai), n. [*Hue*, a gourd, and *wai*, water.] 1. A long-necked *pohue* or calabash prepared to hold water. 2. A water calabash, distinct from calabashes used for other purposes; a large gourd; any kind of bottle used to contain water. Called *huawai* on the island of Lanai.

hulilau (hū'-lī-lā'u), n. 1. General name for calabashes of every description. 2. A calabash used as a receptacle for tapa or garments.

ipu (ī'-pŭ), n. 1. Any cucurbitaceous plant, and its fruit, as melon, pumpkin, etc. 2. A general name for a vessel or container, as dish, cup, mug, etc., each kind being designated by some additional word expressive of its use.

ipuai (ī'-pŭ-ă'i), n. A calabash or vessel for containing food.

ipuala (ī'-pŭ-ă'-lă), n. 1. A box for containing the several articles used in making one's toilet.

ipuauau (ī'-pŭ-ă'u-ă'u), n. A large basin or other receptacle to wash in; a washbasin.

ipuholoholona (ī'-pŭ-hŏ'-lŏ-hŏ-lŏ'-nă), n. 1. A vessel or calabash for bait. 2. A long upright calabash for holding a fisherman's outfit, as lines, hooks, bait, etc.

ipuholoi (ī'-pŭ-hō-lō'i), n. A washbasin. Syn: *ipuauau*.

ipuia (ī'-pŭ-i'a), n. A vessel or dish for containing fish or meat.

ipukai (ī'-pŭ-kă'i), n. A calabash or vessel in which fish or meat is kept or preserved.

ipulaau (ī'-pŭ-lă-ă'u), n. A wooden vessel.

ipulei (ī'-pŭ-lĕ'i), n. 1. A decorated calabash used as a receptacle for leis and choice tapa. (Rev. Elias Bond's annotated copy of Andrews's 1865 dictionary: "*Ipule'i*, something highly valued, as a painted calabash.")

kiaha (kī'-ā'-ha), n. 1. A drinking dish; a cup; a mug; a tumbler. 2. A basin.

kilu (kī'-lu), n. 1. A small gourd or calabash for small, choice things.

kioe (kī'o'e), n. A ladle, dipper, cup; a scoop or spoon made of coconut shell.

koko (kō'-kō'), n. 1. The carrier for a calabash, made of braided strings.

kunono (kū'-nō'-no), n. Small or fine holes in any container, as a calabash.

laulau (lă'u-lă'u), n. 5. The netting in which food is carried. 6. A container generally.

maauau (mā´-ă´u-ă´-u), n. 1. A poi calabash. 2. A special calabash used by poi peddlers.

mamaka (mā´-mă´-ka), n. A stick on which burdens are carried across the shoulders, called also *auamo* and *aumaka.*

maoloha (mă´-ō´-lō´-ha), n. The ancient name of the strings or net for a calabash, equivalent to the modern word *koko.*

mua (mŭ-ā´), n. A bottle-necked calabash, such as were used to drink out of.

oahi (ō-ā´-hi), n. 1. A kind of stone used in polishing canoes and wooden calabashes.

oleole (o´-le-o´-le), n. A frame or skeleton of a structure, set on posts with notches on which to hang calabashes.

omo (o´-mo), adj. 2. A cover to a calabash or pot; a movable cover. Syn: poi.

omoki (o-mo´-ki), n. Same as *umoki.* A cork; a stopper of a bottle; a bung of a casket; the stopper of a calabash.

ooo (o´-o´-o), n. Any small vessel for conveying water to drink.

pa (pā), n. Any material having a flat surface, as a board (see *papa*), a plate, a server, a pan; *pa wili ai*, a poi board; *pa holoi*, a basin to wash in; *pa hao*, an iron pan. (*papa* - flat surface)

pahupalapala (pā´-hu-pā´-lă-pā´-la), n. [*Pahu*, box, and *palapala*, writing.] 1. Originally, a container for the coloring liquid used in printing tapa.

paipu (pā´-ī´-pu), n. 1. A set of empty calabashes. 2. A calabash for packing tapa or clothes to keep them dry in a canoe. 3. Basins used as containers. 4. A bowl for containing food.

papaipu (pā´-pā´-ī´-pu), n. Place for empty calabashes.

papapohaku (pā´-pă-pō-hā´-ku), n. [*Papa*, a flat surface, and *pohaku*, stone.] 1. A flat board on which poi or other food is pounded; the pestle is made of stone and called *he pohaku kui ai*; the board or thick plank is slightly hollowed out like a very flat tray.

papawiliai (pă´-pă-wĭ´-lĭ-ă´i), n. [*Papa*, board; *wili*, to mix; and *ai*, food.] A board for mixing food; a poi board; a very flat tray on which poi is pounded; a kneading trough.

poaha (pō-ā´-ha), n. 1. A circle. 2. A ball wound with a hollow on one side as something to set a calabash on.

poho (pō´-ho), n. 2. A kind of basket. 4. A piece or patch placed over a dent or weak spot.

pohue (pō-hū´-e), n. 1. A broken piece of calabash. 2. A water calabash. 3. A piece of the bitter calabash.

pohue (pō-hū´-e), adj. Of or pertaining to a gourd or calabash.

poi (po'i), n. 1. A cover of any vessel or container, especially the cover or upper gourd of a calabash; hence, 2. The cover of a pot or other vessel.

puliuliu (pŭ´-li'u-li'u), n. A small gourd in which the *laau waiki* (a medicine) was made.

puniu (pū´-nī´-u), n. [*Pu* and *niu*, a coconut.] 1. The shell of a coconut; hence, 2. A small calabash for food.

umeke (ū-mĕ´-ke), n. 1. A poi calabash. (The full form is *umekepoi.*) 2. A circular vessel for holding anything.

umeke (ū´-mē´-ke), n. A large gourd, also the plant; a calabash.

umekelaau (ū´-mē´-kĕ-lā´ă´u), n. A vessel or calabash made of wood.

umekepoi (u-mĕ´-ke-pō´i), n. [*Umeke*, a gourd, and *poi*, a kind of food.] A poi calabash full of food, much valued by Hawaiians.

umoki (u-mo´-ki), n. 1. A stopple of a calabash. Same as *omoki.*

Hawaiian Dictionary
By Mary K. Pukui and Samuel H. Elbert
Honolulu, 1971

'a'aha. Netted carrier for a calabash, made of sennit or *olonā* cord. More commonly called *kōkō.*

'a'a. 3. Bag, pocket.

amo kau. A stick for carrying burdens on the shoulder.

'aumaka. Same as *'auamo*, carrying pole.

'eke. 1. Sack, pocket, bag.

'eke'eke. a. Small bag or sack, pocket, purse.

haka. 1. Shelf, perch, platform; roost, as for chickens; fish spear rack; rack for suspending water gourds and other household objects.

haka ipu. Shelf for calabashes; frame from which calabashes were hung.

hāka'oka'o. Net that enclosed a calabash.

hānai. 3. Body of a *kōkō*-net carrier, and cords attached to it.

hano. 6. Container, as for water or tobacco.

hano wai. Same as *hue wai*, water container.

haona. Same as *hao*, 3, 4; handful, scoopful; receptacle, as a dipper for kava.

hāwele. To tie, bind, lash; net lashing, as for a hue wai, gourd.

hē. 10. Hollow container in which canoe paint was mixed.

hene. 4. Rare var. of *kīhene*, basket.

hiena. 1. Kind of soft porous stone used to smooth and polish utensils; it is harder than the *'ana* stone, which is used on wood.

hīna'i. Basket or container made of braided *'ie* vine, pandanus, or other material; a kind of basket fish trap, as used for shrimps, eels, *hīnālea*, and *'o'opu*. Also called *hīna'i ho'olu'ulu'u*, or *hīna'i ho'omoe i'a.*

hīna'i poepoe. A round basket or container, as braided around a calabash.

hōkeo. 1. Long gourd calabash, as used to hold food, clothing, fishing gear; any cooking pot. *Fig.*, an empty container, a trifle.

hōkelo. Same as *hōkeo*, 1. *Hōkelo ua*, container for catching rain.

hole 'ie. To strip aerial roots of the *'ie'ie* vine for baskets or plaiting.

holo. 6. To sew, as a break in a gourd calabash.

ho'opākākā. To shape into a low, wide door or bowl. 2. A variety of gourd: squat, small, used for meat and fish (*ipu kai*).

hue. 1. Gourd, water calabash, any narrow-necked vessel for holding water.

hue 'awa'awa. Type of bitter gourd, as used for utensils.

hue wai. Gourd water container, bottle.

hue wai 'ihi, hue wai 'ihi loa. Long-necked water container.

hue wai pū'ali. Gourd water container with a constriction about the middle.

hue wai pueo. Water gourd shaped like an hourglass. *Lit.*, owl water gourd.

huini. 3. Wooden peg used in mending bowls. Also *kui lā'au.*

hulilau. 1. A variety of large gourd or calabash, used as a receptacle for tapa or garments, or for food offerings.

ʻie. 1. Aerial root of the *ʻieʻie* vine; the vine itself. 2. A woven basket.

ihiloa. Small, long-necked gourd as used for holding water.

ipu. The bottle gourd (*Lagenaria siceraria*, also called *L. vulgaris*), a wide spreading vine, with large angled or lobed leaves, white, nightblooming flowers, and smooth green and mottled or white fruit varying widely in shape and size. The plant is a native of tropical Asia or Africa. Hawaiians have long used gourds as receptacles, small gourds with thin walls to hold water or food, or for rattles for dances (the *ipu* has a fine tone, halfway between that of *niu* and *laʻamia*), larger ones with thin to thick walls to hold tapa and other articles or to serve as drums. Hawaiians have distinguished between a kind with bitter pulp, used medicinally, and a kind with non-bitter pulp. 3. General name for vessel or container, as dish, mug, calabash, pot, cup, pipe.

ipu ʻai. 2. Calabash or vessel for food or food offering.

ipu ʻaina. Scrap bowl, slop basin, refuse container.

ipu ʻala. Container for perfume or other fragrant matter. *Lit.*, fragrant gourd.

ipu ʻauʻau. Washbasin; container of water for a bath.

ipu ʻaumakua. Large gourd calabash in which food was offered to the *ʻaumakua* family gods.

ipu holoholona. Gourd containing fisherman's gear and bait, or a traveler's possessions. *Lit.*, traveling container.

ipu holoi. Washbasin.

ipu holoi lima. Finger bowl. *Lit.*, container wash hand.

ipu iʻa. Meat dish; fleshpot.

ipu kai. A dish for meat or any dish deep enough to hold gravy (*kai*); gravy boat.

ipu kuaʻaha. Container for sacred objects; gourd calabash covered with sennit net and suspended by a handle composed of four cords; food offerings were placed inside for the god Lono; also called *ipu-o-lono.*

ipu kuha. Spittoon.

ipu lei. Container for leis.

ipu lēʻi. Fishhook container. *Rare.*

ipu mimi. Chamber pot, container for urine.

ipu nui. A large container.

ipu pāwehe. Gourd calabash decorated with designs.

ipu wai. 1. Water container, water bottle.

ipu wai ʻauʻau. Washbasin.

iwi pū niu. Coconut shell.

kaʻele. 1. Empty and hollow, as of a bowl, *poi* board, drum, canoe hull; hull; inside bottom as of a calabash or *poi* board.

kahahānai. 2. Strings securing upper part of the net surrounding a calabash (*kōkō*).

kākai. Handle, as of a bucket, pot, basket, purse; strings by which a netted (*kōkō*) calabash is hung.

kā kāpala. Dye container, probably so called because the edge of the container was hit (*kā*) with the bamboo stamp to dislodge excess dye before printing the tapa.

kākū. 2. Gourd calabash, as used for fishing.

kale ʻai. Watery residue on *poi*-pounding board, which was used to treat *kou* and *milo* wood to be made into utensils, as it was believed to draw out the acid remaining in wood after soaking in the sea.

kāloa. 1. Oval wooden dish or platter.

kamaʻaha. To tie sennit, to bind securely, to form a loop to support a netted calabash; the loop itself.

kana. 2. Horizontal support in houses for carrying poles (*ʻauamo*).

kānoa. Bowl, as for kava.

kā paʻakai. Dish in which fish or meat is salted (short for *kapi paʻakai*).

kā paka. Container for tobacco, pipe, matches.

kāʻumeke. Hanger for *ʻumeke*, bowls.

kepa. 3. Wedge used in repairing wooden bowls, often hammered in obliquely in zigzag pattern. Also call *kepakepa.*

kīʻaha puaniki. Goblet. *Lit.*, holding cup.

kiʻeke. Bag, satchel; basket. *Obs.*

kīhene. Bundle or basket of ti or other leaves, as used to carry sweet potatoes, flowers, etc.

kihi. 4. To plug or patch a calabash or canoe. *Rare.*

kiki. 1. A plug shaped like the *kepa* wedge but with the outer end longer, used in filling cracks in wooden bowls or canoes; to plug a hole, patch a canoe or calabash.

kīkī. 3. Crude temporary basket or bundle, as made of *ʻilima*, ti, or morning-glory plants and used to carry food.

kikikiki. To mend, as a crack in a wooden bowl.

kīlio. 3. Ring of *ʻie*, a vine, sewed to the top of a fishbasket to hold fish in place.

kīʻoʻe. Ladle, dipper, cup; scoop or spoon made of coconut shell.

kilu. 1. A small gourd or coconut shell, usually cut lengthwise, as used for storing small, choice objects, or to feed favorite children from.

kio poi. *Poi* calabash.

koʻi kūkulu. Adze with straight edges, used to shave down the sides of a bowl or canoe.

kōkō. 1. A carrying net, usually made of sennit, as used for hanging calabashes.

kōkō pūʻalu. Netted bag made of sennit, with large plain mesh. Lit., loose net.

kōkō puʻupuʻu. Very fine *kōkō* net for calabash carried by *kahu* of high rank, with chief's food.

kōkō ʻula. Network of red color, as of a spreading rainbow.

kūalani. Sour, especially of calabashes that have held *poi* and have not been soaked in the sun after washing.

kua papa. To hew boards or planks; to hew out a *poi*-pounding board.

kui lāʻau. Wooden peg, especially as made of hardwood and used in mending bowls.

kūmau. 2. Deep wooden bowl with a thick base, as for *poi.*

kū-mauna. 1. *Var.* of *kūmau.*

kūʻoho. 2. Medium-sized, deep bowl.

laha. 2. Gourd calabash painted with patterns.

lawalawaihonua. Type of large wooden bowl.

māʻauʻau. *Poi* calabash as used by *poi* peddlers. *Cf. maʻau*, going from place to place.

māhanakanaloa. Name for large food calabash (root unknown).

māmaka. 1. Horizontal carrying stick, borne over the shoulders.

mua. 2. Bottle-necked gourd, as used for drinking.

nīao. 1. Edge, as of a canoe; groove; rim, as of a bowl.

nuku pueo. Large bottlegourd used for water.

ʻōahi. 2. Rough stone or pumice, as used for polishing surfboards or bowls, or for scraping bristles of a pig.

ʻoai, owai. hōʻoai. 3. Porous stone, as used for polishing canoes and calabashes. *Obs.*

oleole. Rack or branched post on which wooden bowls or netted calabashes were hung.

ʻolo. Long gourd container used as a receptacle, as for kava or water.

ʻolo ʻawa. Coconut shell cut lengthwise as a cup for kava.

ʻolo wai. Gourd water container.

omo. 4. Gourd, as used for a container.

ʻomo. Lid, cover, plug, cork, as of a calabash.

ʻomoki. *Var.* of *ʻumoki*, stopper.

ʻomu. hōʻomu. A dish for fish.

ʻone-wai. Waterpipe; bamboo water container.

oʻoʻo. 2. A small dipper for bailing, as a coconut shell.

ʻōpaka. Cut in evenly matched vertical facets, often eight, as of a bowl, spittoon.

ʻoulo. 3. Gourd container, as for bamboo stamps used for making tapa.

pā. 2. Dish, plate, pan; elongated food bowl used for meat or fish.

paʻahana. 2. Implement, utensil, furnishings.

paʻa ipu kuha. Bearer of the chief's spittoon.

pā hohonu. Soup plate, deep dish (preceded by *ke*).

pā holoi. Wash pan or basin (preceded by *ke*).

pahu palapala. Writing desk; formerly a container for the coloring liquid used in printing tapa. *Lit.*, document box.

pā ipu. 1. Calabash, wood dish in general, cooking utensil, bowl.

pākākā. 1. Low and broad, especially of a wooden bowl or door; a low, wide wooden bowl.

pā lāʻau. 2. Wooden dish or tray (preceded by *ke*).

palapaʻa. Any wooden calabash with a thick base, for example, see *kūmau*, 2.

pālewa. Low wooden bowl.

pa liʻiliʻi. Small dish; saucer (preceded by *ke*).

pānānai. Flat, shallow, as a dish.

papa. 1. Flat surface, stratum, layer, level, foundation, story of a building; class, rank, order, table; sheet, plate, shelf (*rare*).

papa ipu. Shelf for food containers.

papa lāʻau. Board, plank, any large wooden platter.

papa pōhaku. 3. Stone table, stone flat, or stone surface, as for pounding.

papa wili ʻai. Mixing board, food trough, board for kneading *poi*, kneading trough.

pewa. 2. Rectangular patch or wedge used for mending bowls, perhaps so called because of a resemblance to a fishtail.

piko. 6. Bottom round of a carrying net, *kōkō.*

pināʻi. 2. To patch, fill up a crack or hole, as in wood.

pōʻaha. 1. Circle, as of flowers; ring, as of tapa about a sore, that prevents friction; a round support for a calabash made of pandanus or ti leaves wrapped into a ring and bound with a cord.

poho. 3. Patch, as in clothes; a wooden patch inserted into a calabash, as to mend a break; to patch.

poho aho. Container for fishing lines.

poho hoʻoluʻu. Cup of coconut shell, gourd, or stone, containing dye for tapa.

poho kāpalapala. Container for tapa dye.

poho paka. Tobacco pouch, as a tin, coconut shell, or wooden container.

pōhue. 1. General name for gourd plant; potsherd. *ʻUmeke pohue,* gourd bowl.

poʻi. Cover, lid.

poʻia. Same as *poʻi.*

poʻi wai holoi. Washbasin, finger bowl.

pola. 5. Also *bola.* Bowl, cup (preceded by *ke*).

puahala. A medium-sized bowl, as used for serving *poi,* named for a supposed resemblance to a pandanus key (*pua hala*).

puaniki. 2. Small wooden bowl, as for an individual serving of *poi.*

pūhene. 2. Crude basket, as for carrying food. *Obs.*

puka nui. 2. *Var.* of *ʻapua,* a basket; basket of *ʻieʻie* vine aerial roots, for carrying fishing gear.

pūkaula. 2. A bag or bundle carried on the back. *Obs.*

pūkī. 1. Same as *kōkō,* a carrying net.

pūniu. 1. Polished coconut shell or bowl. *ʻUmeke pūniu,* coconut-shell calabash, as for *poi.*

pūʻolo. Bundle, bag, container.

puʻuliʻulī. A variety of small gourd, as used for making feather gourd rattles (*ʻulīʻulī*), medicine cups (*ʻapu*), and individual *poi* containers.

ʻumeke. Bowl, calabash, circular vessel, as of wood or gourd.

ʻumeke ʻai. *Poi* bowl.

ʻumeke ipu kai. Bowl, as for serving meat or salty meat.

ʻumeke kepakepa. Bowl with horizontal flat panels. *Lit.*, wedged bowl.

ʻumeke lāʻau. Wooden bowl.

ʻumeke māna ʻai. Very small bowl, as formerly used for *poi* by favorite children.

ʻumeke ʻōpaka. Bowl with vertical panels with vertical edges between them. See *ʻōpaka,* 1.

ʻumeke palapaʻa. Thick-bottomed wooden calabash. *Lit.*, firm-dabbed bowl, perhaps so called because dabs of *poi* are held firm in this type of calabash that does not upset.

ʻumeke pāwehe. A decorated gourd bowl, as made on Niʻihau.

ʻumeke pohue. Gourd calabash.

ʻumoki. Cork, stopper, bung.

ʻūpoʻi. Same as *poʻi.*

waihona ipu. Place to keep food containers.

NOTES

ABBREVIATIONS TO NOTES

AH	State Archives of Hawaii
BM	Bernice Pauahi Bishop Museum
DB	Daily Bulletin
F	The Friend
FO&Ex	Foreign Office & Executive Files
HA	Honolulu Advertiser
HAA	Hawaiian Almanac and Annual; also known as Thrum's Annual
HEN	Hawaiian Ethnological Notes
HG	Hawaiian Gazette
HMCS	Hawaiian Mission Children's Society
HONAD	Honolulu Almanac & Directory
P	The Polynesian
PCA	Pacific Commercial Advertiser
PP	Paradise of the Pacific
SB	Star-Bulletin
SIG	Sandwich Island Gazette
UH	University of Hawaii Hamilton Library, Pacific Collection

PAGE VI

"Kaiana's high rank -" Day, *History Makers,* p. 62.

"Tyaana -" Portlock, *A Voyage,* p. 360.

"It is only -" Unidentified newspaper, March 5, 1900, GN ETH PAM, 4045, BM.

INTRODUCTION

"The container was -" Malo, *Moolelo Hawaii,* Carter copy, Ch. 33, p. 129, ms, BM. This translation by Marguerite K. Ashford, Honolulu, 1987.

"In no one thing -" Brigham, *The Ancient Hawaiian House,* p. 155.

"It is his predominant characteristic -" Kekahuna, *The Hawaiian Art,* ts, p. 4-C, AH.

"Perhaps the methods -" Ibid., p. 28.

PART I. CALABASHES OF WOOD

THE "AGE OF WOOD"

"Their wooden dishes -" Cook, *A Voyage,* Vol. II, p. 238–239.

"The bowls are -" Beaglehole, *The Journals,* Vol. 3, Part 2, p. 1182.

"The Hawaiians -" Anon., 1915 *Bishop Museum Handbook,* p. 28.

"There was no chief -" Kekahuna, *The Hawaiian Art,* ts, p. 2, 4, AH.

"From their material -" Brigham, *The Ancient Hawaiian House,* p. 152.

"Calabashes and wooden platters -" Kekahuna, *The Hawaiian Art,* ts, p. 2, AH.

"The most highly -" Ibid., p. 6.

"The temperament -" Anon., "Hawaiian Art," *The Bulletin of The Honolulu Academy of Arts,* December 1934, p. 52.

"The Hawaiian bowls -" Ibid., p. 53.

"They make -" Shaler, *Journal,* p. 89.

"Another species -" Dixon, *A Voyage,* p. 276.

"The king brought -" Townsend, *Papers,* Vol. 6, p. 28.

"Maiha Maiha -" Manby, *Log,* ms, microfilm, p. 63, UH.

"He has a big -" Golovnin, *Around the World,* p. 196.

"The islanders make -" Ibid., p. 220.

"At the table -" Ibid., p. 179.

"What we saw -" Ibid., p. 185.

"The poé is served -" Freycinet, *Hawai'i in 1819,* p. 59.

"As for wooden platters -" Ibid., p. 85.

"Indeed, no valuable article -" Wilkes, *Narrative,* Vol. 4, p. 38.

"Everywhere the difference -" Bille, *The Voyage,* ts, p. 80, HMCS.

"Some crockery -" Bullard, ms, p. 2, HMCS

"Kamamalu, Kapiolani -" Bingham, *A Residence,* p. 170.

"Their food was formerly -" Stewart, *Journal,* p. 134.

"Their own native arts -" Mathison, *Narrative,* p. 476.

"The houses of the chiefs -" Beechey, *Narrative,* Vol. 2, p. 417.

"The domestic utensils -" Kotzebue, *A New Voyage,* Vol. 2, p. 222.

"Make very beautiful bowls -" Dampier, *To the Sandwich Islands,* p. 47.

"Kona district -" Bishop, *Reminiscences,* p. 26.

"In the great island-" Raeside, *Sovereign Chief,* p. 294.

"The people are already showing -" Doyle, *Makua Laiana,* p. 101.

"One of the things -" Consul General Wm. Miller to Viscount Palmerston, September 10, 1849. British Consulate 1849 (outgoing), AH.

"The house was filled -" Hall, *Journal,* ms, np., Bancroft Library, Berkeley.

"These people have no money -" Doyle, *Makua Laiana,* p. 101.

"A great call for potatoes -" Ibid., p. 151.

"The discovery of gold -" Judd, *Honolulu,* p. 137.

"In some places -" Doyle, *Makua Laiana,* p. 153.

"Age of Wood - " Brigham, *The Ancient Hawaiian House,* p. 152.

CAPTIONS

"Kamehameha is -" Kuykendall, *The Hawaiian Kingdom,* Vol. 1, p. 29.

TRADITIONAL SHAPES AND SIZES OF WOODEN CALABASHES

"They cannot be considered -" Brigham, *The Ancient Hawaiian House,* pp. 168-169.

"A cover -" Ibid., p. 168.

"After being weaned -" Kekahuna, *The Hawaiian Art,* ts, p. 3, AH.

"Our beautiful as well as our -" Queen Emma to Mr. Williamson, March 25, 1869, notes and copies of letters sent, misc., 1869-1883, M-45, Queen Emma Coll., Nylen-Altman Coll., AH.

"Do not forget about our kou -" Kapiolani to [no addressee], February 3, 1871, Kapiolani letters sent, 1871-1885, M-45, Queen Emma Coll., Nylen-Altman Coll., AH.

"Kapo is taking back -" Queen Emma to Fanny Young, February 13, 1871, Queen Emma to Fanny Young Kekelaokalani (Hipa), 1866-1874, M-45, Queen Emma Coll., Nylen-Altman Coll., AH.

CAPTIONS

"Very handsome -" Prescott, *Hawaii,* p. 28.

"Wooden plates -" Rose, *Hawai'i: The Royal Isles,* p. 178, No. 96.

"The Hawaiians had -" Emory, "Wooden Utensils and Implements," *Ancient Hawaiian Civilization,* p. 127.

"Nowhere else -" Emory, "Wooden Utensils and Implements," *Ancient Hawaiian Civilization,* p. 125–126.

"Calabashes are -" Unidentified newspaper, March 5, 1900, GN ETHN PAM, 4045, BM.

"Poi bowls were -" Emory, "Wooden Utensils and Implements," *Ancient Hawaiian Civilization,* p. 127.

"The Kamehameha Museum -" d'Anglade, *A Tree in Bud,* p. 99.

"The interior is -" Ibid., p. 100.

"The history -" Private collection.

VARIATIONS ON THE TRADITIONAL FORMS

"There were various shapes-" Kekahuna, *The Hawaiian Art,* ts, p. 41, AH.

Kaeppler's theories on Hawaiian ribbed forms - "Genealogy and Disrespect," *RES 3,* Spring 1982, pp. 82-107.

"A more difficult feat -" Brigham, *The Ancient Hawaiian House,* p. 161.

"Within range -" Honolulu Academy of Arts, Accession Card No. 2010.

"Could be old -" Ibid.

"A great number -" Bishop, *Journal,* ms, Vol. 2, p. 19, UH.

"We may glance -" Brigham, *The Ancient Hawaiian House,* p. 167.

"We know that this -" Ibid., p. 172.

"The thirst they have -" Manby, *Log,* ms, microfilm, p. 71, UH.

CAPTIONS

"Can be said -" Kaeppler, "Genealogy and Disrespect," *RES 3,* Spring 1982, p. 94.

"The flat bottoms -" Brigham, *The Ancient Hawaiian House,* p. 167.

"To be sure -" Rose, *Hawai'i: The Royal Isles,* p. 178.

"A more difficult feat -" Brigham, *The Ancient Hawaiian House,* p. 161.

"Na Papa -" Summers, J.S. Emerson Collection, "Fishing," ts, p. 153, BM.

PERSONALIZED ROYAL CONTAINERS

"The chiefs -" Stewart, *Journal,* p. 97.

"Any chief of high rank -" Bishop, *Reminiscences,* p. 13.

"Of the five Kahu -" Anon., 1915 *Bishop Museum Handbook,* p. 29.

"Never spits any where -" Corney, *Voyages,* p. 102.

"I have seen these ipu kuha -" Brigham, *The Ancient Hawaiian House,* p. 186.

"On shoving off -" Nicholson, *From Sword to Share,* pp. 36-37.

"A very ambitious chief -" Choris, *Voyage,* ts, np., AH.

"During our stay -" Turnbull, *A Voyage,* Vol. 2, pp. 67-68.

"A man seated -" Choris, *Voyage,* p. 245.

"The inanimate spittoons -" Anon., 1915 *Bishop Museum Handbook,* p. 29.

"These bowls were much thicker -" Anon., *Preliminary Catalogue of The Bernice Pauahi Bishop Museum* 1893, pp. 15-16.

"The chief came -" Corney, *Voyages,* p. 116.

"When the spittoon was of larger size -" Brigham, *The Ancient Hawaiian House,* p. 187.

"They are exceedingly clean -" Cook, *A Voyage,* Vol. 3, p. 141.

"There was no ceremony -" Ledyard, *A Journal,* p. 114.

"The courses, are served -" Chamisso, ts, pp. 158-181, #22, UH.

"Neat wooden dishes -" Ellis, *Journal,* p. 29.

"An article -" Brigham, *The Ancient Hawaiian House,* p. 182.

"Generally they eat raw fish -" Coke, *A Ride over the Rocky Mountains,* p. 337.

"There were many shapes -" Kekahuna, *The Hawaiian Art,* ts, p. 39, AH.

CAPTIONS

Belonging to Kamehameha - BM Accession Records, No. 1891.01, Govt. Coll., p. 18.

"One of my people -" Cook, *A Voyage,* Vol. 2, p. 243.

"The circumstance of fir -" Vancouver, *A Voyage,* p. 219.

"The things most valued -" Coan, "The Natives of Hawaii," *Publications of the American Academy of Political and Social Science,* p. 12.

"A device -" Brigham, *Old Hawaiian Carvings,* p. 15.

"The old natives -" BM Accession Records, No. 1891.01, Govt. Coll., p. 18.

"Ipu kuha -" Summers, J.S. Emerson Collection, "Food Containers," ts, p. 25, BM.

"A small, round bowl -" Stewart, Old South Seas Leaflets, No. 221, p. 5.

"A third carried -" Campbell, *A Voyage,* p. 155.

"This disposition -" Brigham, *Old Hawaiian Carvings,* p. 15.

"The teeth -" BM Accession Records, No. 1891.01, Govt. Coll., p. 9.

"A small calabash -" Bishop, *Journal,* ms, Vol. 2, p. 101, UH.

FIGURED BOWLS

"These Ava bowls -" Beaglehole, *The Journals,* Vol. 3, Part 2, p. 1182.

"The most curious specimens -" Cook, *A Voyage,* Vol. 3, p. 148.

"Some of them are made -" Beaglehole, *The Journals,* Vol. 3, Part 2, pp. 1182-1183.

"'Awa is a native -" Neal, *In Gardens of Hawaii,* p. 291.

"The Ava is a root -" Dixon, *A Voyage,* pp. 102-103.

"Amongst their religious ceremonies -" Cook, *A Voyage,* Vol. 3, p. 161.

Hawaiian wooden bowls collected on Cook's voyage. Kaeppler, *Artificial Curiosities,* p. 82.

"Captain Clerke made him some suitable -" Cook, *A Voyage,* Vol. 2, p. 246.

"King Teeave -" Beaglehole, *The Journals,* Vol. 3, Part 2, pp. 1227- 1228.

"Sometimes their ava dishes -" Dixon, *A Voyage,* p. 276.

CAPTIONS

"A sauce or gravy dish -" Brigham, *The Ancient Hawaiian House,* p. 175.

"A great number -" Cox, *Hawaiian Sculpture,* p. 51.

"The images are -" Ibid., p. 52.

"The present example -" Brigham, *Old Hawaiian Carvings,* pp. 14-16.

"The next relic -" "Hawaiian Antiquities," *The Islander,* March 12, 1875

THE TRADITIONAL WOODS USED FOR CALABASHES

"Hawaiians developed -" C.S. Judd, "The Woodcraft of the Early Hawaiians," p. 260, F, December 1927, pp. 258-261.

"Dr. W.T. Brigham -" Ibid., p. 261.

"There are a great many kinds -" Kekahuna, *The Hawaiian Art,* ts, p. 19, AH.

"The Hawaiians of today -" C.S. Judd, "The Woodcraft of the Early Hawaiians," p. 261, F, December 1927, pp. 258-261.

"The ancient Hawaiians -" Ibid., p. 259.

"But let us not forget -" Ibid., p. 261.

KOU

"Of large growth -" Brigham, *The Ancient Hawaiian House,* p. 156.

"We saw no wood -" Cook, *A Voyage,* Vol. 2, p. 193.

"In several parts -" Ibid., p. 204.

"The opinion of some botanists -" Brigham, *The Ancient Hawaiian House,* pp. 156-157.

"A tree of considerable size -" Malo, *Hawaiian Antiquities,* Ch. 9, p. 22.

"Those who were skilled -" Ibid., Ch. 33, p. 122.

"Similar in appearance -" HG, December 6, 1876, np.

"Paraoo -" Cook, *A Voyage,* Vol. 3, p. 552.

"Epaee -" Ibid., p. 553.

"The kou is -" HG, February 13, 1867, np.

"Kou trees -" Kamakua, *The Works of People of Old,* p. 47.

"The Trees-" *Hoku O Hawaii,* November 14, 1918.

"It has been a favorite wood -" HG, July 14, 1891, np.

"Vessels made -" Kekahuna, *The Hawaiian Art,* ts, p. 4, AH.

"I wish to inform you -" Kapeau to Minister of Interior, February 17, 1848, Interior Department, misc., AH.

"Dear Sir -" Minister of Interior to Nahaolelua, December 3, 1856, Interior Department, Book 6, p. 428, AH.

"There were two or three -" Bishop, *Reminiscences,* p. 37.

"The houses, which are neat -" Ellis, *Journal,* p. 31.

"This morning, the 17th -" Ibid., p. 67.

"Our road now lay -" Ibid., p. 74.

"Our path ... suddenly turned -" Ibid., p. 133.

"When we had passed -" Ibid., p. 190.

"Between three and four hundred -" Ibid., p. 193.

"Kaimu is pleasantly -" Ibid., p. 196.

"About half-past one -" Ibid., p. 200.

"The shore is nearly barren -" Mann, *Journal,* ms, microfilm, np, UH.

"The beautiful kou -" PCA, July 10, 1875, np.

"A few days since -" Ibid.

"The kou, one of the handsomest woods -" Anon., "Decadence of Hawaiian Forests," HAA, 1875, p. 20.

"Young trees -" Bishop, *Reminiscences,* p. 37.

"On this boat -" Queen Emma to Fanny Young, January 22, 1868, Queen Emma to Fanny Young Kekelaokalani (Hipa), 1866-1874, M- 45, Queen Emma Coll., Nylen-Altman Coll., AH.

"I am directed -" Minister of Interior to H.N. Greenwell, December 22, 1869, Interior Department, Book 10, p. 92, AH.

"If you have -" Queen Emma to Fanny Young, February 14, 1871, Queen Emma to Fanny Young Kekelaokalani (Hipa), 1866-1874, M- 45, Queen Emma Coll., Nylen-Altman Coll., AH.

"Important Sale -" PCA, May 13, 1885, np.

"Another valuable tree -" Anon., "Hawaiian Woods and Forest Trees," HAA, 1883, p. 35.

MILO

"The same geographical range -" Brigham, *The Ancient Hawaiian House,* p. 157.

"The wood of second choice -" Kekahuna, *The Hawaiian Art,* ts, p. 17, AH.

"This was another -" HG, July 14, 1891, p. 1.

KAMANI

"The Kamani -" HG, July 14, 1891, p. 1.

"Another beautiful and durable wood -" Brigham, *The Ancient Hawaiian House,* p. 157.

"The hard, tough wood -" Neal, *In Gardens of Hawaii,* p. 586.

"The kamani is mentioned -" Ibid.

"The tree itself -" Brigham, *The Ancient Hawaiian House,* pp. 157- 158.

KOA

"The calabashes and boards -" Kekahuna, *The Hawaiian Art,* ts, p. 20, AH.

"Many of the modern calabashes -" Castle, *Hawaii Past and Present,* p. 243.

"There is no obstacle -" Kekahuna, *The Hawaiian Art,* ts, p. 20, AH.

CAPTIONS

"Ulukou -" Stokes, "Reestablishing the Kou Tree," *HA,* April 30, 1940, p. ed.

"Wood from this -" BM Accession Records, No. 1891.01, Govt. Coll., p. 7.

"In Hawaiian poems -" Stokes, "Reestablishing the Kou Tree," *HA,* April 30, 1940, p. ed.

"The spherical pod -" Ibid.

"An ornamental tree -" Clark, *Lights and Shadows,* p. 205.

"In earlier days -" Stokes, "Reestablishing the Kou Tree," *HA,* April 30, 1940, p. ed.

"The appearance of Lahaina -" Ellis, *Journal,* p. 42.

"Most of the chiefs -" Ibid., p. 45.

"Its distinguishing feature -" Brigham, *Ancient Hawaiian House,* p. 157.

THE INTRODUCTION OF IRON FOR TOOLS

"Of all the Hawaiian tools -" Anon., *Preliminary Catalogue of The Bernice Pauahi Bishop Museum 1893,* p. 43.

"The wildness of their looks -" Cook, *A Voyage,* Vol. 2, p. 194.

"They seemed only to understand -" Ibid.

"They held it in such estimation -" Ibid., p. 241–242.

"At this time -" Cook, *A Voyage,* Vol. 3, pp. 96-97.

"We were surrounded -" Beaglehole, *The Journals,* Vol. 3, Part 2, p. 1083.

"This is the cheapest Market -" Ibid., Part 1, p. 269.

"The two Forges -" Ibid., Part 2, p. 1141.

"Their own Adzes -" Ibid., p. 1186.

"On our arrival -" Cook, *A Voyage,* Vol. 3, p. 28.

"The eager curiosity -" Beaglehole, *The Journals,* Vol. 3, Part 1, p. 627n.

"These people are fond -" Vancouver, *A Voyage,* Vol. 2, p. 224.

"The fishermen -" Ellis, *Journal,* p. 85.

"Some cloaks -" Portlock, *A Voyage,* p. 78.

"I was as busy and fatigued -" Nicol, *The Life and Adventures,* p. 71.

"A great number -" Cox, *Observations,* p. 51

"Iron is almost -" Fleurieu, *A Voyage,* Vol. 2, p. 11.

"They make ... canoes -" Quimper, ts, p. 5, HMCS,

"They are now so well acquainted -" Manby, *Log,* ms, microfilm, p. 39, UH.

"Though the islanders took knives -" Lisianski, *Around the World,* p. 102. See also: Vancouver, *A Voyage,* Vol. 2, p. 121, "As we approached . . ."

"Of various sizes -" Beaglehole, *The Journals,* Vol. 3, Part 2, p. 1182.

"To five or six gallons -" Campbell, *A Voyage,* p. 143.

"Some of these wooden calabashes -" HG, May 2, 1893, p. 7.

"I was shown -" "Hawaiian Antiquities", *The Islander,* March 12, 1875.

"Though they now use -" Ellis, *Journal,* p. 227

"Axes are rare -" Damon, *Father Bond,* p. 125–126.

CAPTIONS

"They are made -" Arago, *Narrative,* p. 65.

"With these sharp edged adzes -" Bishop, *Reminiscences,* p. 27.

"These workmen -" Freycinet, *Hawai'i in 1819,* p. 87.

"The tool in most general use -" Corney, *Voyages,* p. 143.

THE CRAFTING OF WOODEN CALABASHES

"One of the most important -" Kekahuna, *The Hawaiian Art,* ts, pp. 19-20, AH.

"The native when destitute -" Doyle, *Makua Laiana,* p. 72.

"Cutting it into suitable blocks -" Brigham, *The Ancient Hawaiian House,* p. 159.

"When a dark tone -" Ibid.

FINISHING AND POLISHING

"Where we should saw -" Brigham, *The Ancient Hawaiian House,* p. 164.

"Before finishing -" Kekahuna, *The Hawaiian Art,* ts, p. 24, AH.

Charcoal, bamboo leaf - Malo, *Hawaiian Antiquities,* p. 122.

"When the smoothing had been done -" Kekahuna, *The Hawaiian Art,* ts, pp. 28-29, AH.

"When the insides -" Ibid., p. 30.

"Some of these stained gourd-shells -" Cook, *A Voyage,* Vol. 2, p. 238.

"Another species -" Dixon, *A Voyage,* p. 276.

REPAIRING

"The mending -" Kekahuna, *The Hawaiian Art,* ts, p. 32, AH.

"The demand -" Anon., unidentified newspaper, March 5, 1900, GN ETH PAM, 4045, BM.

"The growing demand -" Anon., "Hawaiian Calabashes," HAA, 1902, p. 153.

"There are six methods -" Kekahuna, *The Hawaiian Art,* ts, p. 32, AH.

CAPTIONS

"Our cabinetmakers -" Arago, *Narrative,* Part 2, pp. 65-66.

"An enterprising German -" P, October 17, 1840, np.

"These nut-trees -" Wilkes, *Narrative,* Vol. 4, pp. 69-70.

"The oil -" Simpson, *Narrative,* Vol. 2, p. 127.

Kukui production between 1840 and 1850 - *HA,* February 21, 1921, p. 1.

"The late intelligent -" PCA, September 19, 1857, np.

Kukui industry - *HA,* February 15, 1929, p. 1.

"Definite Commerce -" Ibid., September 28, 1929, p. 2.

"When this method -" Kekahuna, *The Hawaiian Art,* ts, p. 33, AH.

"In the places -" Ibid., p. 34.

TRADITIONAL CRAFTSMEN

"Reached Waianai -" Pickering, ms, Vol. II, Nov. 21, 1840, Academy of Natural Sciences of Philadephia.

"Unlike the Maori -" Brigham, *The Ancient Hawaiian House,* p. 155.

"I have a few calabashes -" Homer Hayes interview, April 9, 1986.

"According to what I understand -" Kekahuna, *The Hawaiian Art,* ts, p. 20, AH.

"They are not -" Corney, *Voyages,* p. 100. [1896 Edition]

"Wondering what -" Field, *This Life I've Loved,* p. 170–171.

"One day, when I was a child -" Emerson, *Pioneer Days,* p. 166.

"On Wednesday -" *Ke Au Okoa,* May 26, 1867, np. Translated by Carol Silva, Honolulu, 1987.

"I have seen your letter -" Fanny Young to Queen Emma, Lahaina, June 21, 1871, Fanny Young Kekelaokalani (Hipa) to Queen Emma, 1865-1875, M-45, Queen Emma Coll., Nylen-Altman Coll., AH.

CAPTIONS

"In every article -" Campbell, *A Voyage Round The World,* pp. 143.

MODERN WOODEN CALABASHES

Lahaina mission lathe - J. Green to L. Chamberlain, June 18, 1834, Missionary Letters, HMCS.

Green's lathe - R. Armstrong to L. Chamberlain, November 8, 1835, Missionary Letters, David Forbes Notes, HMCS.

Halstead's lathe - R. Armstrong to D. Baldwin, October 23, 1843, Lahaina Restoration Foundation Notes, Vol. 5c, HMCS.

Parke's lathe - Parke obituary, DB, May 29, 1889, np.

Castle's lathe - Third Circuit Probate Minute Book, Vol. 1, p. 2, AH.

"Sofas, Chairs, Bureaus -" P, June 1, 1844, p. 7.

"Turned bed posts -" First Circuit Court, Donnell, Major T., Bkpt. Law No. 1353, Item No. 85, AH.

"Of late years -" Anon., "Hawaiian Calabashes and Bowls," HONAD, 1887, p. 77.

Captain Montressor given bowl by Kamehameha IV - Montressor, *Leaves,* p. 309.

Calabashes in 1876 Philadelphia Exposition - Manning, *Historic Exhibition Catalogues,* ts, p. 183, BM.

"The Honolulu Planing Mill Co. sends -" HG, February 11, 1885, np.

"Four calabashes -" Manning, *Historic Exhibition Catalogues,* ts, p. 70, BM.

"Sir, the undersigned -" Anon. *The Daily Bulletin Hawaiian Hansard,* p. 642.

"If there is anything -" Ibid., p. 675.

$15,000 Kalakaua 1886 Birthday Appropriation - Ibid., np.

"Hookupu -" PCA, March 7, 1871, np.

"Another feature -" Grant, *Scenes in Hawaii,* p. 130.

"They presented money -" Titcomb, ms, SC, Box 3, Folder 3, "Feast and Famine," p. 31, BM, from "Ho'okupu," *Nuhou,* February 28, 1873, np.

"Mr. Wicke is making -" DB, October 15, 1886, np.

"Each division was preceded -" Anon., "Fiftieth Birthday Jubilee of the King," HONAD, 1887, p. 63.

"One of them was led -" Ibid., p. 64.

"This society exhibited -" Ibid.

"The military companies -" Ibid.

"The Enterprise Mill -" DB, November 10, 1886, np.

"A splendid piece -" DB, October 27, 1886, np.

"There is no wonder -" HG, November 16, 1886, p. 5.

"From the morning -" "The Jubilee Birthday," *Kuakoa,* November 20, 1886, HEN, Vol. 1, p. 2863, BM.

"His Majesty was -" PCA, November 17, 1886, np.

"Among the many -" Anon., "Hawaiian Calabashes," HAA, 1902, p. 151.

"Royal acknowledgements -" DB, December 8, 1886.

"Our presentation was -" Mather, *One Summer in Hawaii,* p. 93-94.

"Of late years -" Anon., "Hawaiian Calabashes," HAA, 1902, p. 152.

CAPTIONS

"On parting -" Montressor, *Leaves,* p. 309.

WESTERN CRAFTSMEN

Herrick's arrival - DB, February 25, 1893, np.

C.E. Williams opens store - PCA, July 7, 1859, np.

"Turning Establishment -" PCA, September 21, 1878, np.

"Prepared to do turning -" Ibid.

"An experience of thirty years -" Ibid.

"Mr. W.E. Herrick has now -" DB, May 20, 1889, np.
"Mr. W.E. Herrick has turned out -" DB, February 3, 1886, np.
"Mr. Herrick has just finished -" DB, August 18, 1886, np.
"Mr. Herrick has now for repair -" DB, February 18, 1891, np.
"A novel calabash -" DB, November 11, 1886, np.
"Attentions to our Sovereign -" DB, February 18, 1891, np.
"Besides the large gifts -" Ibid.
"The native sons -" Ibid.
"An old and respected -" DB, February 25, 1893, np.

CAPTIONS

"Some of the stumps -" Wright, *Reminiscences,* p. 4.
"Many fine examples -" Rose, *Hawai'i: The Royal Isles,* pp. 177-178.
"Machine turned -" Ibid., p. 182, no. 120.
"This was on display -" Roger Rose interview, September 27, 1988.
"Annual Meeting -" PCA, February 5, 1889, np.
"Mr. Miller -" DB, November 4, 1886, np.
"An Immense Calabash -" Ibid., July 27, 1887, np.
"More important -" Brigham, *Old Hawaiian Carvings,* p. 10.

CHINESE CRAFTSMEN

Chinese seen by Vancouver, Vancouver, *A Voyage,* Vol. 3, p. 67.
"Here for the first time -" Chamisso, ts, pp. 251-267, #11, UH.
"China carpenter -" William French, William French Ledger No. 3, August 7, 1826-May 15, 1828, p. 62, M-213, Private Collection, AH.
"The houses of the foreign -" Belcher, *Narrative,* Vol. 1, p. 63.
Between thirty and forty Chinese - Census, SIG, May 19, 1838, np.
"We called also -" Lyman, *Around the Horn,* p. 83.
"The Chinese turn their hand -" Gordon-Cumming, *Fire Fountains,* p. 49.
"There is no lack -" Andersson, *A Voyage,* ts, p. 113, HMCS.
"Indeed, some of the finest -" Smiles, *A Boy's Voyage,* p. 234-235.
"The ... storekeepers -" Bird, *Six Months,* p. 161, 170.
"John Chinaman -" PCA, July 20, 1878, np.
"Strolling along -" HG, June 1, 1881, np.
"All along the streets -" DB, August 24, 1883, np.
Chen Mu's signed cabinet- Jenkins, *Hawaiian Furniture,* pp. 242-243.
"What has long been feared -" DB, April 19, 1886, np.

CAPTIONS

"Chinese New Year -" HG, February 2, 1876, np.

JAPANESE CRAFTSMEN

"By the census -" Palmer, *The Human Side of Hawaii,* p. 104.
"As I pass through -" Cameron, *Two Years in Southern Seas,* p. 16.
"My wife -" McSpadden, *Beautiful Hawaii,* p. 160.
Hikohachi Hikokawa - Mrs. Hikokawa interviews, Honolulu, 1980.
Hilo Boarding School History - Lyman, *Notes,* ts, pp. 88-89, Lyman House Museum.
"This is certainly -" *Polk-Husted Directory of Honolulu* 1916, p. 870.
"Calabashes (Bowls) -" Anon., Hilo Boarding School Craft Shop Price List, p. 4.
"He could always turn -" Takeo Doi interview, Hilo, 1986.
Yoichi Watada - Mr. and Mrs. Yoichi Watada interview, Kauai, 1986. Also Mrs. C.E.S. Burns interviews, Honolulu, 1986.
"I made about fifteen -" Ibid.
"I searched -" Ibid.

CAPTIONS

"Plantation life -" Craft, *Hawaii Nei,* p. 63.

LEAF-SHAPED BOWLS

"New and stimulating things -" Lee Cook, "Island Motifs on Textiles," PP, December 1941, p. 45.
"Wooden plates -" *HA,* November 26, 1933, p. 16.
"When prohibition was repealed -" Mary Cook, "George Moody," *Honolulu Beacon,* September 1965, Vol. 5, p. 19.
"He carved hundreds -" SB, April 28, 1956, Sec. Hawaiian Life, p. 4.
"There are more than 20 -" Ibid.

FROM ARTIFACT TO ART

"A few curiosities -" William Lee letter, November 1850, Bancroft Library, Berkeley.
"I regret -" Ibid.
"Every succeeding year -" *Session Laws 1872,* pp. 30-31.
"A number of years ago -" PCA, August 21, 1875, np.
"Many residents possess -" Bird, *Six Months,* p. 68.
"Their home in Honolulu -" Grant, *Scenes in Hawaii,* p. 80.
"There was a collection -" Ibid., p. 200.
"The gathering -" Emerson, HEN, Vol. 1, ts, p. 613, BM.
"During the year -" Ibid., p. 614.
Kalakaua acquires artifacts from natives - Brigham, *Old Hawaiian Carvings,* p. 12.
"On taking our leave -" Grant, *Scenes in Hawaii,* pp. 26-27.
"This sale affords -" PCA, March 1, 1873, np.
"An opportunity -" Ibid.
"Several hundred calabashes -" PCA, April 28, 1877, np.
"Mr. Bartow had large audiences -" PCA, May 5, 1877, np.
"A large collection -" Ibid., March 12, 1884, np.
"The auction -" PCA, March 13, 1884, np.
"There are a great many calabashes -" PCA, May 13, 1885, np.
"High Priced Curios -" PCA, March 15, 1885, np.
"All my native curiosities -" PCA, May 18, 1885, np.
"Sale of Queen Emma's -" DB, February 11, 1886, np.
Hawaiian government purchases at Kanaina's auction, 1877 - Department of Public Instruction, April 30, 1877; May 7, 1877, AH.
"The woman of the house -" Brassey, *A Voyage,* p. 263.
"I made an unsuccessful -" Ibid., p. 272.
"Mr. Rycroft -" DB, August 18, 1887, np.
"A calabash -" DB, May 26, 1892, np.
"Christian Conradt -" PCA, November 1, 1895, np.
"Historic Calabash -" PCA, July 13, 1898, np.
"Rare Calabashes -" PCA, April 24, 1899, p. 3.
"Calabashes are placed -" Unidentified newspaper, March 5, 1900, GN ETH PAM, 4045, BM.
"The old calabashes -" Ibid.
"There has been considerable interest -" Anon., "Hawaiian Calabashes," HAA, 1902, p. 149.
"There are several -" Ibid., p. 153.
"The ancient hand-made bowls -" Brigham, *The Ancient Hawaiian House,* p. 165.
"There are, of course, shops -" Castle, *Hawaii Past and Present,* p. 243.

"If you are fortunate -" Margaret Cullen, "Hawaiian Calabashes," PP, September 1930.

"The old Damon House -" Crawford, *Seven Weeks,* p. 65.

"It was Miss Peabody -" Pitman, *After Fifty Years,* p. 125.

"There were knickknacks -" Anderson, *The Spell of the Hawaiian Islands,* p. 16.

"Here were also -" Ibid., p. 26.

"The calabash, too -" Taylor, "Social Life in Honolulu," *Western Tours,* January 1907, p. 29.

CAPTIONS

"Her home -" Pitman, *After Fifty Years,* p. 125.

"Our hostess -" Ibid., p. 60.

"The alii's - Anon., "Hawaiian Calabashes," HAA 1902, p. 150.

McGuire Probate - Docket No. 11846, Type 3, First Circuit Court, Legal Documents Branch.

"The appraisement -" SB, October 2, 1941, p. 12.

"Then he went -" *HA,* March 27, 1937, p. 1.

"One of the finest -" Unidentified newspaper, March 5, 1900, GN ETHN PAM, 4045, BM.

"Calabashes, mats, spears -" Grant, *Scenes in Hawaii,* p. 200.

"The *kapa* -" Craft, *Hawaii Nei,* p. 57.

"People to-day -" Lawrence, *Old Time Hawaiians,* p. 47.

"We take a trip -" Harlow, *Hawaii by a Tourist,* p. 90.

"Mrs. Charles M. Cooke's -" HAA 1927, p. 104.

FAKES AND DECEPTION

"Much prefer -" Unidentified newspaper, March 5, 1900, GN ETHN PAM, 4045, BM.

"It is seldom -" Brigham, *The Ancient Hawaiian House,* p. 165.

"We remained with them -" Byron, *Voyage of HMS* Blonde, p. 194.

"Observing that several of us -" Dampier, *To the Sandwich Islands,* p. 47.

"The officers of -" Ruschenberger, *Narrative,* Vol. 2, p. 322.

"A Manufacturer of Images -" PCA, November 23, 1872, np.

"In 1865 -" Judd, *Honolulu,* p. 200.

"The Chinese turn their hand -" Gordon-Cumming, *Fire Fountains,* p. 49.

"When I came to Waimea -" Hofgaard letter, September 29, 1926, Catherine Stoddard Notes, Kauai Museum.

"He collects -" LaFarge, *Reminiscences,* pp. 20-21.

CAPTIONS

"In financial matters -" Webster, *Hawaii,* p. 60.

"Kailua was -" Craft, *Hawaii Nei,* p. 155.

"The big dining-hall -" Ibid., p. 156.

PART II. CALABASHES OF OTHER MATERIALS

GOURDS

"Great numbers -" Cook, *A Voyage,* Vol. 2, p. 227.

"Gourd shells they have -" Beaglehole, *The Journals,* Vol. 3, Part 2, p. 1183.

"The conditioning of a Hawaiian -" Dodge, *Hawaiian and Other Polynesian Gourds,* p. 2.

"Gourds grew best -" Handy, *The Hawaiian Planter,* p. 211.

"Among the plants -" "A Plant That it is Wise to Cultivate," *Kuakoa,* March 24, 1922, HEN, BM.

"As the gourd grew big -" Handy, *The Hawaiian Planter,* p. 210.

"The fruit was watched -" "A Plant That it is Wise to Cultivate," *Kuakoa,* March 24, 1922, HEN, BM.

"Extracting the pulp -" Dodge, *Hawaiian and Other Polynesian Gourds,* p. 19.

"The cleaning process -" Handy, *The Hawaiian Planter,* p. 210.

"This is what Keahi Luahine -" Titcomb, ms, SC, Box 5, Folder 1, p. 203, BM.

"They stain their gourd-shells -" Cook, *A Voyage,* Vol. 2, p. 238.

"They have likewise -" Cook, *A Voyage,* Vol. 3, p. 151.

"Many of these -" Dixon, *A Voyage,* p. 273.

"The calabashes -" Freycinet, *Hawai'i in 1819,* p. 85.

"Arapai is-" Ellis, *Journal,* p. 268.

"The calabash -" Ibid.

"The best gourds -" Titcomb, *Hoku o Hawaii,* February 17, 1931, ms, SC, Box 5, Folder 1, p. 192, BM.

"These various types -" Dodge, *Hawaiian and Other Polynesian Gourds,* p. 23.

"Twice a week -" Bishop, *Reminiscences,* p. 15.

Chinese seen by Vancouver - Vancouver, *Voyage,* Vol. 3, p. 67.

"Foreign sailors -" Stokes, "Hawaiian Nets and Netting," in Brigham, *Mat and Basket Weaving,* pp. 130-131.

"Near the palace -" Franchère, *Adventures,* p. 39.

"It might be here mentioned -" Stokes, "Hawaiian Nets and Netting," in Brigham, *Mat and Basket Weaving,* pp. 130-131.

"They 'were surely too remarkable' -" Ibid., p. 132.

"The gourds, which grow -" Cook, *A Voyage,* Vol. 3, pp. 150-151.

"The natives now begin -" Portlock, *A Voyage,* p. 73.

"There is a great quantity -" Gerstaecker, *Narrative,* Vol. 2, p. 90.

"Since there was neither -" Lyman, *Hawaiian Yesterdays,* p. 65.

"Two natives -" Wight, *The Memoirs,* p. 12.

"The road was only -" Bishop, *Reminiscences,* p. 45.

"At that time -" Ibid., p. 60.

"The native population -" Ibid., p. 59.

"All articles of merchandise -" Olmstead, *Incidents,* p. 192.

"The awkwardness -" Gerstaecker, *Narrative,* Vol. 2, p. 91.

"Early in the morning -" Simpson, *Narrative,* Vol. 2, p. 55-56.

"There are some wells -" Evans, *Notes,* p. 105.

"I find it difficult -" Sister Catherine to Azaria Kahalewai, March 27, 1865, 2nd Circuit Court, misc. correspondence, 1865, January to April, AH.

"[The Honolulu mission] kindly -" Wilkes, *Narrative,* Vol. 4, pp. 89-90.

"More allied to a May-day -" Ibid., p. 118.

"It has become -" Martin, *Sarah Joiner Lyman,* p. 114.

"Some on horseback -" Anon., "Account of a Visit to the Volcano of Kirauea, in Owyhee, Sandwich Islands, in September 1844," *Blackwoods Magazine,* November 1845, p. 591.

"It was surprising -" Wood, *Wandering Sketches,* pp. 162-163.

"He, with a load -" Bille, *The Voyage,* ts, p. 168, HMCS.

"Each was provided -" Wise, *Los Gringos,* Part 2, pp. 331-332.

"The Ohio left -" Martin, *Sarah Joiner Lyman,* pp. 125-126.

"Visitors to the islands -" Brassey, *Voyage in the* Sunbeam, p. 259.

"To carry all this luggage -" Geiger, *A Trip,* ts, p. 15, AH.

"The furniture of it -" Bloxam, *Diary,* p. 41.

"Two or three old chairs -" Paulding, *Journal,* pp. 201-202.

"It is the custom -" Judd, *Honolulu,* p. 111.

"These calabashes serve -" Bille, *The Voyage,* ts, p. 126, HMCS.

"Around the walls -" Andersson, *A Voyage,* ts, p. 121, HMCS.

"In the second hut -" Ibid.

"The houses -" Ibid., p. 114.

"Around the room -" Baxley, *What I Saw,* pp. 612-613.

"The family took -" Vincent, *Through and Through the Tropics,* p. 84.

"Nalemanu, a great man -" Bird, *Six Months,* p. 91.

"I was surprised -" Ibid., p. 92.

"At Hamoa in Hana -" Handy, *The Hawaiian Planter,* p. 211.

"The Governor owned -" Damon, *Koamalu,* p. 741.

REPAIRING GOURDS

"On other occasions -" Cook, *A Voyage,* Vol. 2, p. 238.

"It would perhaps be well -" Kekahuna, *The Hawaiian Art,* ts, p. 35, AH.

CAPTIONS

"Instead of baskets -" Wilkes, *Narrative,* Vol. 3, pp. 389- 390.

"Gourds were -" Kamakau, *The Works,* p. 46.

"All their cooking -" Walpole, *Four Years in the Pacific,* p. 247.

"Na Huewai -" Anon., *Preliminary Catalogue of the Bernice Pauahi Museum 1893,* p. 20.

"The canoes gathered -" Titcomb, ms, SC, Box 5, Folder 1, p. 203, BM.

"A young woman -" Arago, *Narrative,* Part 2, p. 92.

"Small gourds -" Ruschenberger, *Narrative,* Vol. 2, p. 331.

"The koko puu puu -" Stokes, "Hawaiian Nets and Netting," in Brigham, *Mat and Basket Weaving,* pp. 129-130.

"One cannot but -" Wilkes, *Narrative,* Vol. 3, pp. 389-390.

"Auamo or Mamaka Kii -" Summers, J.S. Emerson Collection, "Carrying Poles," ts, p. 3, No. 356, BM.

Burden pole costing $1 - Ibid., No. 337.

"In one Corner -" Beaglehole, *The Journals,* Vol. 3, Part 2, p. 1176.

"Their household -" Campbell, *A Voyage,* p. 130.

"When the house -" Ellis, *Journal,* p. 322.

"The koko pualu -" Stokes, "Hawaiian Nets and Netting," in Brigham, *Mat and Basket Weaving,* p. 128.

"The fisherman's huewai -" Brigham, *The Ancient Hawaiian House,* p. 141.

"While a fisherman -" Ibid., pp. 189-190.

"He was sitting -" Mathison, *Narrative,* p. 423.

"Gourd shells -" Beaglehole, *The Journals,* Vol. 3, Part 2, p. 1183.

"Long thin varieties -" Brigham, *The Ancient Hawaiian House,* p. 141.

"Gourds used-" Dodge, *Hawaiian and Other Polynesian Gourds,* p.34.

"Death still rages -" G. Rowell to D. Baldwin, January 30, 1849, MCHS.

COCONUTS

"The coconut is -" Brigham, *The Ancient Hawaiian House,* p. 147.

"The Cocoa nut shells they use -" Beaglehole, *The Journals,* Vol. 3, Part 2, p. 1183.

"They brought us out -" Ibid., p. 1164.

"Its fruit presents -" Dampier, *To the Sandwich Islands,* p. 47.

"The Hawaiians made -" Brigham, *The Ancient Hawaiian House,* p. 147.

"Here we may mention -" Ibid., p. 152.

"Natives in remote districts -" Doyle, *Makua Laiana,* p. 154.

"This is the news -" Queen Emma to Fanny Young, January 29, 1871, Queen Emma to Fanny Young Kekelaokalani (Hipa), 1866-1874, M-45, Queen Emma Coll., Nylen-Altman Coll., AH.

"A touch -" Rose, *Hawai'i: The Royal Isles,* p. 183, No. 128.

"As the coconut shell takes -" Brigham, *The Ancient Hawaiian House,* p. 149.

"One thing that made the table -" Pitman, *After Fifty Years,* p. 60.

"When the time came -" Howell, *An Island Paradise,* p. 47.

"At Mr. Nolte's -" *Saturday Press,* July 14, 1883, np.

"A Souvenir -" PCA, July 24, 1883, np.

"A German -" Ibid.

"There are also a large number -" PCA, May 29, 1885, np.

"Statues, calabashes, canes -" DB, April 2, 1886, np.

Otremba death - SB, August 9, 1910, p. 7.

"An adept -" PCA, July 12, 1886, np.

"Engraving Establishment -" DB, September 18, 1886, np.

"Native Genius -" Ibid.

"He has in various stages -" Ibid.

"He certainly has claims -" Ibid.

"I have now placed -" Samuel Nowlein to Minister of Foreign Affairs, September 1, 1887, FO&Ex, "Hawaiian Youths Abroad: Italy, 1887," AH.

"Notify those in Italy -" Cabinet meetings minutes (February 21, 1888), 1887-1890, p. 25, AH.

"The boy reached here -" D.A. McKinley to Jonathan Austin, July 27, 1888, FO&Ex, "Hawaiian Youths Abroad: Italy, 1888," AH.

"I had to pay debts -" J.M. Herring to Police Marshal, April 17, 1893, Marshal's misc. letters, 1893, AH.

Herring remained in San Francisco - PCA, March 20, 1893, np.

"After his return -" DB, March 20, 1893, np.

"In with the radical element -" Ibid.

"The deed of shooting -" Minutes, Council of State, July 1, 1898, pp. 136-137, AH.

"Glossy bowls -" Mather, *One Summer in Hawaii,* p. 140.

Wicke takes over father's shop - DB, February 1, 1887, np.

"Mr. Wiki -" Brewer, *Diary,* ts, p. 38, AH.

"*Poi*- bowls -" Pitman, *After Fifty Years,* p. 93.

"Territorial Tree -" SB, March 18, 1930, p. 15, C-4.

CAPTIONS

"The men -" Iselin, *Journal,* p. 65.

"A tobacco pipe is hung -" Corney, *Voyages,* p. 110.

"Another gracious act -" von Holt, *Stories of Long Ago,* p. 103.

FIBER

"For solidity -" Brigham, *Mat and Basket Weaving,* p. 60.

"'Born is the tangled ieie' -" Ibid., p. 61.

"The many long, narrow, aerial roots -" Neal, *In Gardens of Hawaii,* p. 54.

"Exactly how these were made -" Brigham, *Mat and Basket Weaving,* p. 63.

"Cook Collection." Kaeppler, *Artificial Curiosities,* p. 86.

"One works in the [ieie] -" Freycinet, *Voyage Autour du Monde,* Vol. 3, Historique, p. 613. Translated by Carol Silva, Honolulu, 1987.

"Before we left -" Ellis, *Journal,* p. 213.

CAPTIONS

"Used for containing -" BM Accession Records, No. 1891.01, Govt. Coll., pp. 16-17.

"The hinai poepoe -" Anon., *The Hawaiian Portion of the Polynesian Collections in the Peabody Museum of Salem,* p. 28.
"In the economic system -" HAA 1895, p. 110.
"The examples of Hawaiian basketry -" Dale Kronkright interview, June 1988.
"Some of the finest -" Rose, *North American and Pacific Basketry,* p. 54.

PART III. CALABASHES, FOODS, AND FEASTING

POI, THE STAFF OF LIFE

"The food of these natives -" Ruschenberger, *Narrative,* p. 373.
"The Hawaiian poi -" Beaglehole, *The Journals,* Vol. 3, Part 1, p. 283n4.
"To see the natives -" Simpson, *Narrative,* Vol. 2, p. 34.
"They frequently make a pudding -" Portlock, *A Voyage,* p. 192.
"The want of their favourite dish -" Beechey, *Narrative,* Vol. 1., p. 233.
"Instead of partaking -" Paulding, *Journal,* p. 229.
"Tarrow, which is the principal -" Corney, *Voyages,* p. 108.
"The oven -" Ellis, *Journal,* p. 147.
"Several thicknesses of [ti leaves] -" Titcomb, "Imu" (First Draft), ms, SC, Box 3, Folder 1, p. 3, BM.
"The quantity required -" Walpole, *Four Years,* pp. 296-297.
"The consistency -" Duthie, *A Bishop in the Rough,* p. 165.
"Taro ... is always eaten -" Elwes, *A Sketcher's Tour,* p. 186.
"They have -" Holman, *Journal,* p. 19.
"Usually they are particular -" Cannon, "My First Mission," in Nibley, *Three Mormon Classics,* p. 61.
"All unpleasant -" Mary Pukui (Wiggen), HENI, Vol. 1, p. 999, BM.
"Their happiest -" Ingram, "The Hawaiians," *The Chautauquan,* September 1891, pp. 755-756.
"I tasted -" Bloxam, *Diary,* p. 23.
"The taste -" Cronise, "Hawaii and Hawaiians," *Commercial Traveller's Home Magazine,* January 1896, p. 14.
"The *poi* is made -" Pitman, *After Fifty Years,* p. 61.
"Poi can be purchased -" "Poi Making in Hawaii," PP, October 1930, p. 12.
"Our friend 'Kentuck' -" PCA, April 16, 1863, np.
"Poi making -" HG, July 27, 1881, np.
"Poi is made by the Chinese -" Grant, *Scenes in Hawaii,* p. 35.
"The adhesive quality -" Silvers, *The Land of the O-o,* p. 110.
"There are within the limits -" Report of the Board of Health to the Legislature of 1888, p. 56, AH.
"I have been having -" Crawford, *Seven Weeks in Hawaii,* p. 67.
"It is served generally -" Wetmore, *Sounds from Home,* p. 40.
"Nearly every one visiting -" Crawford, *Seven Weeks in Hawaii,* p. 67.
"I don't know whether you have ever -" Reprinted from Chicago News, np., in PCA, February 16, 1884, p. 9.
"Nine poi factories -" SB, September 1932, Section 3, p. 1.

CAPTIONS

"He seats himself -" Townsend, *Sporting Excursions,* Vol. 2, p. 43.
"The natives -" Ingram, "The Hawaiians," *The Chautauquan,* September 1891, pp. 755-756.
"*Umeke poi* -" see p. 250.
"All *poi* -" Craft, *Hawaii Nei,* p. 59.
"It looks -" Webster, *Hawaii,* p. 57.
"Dry land taro -" Titcomb, ms, SC, Box 664, Folder 2, p. 9, BM.
"In regard to cheapness -" Simpson, *Narrative,* Vol. 2, p. 123.

LUAU AND PAINA

"Their supper scene -" Bingham, *A Residence,* p. 193.
"The principal dish -" PCA, March 13, 1875, p. 3.
"It is so important a food -" Titcomb, "Greens," ms, SC, Box 3, Folder 1, p. 2, BM.
"Before serving -" Titcomb, ms, SC, Box 5, Folder 3, p. 261, BM.
"A small pig -" Bille, *The Voyage,* ts, p. 127, HMCS.
"The navigator -" Sparks, *The Life,* p. 95.
"Hostesses of that era -" Yardley, *HA,* March 23, 1994, p. D7.
"I never could imagine -" Pitman, *After Fifty Years,* pp. 59-60.
"A koa-wood plate -" McSpadden, *Beautiful Hawaii,* pp. 54-55.
"In America -" Doyle, *Makua Laiana,* p. 165.
"If now you look -" Nordhoff, *Northern California,* pp. 86-87.
"He pointed out -" Knox, *The Boy Travellers,* p. 16.
"I have never seen -" Mary Pukui (Wiggin), HEN, Vol. 1, p. 998, BM.
"Tables were draped -" Grant, *Scenes in Hawaii,* pp. 133-134.
"The feast was laid -" Howell, *An Island Paradise,* pp. 43-44.
"A long, low platform -" PCA, October 7, 1882, p. 5.
"Tamaahmaah -" Kotzebue, *Voyage,* Vol. 1, p. 313.
"Now prepare for a shock -" Pitman, *After Fifty Years,* p. 61.
"Her majesty proceeded -" Silvers, *Land of the O-o,* p. 297.
"Knives, forks, and spoons -" PCA, February 11, 1882, p. 2.
"At every second or third -" Grant, *Scenes in Hawaii,* pp. 133-134.
"We saw but few hogs -" Manby, *Log,* ts, microfilm, p. 144, UH.
"They are, in general, fed -" Cook, *A Voyage,* Vol. 3, p. 118.
"In their feasts -" Ellis, *Journal,* p. 247.
"The greatest dainty -" Bishop, *Journal,* ms,Vol. 2, p. 23, UH.
"Near my place -" Ruschenberger, *Narrative,* Vol. 2, p. 336.
"The whole party -" Reynolds, *Voyage,* p. 411.
"Food,-" SIG, September 24, 1836.
" 'And which is the dog?' -" Taylor, *A Voyage,* Vol. 2, pp. 245-246.
"Two long tables -" P, November 28, 1840, p. 99.
"The aboriginal, or poë dog -" Bennett, *Narrative,* Vol. 1, pp. 246-247.
"The dinner -" Anon., "Holiday Observances in Monarchial Days," HAA, 1930, p. 103.
"Beef, pork, fish, and poi -" Ibid., p. 104.
"Reports an undated note -" PP, October 1920, p. 19.
"I was most fortunate -" Anderson, *Seeing Hawaii,* p. 99.
"271 hogs -" Anon., "Holiday Observances in Monarchial Days," HAA, 1930, p. 104.
"For the Luau -" PCA, February 11, 1882, p. 3.
"Pigs, in almost continual streams -" DB, October 22, 1886, np.
"The guests began -" DB, November 24, 1886, np.

CAPTIONS

"The first course -" Silvers, *Land of the O-o,* p. 142.
"We took our seats -" Ibid.
"Invitations to a dinner -" Craft, *Hawaii Nei,* p. 39.

PAGE 270

"The preparation of poi -" Craft, *Hawaii Nei,* p. 58.

ABRIDGED BIBLIOGRAPHY

Anderson, Isabel. *The Spell of the Hawaiian Islands.* Boston, 1916.

Anderson, John. *Seeing Hawaii on American Pluck.* Los Angeles, 1922.

Anderson, Mary. *Scenes in the Hawaiian Islands and California.* Boston, 1865.

Andrews, Lorrin. *A Dictionary of the Hawaiian Language.* Honolulu, 1865.

d'Anglade, M. G. Bosseront. *A Tree in Bud.* Honolulu, 1987.

Arago, Jacques Etienne Victor. *Narrative of a Voyage Around the World.* 2 vols. London, 1823.

Baxley, Henry. *What I Saw on the West Coast of South and North America and at the Hawaiian Islands.* New York, 1865.

Beaglehole, John. *The Journals of Captain James Cook on His Voyages of Discovery.* 4 vols. Cambridge, 1955.

Beechey, Frederich. *Narrative of a Voyage to the Pacific and Beering's Straits.* 2 vols. London, 1831.

Belcher, Edward. *Narrative of a Voyage Round the World.* 2 vols. London, 1843.

Bennett, Frederick. *Narrative of a Whaling Voyage Round the Globe.* 2 vols. London, 1840.

Bingham, Hiram. *A Residence of Twenty-one Years in the Sandwich Islands.* Hartford, 1847.

Bird, Isabella. *Six Months in the Sandwich Islands.* Honolulu, 1964.

The Bernice Pauahi Bishop Museum. *A Preliminary Catalogue of Polynesian Ethnology and Natural History, Part 1.* Honolulu, 1892.

—. *Bishop Museum Handbook, Part 1: The Hawaiian Collections.* Honolulu, 1915.

Bishop, Sereno. *Reminiscences of Our Hawaii.* Honolulu, 1916.

Bloxam, Andrew. *Diary of Andrew Bloxam.* Honolulu, 1925.

Brassey, Anne. *A Voyage in the* Sunbeam. Chicago, 1881.

Brigham, William. *Mat and Basket Weaving of the Ancient Hawaiians.* Honolulu, 1906.

—. *Old Hawaiian Carvings.* Memoirs of the Bernice Pauahi Bishop Museum, Vol. II, No. 2. Honolulu, 1906.

—. *The Ancient Hawaiian House.* Honolulu, 1908.

Buck, Peter. *Arts and Crafts of Hawaii.* Honolulu, 1957.

Byron, George. *Voyage of the* HMS Blonde *to the Sandwich Islands in the Years 1824-1825.* London, 1826.

Cameron, Charlotte. *Two Years in Southern Seas.* London, 1923.

Campbell, Archibald. *A Voyage Round the World from 1806 to 1812.* Honolulu, 1967.

Castle, William, Jr. *Hawaii — Past and Present.* New York, 1917.

Clark, Joseph G. *Lights and Shadows of Sailor Life.* Boston, 1848.

Coan, Titus Munson. "The Natives of Hawaii: A Study of Polynesian Charm." Publications of the American Academy of Political and Social Science, No. 395. Philadelphia, 1901.

Coke, Henry. *A Ride over the Rocky Mountains to Oregon and California.* London, 1852.

Cook, James. *A Voyage to the Pacific Ocean.* 3 vols. London, 1785.

Corney, Peter. *Voyages in the Northern Pacific.* Honolulu, 1896.

Cox, J. Halley, with William H. Davenport. *Hawaiian Sculpture.* Honolulu, 1974.

Cox, John. *Observations Made During a Voyage... in the Brig* Mercury. London, 1791.

Craft, Mabel. *Hawaii Nei.* San Francisco, 1899.

Crawford, Minnie. *Seven Weeks in Hawaii.* Los Angeles, 1920.

Damon, Ethel. *Father Bond of Kohala.* Honolulu, 1927.

—. *Koamalu.* Honolulu, 1931.

Dampier, Robert. *To the Sandwich Islands on the* H.M.S. Blonde. Honolulu, 1971.

Day, A. Grove. *History Makers of Hawaii.* Honolulu, 1984.

Dixon, George. *A Voyage Round the World.* London, 1789.

Dodge, Ernest. *Hawaiian and Other Polynesian Gourds.* Honolulu, 1978.

Doyle, Emma. *Makua Laiana, the Story of Lorenzo Lyons.* Honolulu, 1945.

Duthie, Rev. David. *A Bishop in the Rough.* London, 1909.

Ellis, William. *Journal of William Ellis.* Honolulu, 1963.

Elwes, Robert. *A Sketcher's Tour Round the World.* London, 1854.

Emerson, Oliver. *Pioneer Days in Hawaii.* Garden City, New York, 1928.

Emory, Kenneth. "Wooden Utensils and Implements," in *Ancient Hawaiian Civilization.* Rutland, Vermont, 1965.

Evans, Robert. *Notes on Land and Sea.* Boston, 1922.

Field, Isobel. *This Life I've Loved.* New York, 1938.

Fleurieu, Charles. *A Voyage Round the World.* 2 vols. London, 1801.

Franchère, Gabriel. *A Voyage to the Northwest Coast of America.* Chicago, 1954.

Freycinet, Louis de. *Hawai'i in 1819: A Narrative Account.* Bishop Museum Pacific Anthropological Records, No. 26. Honolulu, 1978.

—. *Voyage Autour du Monde.* "Historique." 3 vols. Paris, 1839.

Gerstaecker, Frederich. *Narrative of a Journey Round the World.* 3 vols. London, 1853.

Golovnin, Vasilii. *Around the World on the* Kamchatka. Honolulu, 1979.

Gordon-Cumming, Constance. *Fire Fountains.* London, 1883.

Grant, Minnie. *Scenes in Hawaii.* Toronto, 1888.

Handy, Edward. *The Hawaiian Planter.* Honolulu, 1940.

Harlow, Grace. *Hawaii by a Tourist.* Los Angeles, 1928.

Holman, Lucia Ruggles. *Journal of Lucia Ruggles Holman.* Connecticut, 1986.

Howell, Henry. *An Island Paradise.* Toronto, 1892.

Iselin, Isaac. *Journal of a Trading Voyage Around the World.* 1805-1808. New York, n.d.

Jenkins, Irving. *Hawaiian Furniture and Hawaii's Cabinetmakers.* Honolulu, 1983.

Judd, Laura. *Honolulu: Sketches of the Life ... in the Hawaiian Islands from 1828 to 1861.* Honolulu, 1928.

Kaeppler, Adrienne. *Artificial Curiosities.* Honolulu, 1978.

Kamakau, Samuel. *The Works of the People of Old.* Honolulu, 1976.

Knox, Thomas. *The Boy Travellers in Australasia.* New York, 1889.

Kotzebue, Otto von. *A Voyage of Discovery in the South Sea, and to Beering's Straits.* 3 vols. London, 1821.

—. *A New Voyage Round the World.* 2 vols. London, 1830.
Kuykendall, Ralph S. *The Hawaiian Kingdom.* 3 vols. Honolulu, 1958.
LaFarge, John. *Reminiscences of the South Seas.* London, 1914.
Lawrence, Mary. *Old Time Hawaiians and Their Work.* Boston, 1912.
Ledyard, John. *A Journal of Captain Cook's Last Voyage.* Chicago, 1963.
Lisianski, Urey. *A Voyage Around the World.* London, 1814.
Lyman, Chester. *Around the Horn to the Sandwich Islands and California, 1845-1850.* New Haven, Conn., 1924.
Lyman, Henry. *Hawaiian Yesterdays.* Chicago, 1906.
Malo, David. *Hawaiian Antiquities.* Honolulu, 1898.
Martin, Margaret. *Sarah Joiner Lyman.* Honolulu, 1970.
Mather, Helen. *One Summer in Hawaii.* New York, 1891.
Mathison, Gilbert. *Narrative of a Visit to Brazil, Chile, Peru, and the Sandwich Islands.* London, 1825.
McSpadden, Joseph. *Beautiful Hawaii.* New York, 1935.
Montressor, C. *Leaves from Memory's Log-book and Jottings from Our Journals.* London, 1887.
Neal, Marie. *In Gardens of Hawaii.* Honolulu, 1965.
Nibley, Preston. *Three Mormon Classics.* Salt Lake City, 1945.
Nicholson, Henry. *From Sword to Share; or a Fortune in Five Years at Hawaii.* London, 1881.
Nicol, John. *The Life and Adventures of John Nicol, Mariner.* Edinburgh, 1822.
Nordhoff, Charles. *Northern California, Oregon and the Sandwich Islands.* New York, 1874.
Olmsted, Francis. *Incidents of a Whaling Voyage.* New York, 1841.
Palmer, Albert W. *The Human Side of Hawaii.* Boston, 1924.
Paulding, Hiram. *Journal of a Cruise of the United States Schooner* Dolphin. New York, 1831.
Peabody Museum of Salem. *The Hawaiian Portion of the Polynesian Collections in the Peabody Museum of Salem.* Salem, 1920.
Pitman, Almira. *After Fifty Years.* Norwood, 1931.
Portlock, Nathaniel. *A Voyage Round the World.* London, 1789.
Pukui, Mary K. and Samuel H. Elbert. *Hawaiian Dictionary.* Honolulu, 1971.
Raeside, J. *Sovereign Chief: A Biography of Baron de Thierry.* Christchurch, 1977.
Reynolds, Jeremiah. *Voyage of the United States Frigate* Potomac. New York, 1835.
Rose, Roger G. *Hawai'i: The Royal Isles.* Honolulu, 1980.
—. *North American and Pacific Basketry.* Honolulu, 1984.
Ruschenberger, William. *Narrative of a Voyage Round the World.* 2 vols. London, 1838.
Shaler, William. *Journal of a Voyage Between China and the Northwest Coast of America.* California, 1935.
Silvers, Ash. *The Land of the O-o.* Cleveland, 1892.
Simpson, George. *Narrative of a Journey Round the World.* 2 vols. London, 1847.
Smiles, Samuel. *A Boy's Voyage Round the World.* London, 1871.
Sparks, Jared. *The Life of John Ledyard.* Cambridge, 1828.
Stewart, Charles. *Journal of a Residence in the Sandwich Islands.* London, 1830.
Taylor, Fitch. *A Voyage Round the World and Visits to Various Foreign Countries.* 2 vols. New Haven, Conn., 1848.
Townsend, Ebenezer. *Extracts from the Diary of Ebenezer Townsend Jr.* Hawaiian Historical Society Reprints, No. 4. Honolulu, n.d.
Townshend, John. *Sporting Excursions in the Rocky Mountains.* 2 vols. London, 1840.
Turnbull, John. *A Voyage Round the World.* 3 vols. London, 1805.
Vancouver, George. *A Voyage of Discovery.* 3 vols. London, 1798.
Vincent, Frank. *Through and Through the Tropics.* New York, 1875.
von Holt, Ida. *Stories of Long Ago.* Honolulu, 1953
Walpole, Frederich. *Four Years in the Pacific.* London, 1849.
Webster, Charles [Conflagration Jones]. *Hawaii ... A Snapshot.* Chicago, 1893.
Wetmore, Mary. *Sounds from Home.* Cincinnati, 1898.
Wight, Elizabeth. *The Memoirs of Elizabeth Kinau Wilder.* Honolulu, 1909.
Wilkes, Charles. *Narrative of the United States Exploring Expedition.* 5 vols. Philadelphia, 1845.
Wise, Henry. *Los Gringos.* 2 vols. New York, 1849.
Wood, William. *Wandering Sketches of People and Things.* Philadelphia, 1849.

MANUSCRIPTS

Andersson, Nils. A Voyage Around the World with the Swedish Frigate *Eugenie*, 1851-1853. Translated by Father Reginald Yzendoorn from *Kaliforniën och Oceaniën.* Stockholm, 1854. Typescript, HMCS.
Bille, Steen. *The Voyage of the Corvette* Galathea. Translated from W.V. Rosen's German edition. Unpublished typescript, HMCS, 1922.
Bishop, Francis. *Journal* [surgeon of the British whaling vessel *Recovery*, 1832-1835]. Manuscript, 3 vols., UH.
Brewer, Helen. *Diary of Mrs. Joseph Brewer's Trip to Hawaii, December 1881 to April 1882.* Unpublished typescript, AH.
Bullard, Charles. *Letterbook of Charles B. Bullard, Supercargo* [trading master] *for Bryant and Sturgis at the Hawaiian Islands and at Canton, March 20, 1821-July 11, 1823.* Unpublished typescript, HMCS.
Chamisso, Adelbert von. Excerpts from *Chamissos Werke (Chamisso's Work)*, Vol. 3. Translated from the German by Maria and Helmuth Hormann. Unpublished typescript, UH, 1970.
Choris, Louis. *Voyage Around the World.* Chapter on the Sandwich Islands. Translated by Victor Houston. Unpublished typescript, AH, n.d.
Geiger, Hezekiah. *Trip by H.R. Geiger, Ph.D., LLD.* Springfield, Ohio, 1874. Unpublished typescript, AH.
Hall, Gordon. *Journal of a Whaling Voyage, 1844-1847.* Manuscript, Bancroft Library, Berkeley, California.
Kekahuna, Henry. *The Hawaiian Art of Making Wooden Calabashes.* Unpublished typescript, M-445, Folders No. 2 and 3, Calabash, Henry E.P. Kekahuna Collection, AH, n.d.
Lyman, Nettie. *Notes on the Hilo Boarding School, 1836-1935.* Unpublished typescript, Lyman House Museum.
Manby, Thomas. *The Log of the Proceedings of His Majesty's Armed Tender* Chatham, *Lieut. R.W. Broughton and Lieut. P. Pugett, Commanders, Commencing the 27th of September and Ending the 8th of October 1794.* Manuscript, microfilm, UH.
Mann, Horace. *Journal, May 5th-July 28, 1864.* Manuscript, microfilm, UH.
Manning, Anita. *Historic Exhibition Catalogues Index.* Unpublished typescript, 2 vols., BM, 1982.
Pickering, Charles. *Journal Kept on the United States Exploring Expedition, August 13, 1840 to April 8, 1841.* Unpublished manuscript, 2 vols., Ms. Coll. No. 308, Library of the Academy of Natural Sciences of Philadelphia.
Quimper, D. Manuel. *The Sandwich Islands.* Madrid, 1882. Translated by Lee Clark, Honolulu, 1937. Unpublished typescript, HMCS.
Wright, Anna. Reminiscences of Lihue and Koloa, Kauai. Unpublished typescript, Kauai Historical Society, Kauai Museum, n.d.

Index

CREDITS

Calabashes not listed here are from private collections. Multiple objects in same photo are listed top to bottom and left to right.

Dust jacket, back cover.
Calabash Support Ring -
Bishop Museum, C.6374,
Gift of Carrie Robinson and Frank Kalaimamahu.

Page xiv
Woven Container - Bishop Museum, 3844.
Covered Gourd - Bishop Museum, 1077.
Decorated Gourd - Bishop Museum, 9285, Deverill Collection.
Wooden Bowl - Bishop Museum, C.5634, Henriques Collection.
Coconut Cup - Bishop Museum, B.2677, Damon Collection.

Page 4
Wooden Bowl, British Museum; Museum of Mankind, 6269.
Wooden Cover, British Museum; Museum of Mankind, 6891.
Figured Bowl, British Museum; Museum of Mankind, HAW 47.

Page 6
Vienna Museum of Ethnology, 173.
Vienna Museum of Ethnology, 174.
Vienna Museum of Ethnology, 175.

Page 11
Painting courtesy Honolulu Academy of Arts.

Page 12
Bishop Museum, 2294,
Hawaii National Museum Collection.
Bishop Museum, 2290,
Hawaii National Museum Collection.
Bishop Museum, 4004,
Hawaii National Museum Collection.
Bishop Museum, 1355,
Hawaii National Museum Collection.
Bishop Museum, 3898,
Hawaii National Museum Collection.

Page 13
Bishop Museum, 2293,
Hawaii National Museum Collection.
Bishop Museum, 2291,
Hawaii National Museum Collection.
Bishop Museum, 2292,
Hawaii National Museum Collection.
Bishop Museum, 2295,
Hawaii National Museum Collection.
Page 20
Honolulu Academy of Arts, 2035,
Mrs. C.M. Cooke Collection.
Honolulu Academy of Arts, 2044,
Mrs. C.M. Cooke Collection.
Honolulu Academy of Arts, 4944,
Gift of Mrs. W.F. Giddings.

Page 23
Honolulu Academy of Arts, 3756,
Mrs. C.M. Cooke Collection.

Page 24
Background Bowl,
Honolulu Academy of Arts, 2050,
Mrs. C.M. Cooke Collection.

Page 29
Bishop Museum, 5028,
Queen Emma Collection.

Page 30
Bishop Museum, 2635,
Damon Collection.

Page 31
Hawaii State Archives Photo.

Page 32
Kauai Museum, Loan, Dora Jane Cole.

Page 33
Bishop Museum Photo.

Page 34
Bishop Museum, 640.
Bishop Museum, 1357,
Government Collection.
Bishop Museum, 728,
Queen Emma Collection.
Bishop Museum, 628,
Queen Emma Collection.
Bishop Museum, 610.
Bishop Museum, 1356,
Government Collection.

Page 37
Background Bowl -
Bishop Museum, C.9557,
Gift of J.M. McCandless.

Page 38
Foreground Bowl -
Bishop Museum, B.6887,
Kapiolani-Kalanianaole Collection.

Page 40
Bishop Museum, 488.
Bishop Museum, 462.

Page 41
Bishop Museum, 1146,
Hawaii National Museum Collection.

Page 42
Bishop Museum, 157,
Emerson Collection.
Bishop Museum, 158,
Emerson Collection.

Page 43
Bishop Museum, B.142,
Gift of Agnes Judd.
Bishop Museum, 1986.287.43,
Gift of Maner Hite.
Bishop Museum, 10,297, Princess Kaiulani Collection.

Page 44
Bishop Museum, 675.
Bishop Museum, 700.
Bishop Museum, 683.
Bishop Museum, 678.

Page 47
Bishop Museum, 6927,
Hawaii National Museum Collection.

Page 51
British Museum; Museum of Mankind, 55.12-20-50.
British Museum; Museum of Mankind, 1920.10.23.1.

Page 52
Bishop Museum, B.7006,
Kapiolani-Kalanianaole Collection.
Bishop Museum, 5009,
Emerson Collection.
Bishop Museum, 706.
Bishop Museum, 708.

Page 53
Bishop Museum, 4143,
Hawaii National Museum Collection.

Page 54
Bishop Museum, 9069,
Gift of F. Haenisch.
Bishop Museum, 636,
Queen Emma Collection.
Bishop Museum, 637.
Bishop Museum, C.9635,
Gift of Mrs. Reginald Carter.

Page 55
Bishop Museum, 4144,
Queen Emma Collection.
Bishop Museum, 3997,
Hawaii National Museum Collection.

Page 56
Bishop Museum, 620.

Page 57
Bishop Museum, 624.
Bishop Museum, 626.
Bishop Museum, 614.

Page 58
Gourd - Saffron Walden Museum,
England, LN190.
University Museum of Archaeology
and Ethnology, Cambridge, England,
22,916.

Page 61
Background Bowl - C.5637,
Henriques Collection.
Figured Bowl - Bishop Museum, 5181,
Queen Emma Collection.
Spittoon - Bishop Museum, 701,
Queen Emma Collection.

Page 62
Photograph by K. Stowell.

Page 63
British Museum; Museum of Mankind,
HAW46.
British Museum; Museum of Mankind,
VAN.297.

Page 64
British Museum; Museum of Mankind,
HAW48.
British Museum; Museum of Mankind,
1904-95, Gift of C. Dove.

Page 65
British Museum; Museum of Mankind,
54.12-27.119.

Page 67
Bishop Museum, D.565, Gift of
Richard Nishino and Rodney Minami.
Bishop Museum, 9073.

Pages 68, 69
Bishop Museum, 408.

Page 82
Bishop Museum, 3107,
Emerson Collection.
Bishop Museum, D.2643.
Bishop Museum, 3102,
Emerson Collection.

Page 87
Bishop Museum, 1970.10.24,
Gift of Mrs. W.F. Giffard.
Bishop Museum, 3115,
Emerson Collection.
Bishop Museum, C.452,
Gift of Eliza Mackenzie.

Page 88
Bishop Museum, 4747.
Bishop Museum, 4745.
Bishop Museum, 682,
Queen Emma Collection.

Page 92
Bishop Museum, 472.
Bishop Museum, 5595.

Page 94
Bishop Museum, 4743.
Bishop Museum, 4005.
Stones from Bishop Museum -
1983.48.47, Gift of Vivian Klammer.
1983.48.41, Gift of Vivian Klammer.
B.7158, Kapiolani-Kalanianaole
Collection.
3019, Emerson Collection.
B.9535.
1976.201.12, Gift of Roy Yamaguchi.

Page 106
Bishop Museum, C.2929,
Gift of Mrs. Gay.
Bishop Museum, C.9548,
Gift of V. Houston.
Adze - Bishop Museum, 3103,
Emerson Collection.
Stones from Bishop Museum - 3067,
Emerson Collection.
C.5392, Henriques Collection.

Page 110
Bishop Museum Photo.

Page 114
Bishop Museum, 592.
Bishop Museum, 595,
Queen Emma Collection.

Page 117
Sotheby's London, 1988.

Page 119
Bishop Museum, HH 1797,
Fagan Collection.

Pages 120, 121
Hawaii State Archives Photo.

Page 123
Bishop Museum, B.6959,
Kapiolani-Kalanianaole Collection.

Page 128
Bishop Museum, B.6963,
Kapiolani-Kalanianaole Collection.

Page 129
Bishop Museum, B.6996,
Kapiolani-Kalanianaole Collection.

Page 131
Bishop Museum, 5010,
Hawaii National Museum Collection.
Friends of Iolani Palace, F.520.1.

Page 133
Bishop Museum, B.6962,
Kapiolani-Kalanianaole Collection.
Bishop Museum, 3211.
Bishop Museum, 3049,
Gift of Mrs. W. Westervelt.

Page 135
Bishop Museum, B.6958,
Kapiolani-Kalanianaole Collection.
Bishop Museum, B.6960,
Kapiolani-Kalanianaole Collection.

Page 136
Bishop Museum, 587.
Bishop Museum, 586.
Bishop Museum, 588.

Pages 140, 141
Friends of Iolani Palace, F.520.1,
Gift of the Kawananakoa Family.

Page 145
Photo courtesy of Hikokawa Family.

Page 148
Photo by Augie Salbosa, courtesy of
Hawaii State Department of Land and
Natural Resources.

Page 154
Grove Farm Homestead Museum.

Page 157
Bishop Museum Photo.

Page 160
Hawaii State Archives Photo.

Page 161
Hawaii State Archives Photo.

Page 165
Bishop Museum Photo.

Page 167
Kauai Museum Photo.

Pages 168, 169
Honolulu Academy of Arts,
Mrs. C.M. Cooke Collection.

Page 170
Bishop Museum Photo.

Page 176
Bishop Museum, 7651.
Bishop Museum, 4297.
Bishop Museum, C.1116,
Emerson Collection.

Page 178
Covered Gourd Top -
Bishop Museum, 1079.
Covered Gourd Body -
Bishop Museum, 2666.
Bishop Museum, 10,997.
Bishop Museum, 1104.
Bishop Museum, D.98,
Gift of George Ii Brown, Jr.

Page 182
Bishop Museum, 1097,
Emerson Collection.
Stopper - Bishop Museum, B.1455,
Gift of James Munro.
Bishop Museum, 1077.

Page 183
Background Bowl -
Bishop Museum, 1977.206.01a.
Stopper - Bishop Museum, B.1455,
Gift of James Munro.

Page 185
Grove Farm-Homestead Museum.
Kauai Museum, P.240,
McBride Collection.
Honolulu Academy of Arts, 3628,
Mrs. C.M. Cooke Collection.
Honolulu Academy of Arts, 4153,
Gift of Estate of Mrs. C.M. Cooke.

Page 186
British Museum; Museum of Mankind,
HAW51.
British Museum; Museum of Mankind,
HAW51A.

Page 187
Vienna Museum of Ethnology, 176.
Vienna Museum of Ethnology, 177.

Page 189
Bishop Museum, B.1516,
Queen Emma Collection.

Page 190, 191
Koko - Bishop Museum, 7966.
Gourd - Bishop Museum, 4298,
Emerson Collection.
Koko - Bishop Museum, B.6955,
Kapiolani-Kalanianaole Collection.
Gourd - Bishop Museum, 1081.
Gourd Cover - Bishop Museum, 3923,
Hawaii National Museum Collection.
Pole - Bishop Museum, 9524.

Page 193
Bishop Museum, 9475,
Deverill Collection.
Bishop Museum, 10308,
Kaiulani Collection.
Bishop Museum, 147,
Emerson Collection.
Bishop Museum, 144,
Emerson Collection.
Bishop Museum, C.9051.

Page 195
Bishop Museum, Hawaiian Hall.

Page 197
Bishop Museum, 3994,
Hawaii National Museum Collection.
Bishop Museum, 10,990.
Bishop Museum, 3871,
Emerson Collection.
Bishop Museum, 3880.

Page 199
Bishop Museum, B.6869.
Bishop Museum, 10,988.
Bishop Museum, 10,987.
Bishop Museum, 6873.
Cover- Bishop Museum, 3869.

Page 201
Kauai Museum, 81,
Eric Knudsen Collection.
Kauai Museum.

Page 204
Bishop Museum, 1074,
Emerson Collection.
Bishop Museum, 3983.

Page 209
Bishop Museum, B.2657,
Damon Collection.
Bishop Museum, 2658.
Bishop Museum, 10,499, Princess
Kaiulani Collection.

Page 215
Bishop Museum, HH 1801,
Fagan Collection.

Page 217
Foreground Bowl - Bishop Museum,
1940.65.02, Gift of A. Farenholt.

Page 218
British Museum;
Museum of Mankind, HAW49.
British Museum;
Museum of Mankind, HAW50.
British Museum;
Museum of Mankind, HAW163.

Page 221
Bishop Museum, 1404,
Emerson Collection.
Bishop Museum, 3890.
Bracelet - Bishop Museum, D.02325.
Lei - Bishop Museum, 02830, Emerson
Collection.
Palaoa - Bishop Museum, 01338.
Cape - Bishop Museum, 1925.002.01,
Gift of Walter Dillingham.

Page 223
Bishop Museum, 1404,
Emerson Collection.

Page 224
Bishop Museum Photo.

Page 228
Bishop Museum Photo.

Page 229
Bishop Museum Photo.

Page 232
Painting courtesy Drs. Ben and A. Jess
Shenson.

Page 233
Bishop Museum Photos.

Page 238
Bishop Museum Photo.

Page 239
Bishop Museum Photo.

Page 270
Bishop Museum, 1984.414.02a,
Gift of Mrs. Oscar Winne.
Bishop Museum, D.4376,
Gift of Martha Bolster.
Dark Poi Pounder -
Bishop Museum, 9118,
Gift of C. Dove.
White Poi Pounder -
Bishop Museum, 4094.

ABOVE: *The thick wooden platters in this picture were made to hold taro corms while stone pestles were employed to pound them into smooth liquid poi. The board in the foreground is 37" long. The longer board resting on its side in the background is 53 1/2" long and was meant to be used by two men working independently at either end at the same time. By the turn of the century, pounding poi by hand was done only in a few country areas. Mabel Craft, visiting in the 1890s wrote: "The preparation of* ***poi*** *has fallen on evil days. In Honolulu it is made by Chinese almost exclusively. Much of it is pounded by machinery, and it is only in remote country districts that one may see the* ***taro****-beaters with trough and stone pestle, pounding the tough root which is their staple of life."*

ACKNOWLEDGEMENTS

This book is the direct result of Juliet Rice Wichman's dream of publishing a study on Hawaiian calabashes. Her enthusiasm and commitment to this project led her to make a personal donation to the Kauai Museum, enabling her dream to become a reality. Although she did not see the book in final form, we spent many enjoyable hours together developing the concept. The Hawaiian Calabash is a gift from Juliet Rice Wichman to the people of Hawaii.

This book is also a special joint project of the Kauai Museum and the Bernice Pauahi Bishop Museum Department of Anthropology. Yosihiko Sinoto, director of the department, enthusiastically supported the project from its inception. He not only provided access to the Bishop Museum's collections, but also made it possible to include material from museums in Europe. The support of Dr. Sinoto, one of the most renowned Pacific Rim archaeologists, was an inspiration and unbounded resource to me. The majority of pieces included in the book were photographed at the Bishop Museum. Toni Han, head of the Ethnology Department, was responsible for coordinating all of our photographic efforts at the museum. Bishop Museum ethnologist Roger Rose read the manuscript for historical accuracy and offered valuable insights, knowledge, and many corrections.

The high quality of photography in this book reflects the skill and commitment of the project photographer, Hugo de Vries. Hugo generously gave many hours of his time to ensure the quality of every photograph taken and photographed many more pieces than originally anticipated. I personally found that, in addition to possessing fine technical skills, Hugo is a delight to work with.

Cindy Turner collaborated with the book design and assisted her husband, Hugo de Vries, with much of the photographic work. Chris Fayé was the project illustrator.

Poet Frank Stewart was once again my indispensable copy editor. My good friend, David Forbes, one of Hawaii's outstanding authorities on Hawaii's history, contributed research. Sarah Collins and Allan Ziegler provided bone identification for inlaid refuse containers.

Many museums participated in this project. I thank Dorota Starzecka and Jill Hassel of the Museum of Mankind in London; Hanns Peter of the Museum of Ethnology in Vienna; David Phillipson and Qwil Owen of the University Museum of Archaeology and Ethnology, Cambridge; and Len Pole, Saffron Walden Museum, Essex. Christine Davies of Sotheby's, London, allowed us to use a photograph of a container owned by King Kamehameha IV.

In Hawaii, I thank Alice Guild and Jim Bartels of Iolani Palace; Barnes Reznik, Grove Farm Homestead Museum; and George Ellis, Sanna Deutsch, Hilde Randolph, and Tibor Franyo, with the Honolulu Academy of Arts. Ginger Alexander of the Kauai Museum was responsible for all the bookkeeping.

Regional Manager Thomas Rupp coordinated efforts of the Ralph Wilson Plastics Company in donating backdrop materials and sending them to Europe so that backdrops used in all of the photographs would be consistently Wilsonart laminates. All second edition photographs with solid color backgrounds were also done on Wilsonart.

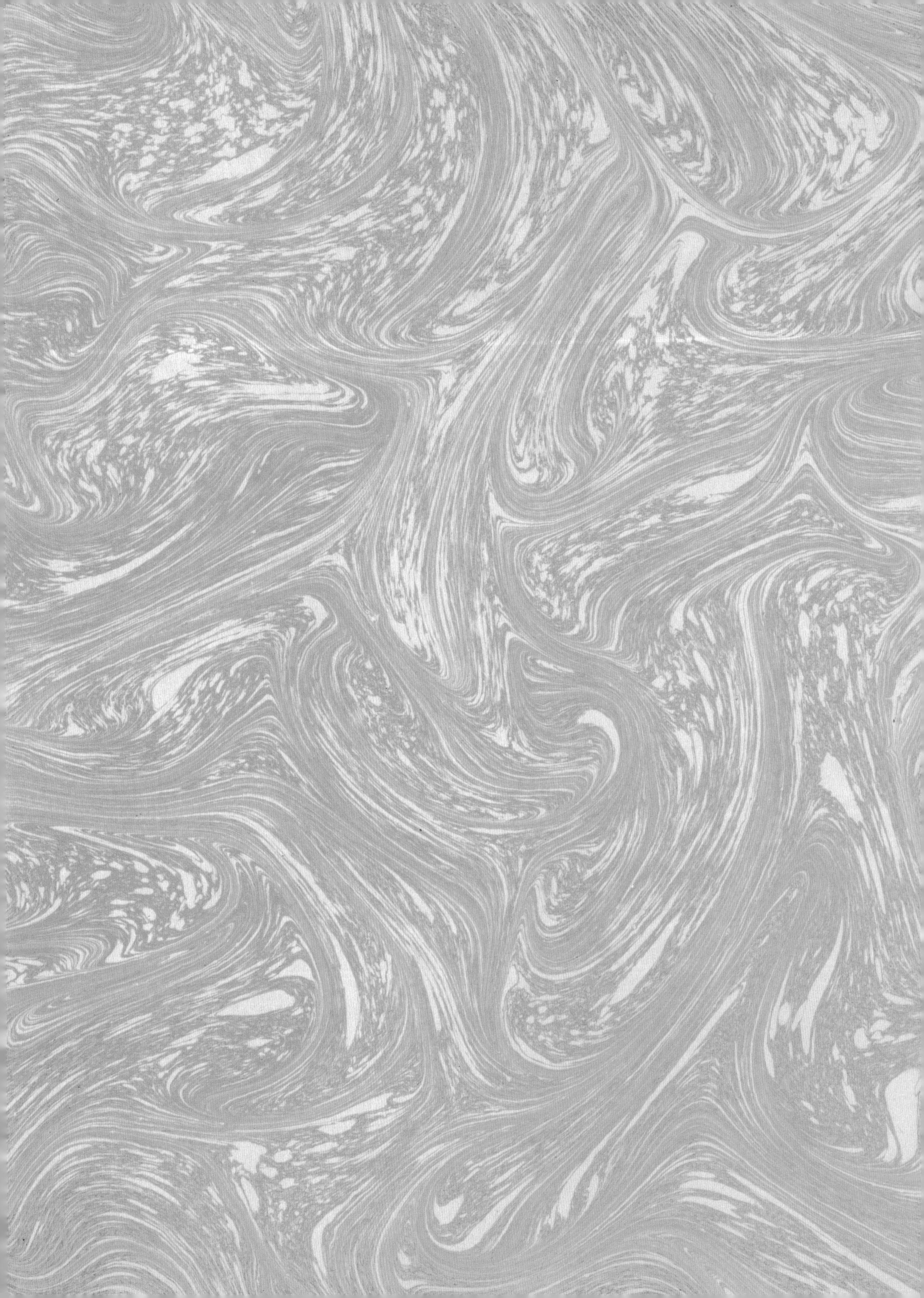